Love and Pomegranates

Love and Pomegranates

Artists and Wayfarers on Iran

Edited by

Meghan Nuttall Sayres

www.nortiapress.com

2321 E 4th Street, C-219
Santa Ana, CA 92705
contact @ nortiapress.com

Cover photograph by Aphrodite Désirée Navab
Cover design by Gaelen Sayres
Text design by Russ Davis at Gray Dog Press (www.graydogpress.com)

ISBN: 978-0-9848359-9-7
Library of Congress Control Number: 2012956356

Nortia Press is distributed to the trade by
Consortium Book Sales & Distribution
Fax: (800) 351-5073
Phone: (800) 283-3572
Email: orderentry@perseusbooks.com

Printed in the United States of America

For
Manda Jahan

To
Iranians Everywhere

With
Special Thanks To

Brian H. Appleton

A Note about the Text and Persian Words

You will find a square ■ at the end of several of the essays, poems, etc. This indicates that the author has provided additional material related to the piece, which is featured at the back of the book under Notes.

In most cases we chose the phonetic spellings for the Persian words; however, for several names we chose common transliterations instead, such as Hafiz and Rumi.

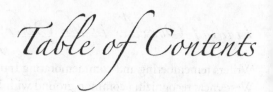

Table of Contents

Finding Ourselves in the Other *p.35*

Writers remembering and commemorating Iranians they've known and loved. Westerners recognizing common ground with Iranians or feeling at home in Iran. Iranians of the Diaspora explore what it means to be Iranian in their new homelands. Those living in exile yearn for the people and traditions they miss.

Tasting Home p.101

Iranians of the Diaspora celebrate and maintain ties with their culture through food.

Art and Culture p.117

Contributors express their abiding appreciation for Iranian art, literature, music, and religion.

Islam and Other Faiths p.175

Writers explore Islam, Sufism, Zoroastrianism and other spiritual paths and how these faiths enrich or influence their lives.

A New Path Forward p.199

More Love Online...

We couldn't fit all of our contributors' work into our physical book; however, their essays, interviews and poems (presented alphabetically) are featured online at loveandpomagranates.com as well as other e-formats. We invite you to share your story on our blog.

"Forty Days in a Wilderness of Heartland," a poem by Brian H. Appleton on missing Iran.

"My Grandmother's Fesenjoon," a recipe contributed by Neilufar Naini in memory of Majideh Massumi.

"An Iranian Seder in Beverly Hills," by Joan Nathan.

"Norooz in New Jersey," a poem by Roger Sedarat about the Persian New Year.

"Modern Iranian Amulets," an excerpt by Bill Wolak and Mahmood Karimi-Hakak, exploring amulets, good luck charms, and protection from jinn.

"Reaching Out in Friendship, A Civilian Diplomat in Iran," by Bill Wolak, on the importance of cross-cultural experiences.

*X*enophon, an Athenian mercenary and adventurer who wrote a glowing biography of Cyrus the Great, wasn't always sure he wanted to travel to Iranian lands. After all, the Athenians had fought Iran at the epic battles of Marathon and Salamis, both traumatizing and foundational moments in the history of Western civilization. Though Xenophon lived a full century after those close calls, he felt enough trepidation to seek out no other than Socrates, who advised him to consult the oracle.[1]

Of course, Xenophon knew little of Iran before he headed east, and we today seem to know less still. Iran's political battles appear to us in shocking sound bites on the nightly news, usually following a brash statement from an Iranian politician, translated literally to cause the most alarm. In a country where regular greetings include phrases like, "I will sacrifice myself for you," and "step on my eye," it doesn't take much to take things out of context. Yes, we know very little about Iran, but the little we do know seems to make us want to proceed with caution, as Xenophon did before starting on his long journey some 2,200 years ago.

So what should we know about this land before embarking on our trip? The history and character of Iran is too vast to cover in a book, let alone a few pages, but some basic facts are essential. To start with, Iran is a very old country. It dates back some 2,500 years as a Persian-speaking nation that has for centuries been centered in the Iranian Plateau, a region that extends east from the Zagros Mountains on the border with Iraqi Kurdistan nearly to the Indus river. In contrast to Iran's longevity, most modern-day countries in the Middle East are in one way or another products of European colonial influence, with their national identity consciously honed by their leaders only in the last century.

Unlike most of its neighbors Iran is not an Arab country, but a diverse collection of ethnicities, which has traditionally been dominated by ethnic Persian culture and language, with origins in central Iran. Persia, or Pars, was a hub of Zoroastrian religious life in pre-Islamic Iran, and it was this name that the Greeks used for all of Iran. Until the 1930s, when leader Reza Shah asked the West to stop calling his country "Persia," most maps in Europe and the United States were still using the "P" word. Today, ethnic Persians comprise a plurality of the country, with Azeri Turks, Kurds, Luris, Baluchis, Arabs, and others making up the rest of the Iranian quilt.

Religion has also made Iran unique in the region. Iran today is a predominantly Shi'i Muslim country in a region that is mostly Sunni. Iranians usually tend to play down the differences between themselves and Sunnis, though many of their neighbors—particularly the more radical Sunnis—remain skeptical, even hostile to Shi'ism and Iran. Given Iran's unique character and history, and given its sheer size (70 million) it has had to go out of its way to reassure Arab countries that it is not hostile toward them. In fact, many of Iranian leaders' aggressive anti-American and anti-Israeli statements play well with the people of the region, and have ironically led to the increased popularity and security of an otherwise isolated Iran.

Iran's history begins with the reign of Cyrus the Great, who in 539 BC captured Babylon and famously freed the slaves and ordered the Temple of Jerusalem rebuilt. It was Cyrus, or at least the collective memory of him, that instilled in Iran a profound sense of what benevolent rule looks like. In the narrative of Iranian nationalism, Cyrus's cuneiform cylinder of laws is considered the first human rights charter.[2] This was at the dawn of the Achaemenid Empire, whose ruins at the winter palace of Persepolis still stand as a testament to the grandeur and achievements of the Iranian superpower. Its majestic sandstone pillars, its walls carved with images of Cyrus's adoring subjects, exemplify the architectural, engineering, and artistic genius of ancient Iran.

By the last pre-Islamic state (the Sasanian Empire, 224-651 AD) Iran's Zoroastrian faith became a codified, hierarchical, and priestly institution. Today, remnants of Zoroastrian practice are still felt, and the Persian New Year is a pagan holiday that comes second to none in Iran. Zoroastrians made use of earth, fire, and water in their rituals, and venerated a plethora of deities. Above all, however, was the supreme creator Ohrmazd (Ahura Mazda), whose importance makes the faith almost monotheistic in character. It was during the Sasanian era that the neighboring Byzantine Empire was codifying Christianity, and the Jewish communities of Iranian-ruled Babylon were doing the same with Judaism. Organized, monotheistic religion, as we know it and understand it today, was born in the Fertile Crescent at this time.

But there was another religion that would emerge in late antiquity: Islam. The Muslim faith began with the first revelations of the Prophet Muhammad in 610 AD, and soon formed the basis for a new Arab state. After Muhammad, the Muslim Empire—called the Caliphate—engaged in a lighting-fast military campaign that brought down Sasanian Iran and ushered in a new era in the Middle East. A gradual period of conversion began in Iran, and today the country is predominantly Muslim.

Iran, often called a land that conquers its conquerors, did manage to leave its mark on the Muslim faith: Islam eventually adopted the Zoroastrian staples of land endowment (Arabic: *waqf*) and the office of a religious judge (*qadi*). As time passed, Iranian-Islamic architecture—with its its non-representational geometric art and iconic blue tiles decorated with Quranic calligraphy—blossomed in Central Asian hubs such as Bukhara and Samarqand (modern-day Uzbekistan); and Iranian poets (Hafiz, Sa'di, Ferdowsi, etc.), philosophers (Mullah Sadra, al-Ghazali, etc.) and scientists (Khayyam, Ibn

Sina, etc.) seamlessly married Iranian aesthetics with Islamic theology and morals over the course of the centuries.

Politically, Iran saw periods of national revival and decline. By the time we get to the nineteenth century, however, Iran was thoroughly weak and divided, and left open to British and Russian exploitation of its economy and natural resources. This led to a series of popular movements to rid Iran of foreign intervention, which in 1905-6 touched off a period called the Constitutional Revolution—mass protests and grassroots civic action that led to the creation of a parliament and a written constitution.

During this time many in Iran had viewed the British as the source of most of the country's ills, but the transition of world power into US hands later in the century led to a rise in anti-Americanism. This was especially true when in 1953 the CIA orchestrated the toppling of prime minister Mohammad Mosaddeq. In protest against poor royalties and general mistreatment, Mosaddeq had nationalized the Anglo-Iranian Oil Company just two years prior, dealing a financial blow to Great Britain and prompting fears in Washington about the potential for a communist takeover.

After the coup, Mohammad Reza, the *shah*, or king of Iran, began to crack down on the nationalist opposition using his notorious secret police, the SAVAK. Iran became increasingly dictatorial, and in 1975 Amnesty International declared that the Shah "retains his benevolent image despite the highest rate of death penalties in the world, no valid system of civilian courts and a history of torture which is beyond belief."[3]

So long as the oil flowed to the West, however, US administrations looked the other way and continued friendly relations with Iran. Protests against the government became increasingly extremist and anti-American in nature, and Iran witnessed the emergence of a radical and politically charged clergy, along with secular militant groups seeking nothing short of revolution.

Revolution finally came in 1979, and Iranians got their political independence—but at great cost. That year, a group of students overran the US embassy and took hostages, keeping 52 of them for 444 days. In the meantime, neighboring Iraq planned an invasion to take advantage of Iran's internal unrest and international isolation. The Iran-Iraq War lasted eight years (1980-88) and proved to be one of the most serious existential threats in Iran's long history: Both world superpowers, the Soviet Union and the United States, joined forces with most neighboring Arab states to support Iraq. Iran hung on and the borders remained unchanged, but in the process an estimated one million lost their lives on both sides.

Just as the previous political system had done, the Islamic Republic of Iran has inspired increasing discontent, particularly around the strict enforcement of their version of Islamic law—which could include beatings and imprisonment for public displays of affection by unmarried couples, and in most extreme cases the death penalty for adultery and homosexuality. While Iran's government is on many fronts less politically restrictive than that of the shah, women and religious minorities have been worse off, given the state's interpretation of Islamic governance as male-dominated and compulsively "moral."

There are, however, positive developments in the society. Despite government quotas that have been established to bar women from several fields of study, women still

Love and Pomegranates

make up the majority of university students, and women hold positions at every level in the public and private sectors: many are university professors, business CEOs and parliamentarians, and Iran has had a female vice president. In the area of health care, Iran has also made great strides. The country's revolutionary methods of rural health are now serving as models for access in remote parts of the southern United States. Iran's long artistic history, which is at the heart of its age-old identity, flourishes today. The work of Iranian writers, artists, and especially the country's great filmmakers, have left an indelible mark on global culture—illuminating bookshelves, gallery walls, and movie screens in such cities as Dubai, New York, and Cannes.

This youthful and creative energy of Iran has only fueled opposition sentiment in the political realm, which reached fever pitch following the elections of June 12, 2009, when president Mahmoud Ahmadinejad was proclaimed the winner before the national vote could realistically have been counted. While Iran does not have a democracy, and real power officially lays in the clerical position of the Supreme Leader, the presidency has always been an important mechanism for citizens to express their political preference. The lack of respect for the voters ignited unrest on a scale not seen since the 1979 revolution.

The story of Iran is still being written. Politically, it remains divided, with its citizens clinging to different versions of what Iran should be, but all of them embracing the concept of justice, as they see it, and as established in the narratives of great leaders like Cyrus the Great. It is only fitting that the memory of Cyrus was the vehicle for Xenophon's writings on Iranian virtue. It wasn't a complete picture of the nation, to be sure, but it was an important part of the story, lost amidst the vitriolic memories espoused in Athens and the West. Xenophon's stories, not unlike those told by the authors of this book, are simply the other side of the coin.

Today, Iran continues to play a unique role in the Middle East, not only as a non-Arab, non-Sunni country, but as one that inspires both awe and consternation, with its controversial nuclear program and its aggressive tone toward the West. Iran is, and will likely always be, at the center of the world's attention—just as it was when Xenophon and Socrates sat down for a talk over two thousand years ago. ■

Nathan Gonzalez
Orange County, California
January 28, 2013

xviii

Iason Athanasiadis

Introduction

*P*rior to my first trip to Iran in March 2005, when I was invited to speak at the country's First International Children's Book Festival, I had looked for a book to help relieve doubts about my decision to go. At first, I found none. Then a friend gave me a copy of Alison Wearing's *Honeymoon in Purdah.* Wearing's account of her travels in Iran during the summer of 2000 helped me to deconstruct the myth that Iran is a haven of sequestered women and armed masked martyrs. Her book—infused with humor—showed me that I, too, would be welcomed there.

Love and Pomegranates: Artists and Wayfarers on Iran came about because my friends, colleagues and I have developed a profound appreciation of Iranian culture and an abundance of stories about the friendships we made and the generosity we received in Iran. On our journeys we found another Iran, one that lies in stark contrast to the ominous picture of their culture painted by the American and other Western mainstream media, which has repeatedly tainted our collective perspective on Iran. A recent study discovered that half of Americans view Iran as a threat and opinions of that country have worsened in recent years; yet, two thirds of us have never met an Iranian. Perhaps the study suggests that the media's focus on our nation's foreign policies and on the idea of national security prevents us from considering the richness of Persian history and culture, which reflects a long-held tradition of peace and hospitality.

Perhaps the bias against Iranians is bound up in a bias against Muslims. After the capture and killing of Osama Bin Laden in 2011 polls revealed that the perceived threat from Muslims living in the United States and abroad increased significantly. While many Iranians in the US and Iran are Muslim, they are also secular, Christian, Jewish, Zoroastrian, Bahai, or follow other spiritual paths. An Iranian acquaintance of mine living in Tehran attends her father's mosque and her mother's Catholic church. Dr. Carl

Love and Pomegranates

Ernst, a professor of Islamic Studies at University of North Carolina at Chapel Hill estimates that there are at least 300,000 Christians in Iran today. Historically, in Sasanian Iran, Christianity was a prominent religion and home to a number of Eastern churches that were considered heretical by the Byzantines.

Whatever the cause, the purpose of this anthology is to counter an insufficient understanding of a nation and its people. We hope this anthology of essays, interviews, poems and blogs from people who have traveled or lived in this country of golden deserts, cypress-scented mountains, and inexpressibly-beautiful tiled mosques, will help readers to better interpret the disinformation and stereotypes about Iran that might eclipse what the human heart may discover: a warm, educated and artistic people, whose dreams are much like our own. We are hopeful that this collection will help to inspire others to get to know their Iranian neighbors at home and perhaps even travel to Iran.

Indeed, I made many new friends and acquaintances in Iran. So have all the contributors to this collection. This volume is enriched by their varied backgrounds; here are voices of botanists, a Persian *dafs* musician, a radio show host, professors of Persian history and literature, filmmakers, grandmothers, teachers, carpet dealers, adult and children's book writers. Many are of Western ancestry and thus have little or no familial ties with Iran. Few knew each other prior to submitting their work for this anthology. I think of each of them as "missionaries in reverse," a term borrowed from musician Cameron Powers, who has traveled in the Middle East connecting with people through the love of music as founder of Musical Missions of Peace. The American contributors in this anthology did not go to Iran to promote Western culture or to preach any religion. They went to learn from our supposed foe, to enrich and enlighten their own lives through their experiences. Reading their work, I felt a rind peeling back and seeds of a new garden spilling over me—a leafy space where a fresh breeze of conversation flows. Their testimonies bestow a pomegranate-like radiance by which others may see.

The Iranian contributors' memories and praise for Iran spoke of love: of friends and relatives missed; of a deep yearning for the sands of their homeland; of Persian cooking, art, classical literature, music and traditions.

Many of the contributors visited Iran for a few weeks, others worked and lived there for several years. Some grew up in Tehran, but now live in the United States and other Western countries. A few of them have always lived in Iran. What the non-Iranians have in common are fond memories of those they've met during their stays in Iran. As Rowan Storm writes in her blog, "These everyday meetings with vulnerable and open-hearted people are what provide the foundation for making a difference in this world." The Iranian voices of the diaspora and of those living in Iran give us a seldom-heard view of their homeland, one which defies the bleak picture painted by some expats whose voices have become hostages of yesterday's demons. The Iranian writers in this collection move beyond the past with an open mind, give us the opportunity to hear their questions and know their assessment of us, from which we may grow.

Dr. Martin Luther King said during the Vietnam War, "The world now demands of America a maturity we may not be able to achieve." He called for a worldwide fellowship "that lifts neighborly concern beyond one's tribe, race, class and nation," and for "an all-embracing and unconditional love for all men." The writers in this anthology from both East and West, who have made an effort to find themselves in others, help show our diplomats and public officials a path toward that maturity. The synchronicity, the friendships, and forces that drew these writers from many different continents together in this book is—to borrow a notion from the late Cistercian monk Thomas Merton—"an epiphany of certainties we could not know in isolation." An epiphany that affirms a deep belief that there is a more sympathetic way to live and gaze upon this world. President Barack Obama's rhetoric toward Iran seems to suggest a willingness to undertake a small but crucial step toward Dr. King's dream of a mature America. One that may lead the world to a more inclusive vision of compassion.

In This Collection

Within, you will find a communion of spirits among new voices from many countries: America, Iran, Greece, New Zealand, Britain, Turkey, and more. Original essays will take you, among many other destinations, into a bakery in Tehran to bake bread; on a journey from Tabriz to the Turkish-Iranian border in search of a lost passport; alongside a painter whose work is transformed at the foot of Hafiz's shrine in Shiraz; into the heart of an Iranian poet as she questions her new American identity; high into the Alborz Mountains to discover flowering lamb's ear (*Stachys byzantina*) in its native haunts; deep into the woods on a dark winter night to witness a Zoroastrian fire ritual; and beneath a bridge over the River Zayandeh to smoke *hookah*.

Love and Pomegranates opens with the section *First Impressions and Persian Hospitality* which captures immediate reactions to Iran as written in blogs as well as reflective essays on returning to Iran after a prolonged absence. It also holds stories of Iranians of the diaspora stepping foot on the soil of their ancestors for the first time and tales of random acts of kindness experienced by Westerners, such as a spontaneous all-day tour with a stranger. Natives talk about tourists they've hosted or welcomed to their country. In the section *Finding Ourselves in the Other* Westerners talk about Iranians they've known and loved, and about finding common ground with others they've just met. Iranians living outside of Iran write about their adjustment to their adopted countries, their nostalgia for the traditions of their homeland and what it means to be part of the diaspora. The sections *Arts and Culture* and *Islam and Other Faiths* share stories by artists and scholars who traveled to Iran in pursuit of their muse or work. They express their admiration for Iranian musicians, painters, writers, Islamic saints, Sufis, nature, art and architecture. *A New Path Forward* touches upon the United States' past and current relationship with Iran. It includes thoughts on how the West might move toward a better understanding of Iranians at home and abroad through cultural, academic and medical exchanges, as well as other creative avenues.

A theme running through many of these essays by contributors from both East and West, involves having experienced in Iran a sense of ecstasy—a communion with a larger reality, a universal light. It seemed fitting to include in this collection poems by the classical Persian Sufi poets Hafiz, Sa'di, Khayyam, Ferdowsi, 'Attar, Rumi and others, writers who call us to a deeper consciousness and who remind us that only love will help us evolve. No book celebrating the richness of Iranian culture could be without them. In keeping with Persian tradition, some of the selections of these poems were made by the contributors opening books by their favorite poets to a random page. This age-old practice has proven that the words found in the poetry offer wisdom or even an anecdote for whatever question or problem the reader or seeker might be experiencing at the time. We encourage you to read this collection in a similar spirit of openness.

It is my hope that the depiction of life in Iran in this anthology will lift you out of this period in history in which we sometimes reduce people and nations to simplistic groupings of good and evil. *Love and Pomegranates* is a gesture of peace. ∎

Meghan Nuttall Sayers

Bazaar ~ Fahimeh Amiri

First Impressions
and Persiah Hospitality

The Fragrance of Naan

Shahrokh Nikfar

In March 2000, Shahrokh Nikfar, a US citizen who was born and raised in Tehran, returned to his homeland for the first time in 21 years, having left just prior to the 1979 revolution.

I am dead against it!" Nahid had said. From the moment I had brought up the idea of going to Iran, my sister began to worry. For a month before my trip, she called me nearly every day to discourage me. And there her voice was again, warning me at an altitude of 30,000 feet, on a plane bound for Tehran.

"This is not the same Iran we grew up in. That Iran has been lost and the people have changed. Iran has turned into a dungeon and you will be lucky if you get back alive!"

I tossed and turned in my seat, trying to shut out her voice. But admittedly I had my own reservations and worries to struggle with. I wondered if my relatives in Iran would resent me for moving to America, or call me an anti-revolutionary and turn me over to the authorities.

The temperature in the cabin seemed to drop. I felt cold even after pulling the flimsy blue blanket over me. I leaned against the window and decided to focus on something positive: the event that inspired my trip—the welcome back party I attended for my friend Saeed and his wife Shelly, just after they returned from Iran. I had expected a story of doom and gloom. But when I asked Saeed if the Iranian officials gave them a hard time, he said no.

"In fact, we felt ignored by them." He told me they were met with hospitality everywhere they went. I was surprised by his answer, attributing this warmth to the nature of his Iranian relatives. But then his story changed. "A pick pocket stole my wife's purse!" he said. "So we went to the police station to report it."

Uh-oh! I thought to myself; what an idiot. Didn't he know he should have avoided all contacts with anybody who carried a gun or had any affiliation with the Islamic Republic?

"What did they do to you?" I braced myself for the inevitable story of how they were abused and mistreated once it became known that they were from America.

"Nothing," he said. "In fact, they were so embarrassed that a guest in their country was robbed, they passed around a hat and got a collection to reimburse my wife for what she had lost."

"What?" I said, almost yelling. "Are you making this up?"

"No, Shahrokh. That's what happened!" Saeed spoke about how wonderful everyone was and how much fun they had in Iran. Remembering that night, as I looked into the darkness outside of the airplane window, my sister's voice faded away as I slowly fell asleep.

When we landed at the airport in Tehran, the cabin filled with movement. In what seemed like an orchestrated effort, the female passengers started covering themselves with headscarves and raincoats to hide their hair and flesh. Once off the plane, I joined a line for customs. It all seemed normal, but I felt the collective anxiety. As I moved up the line, I saw a bearded man wearing a suit but no tie, a look that designates one's position as an official with the Islamic Republic. I had heard they had the authority to whisk anyone away, never to be heard from again. The official seemed to be inspecting the passengers, as if he were waiting to catch someone making a false move. I tried not to look at him, but felt him watching me. I couldn't help but feel like something bad was about to happen. Sure enough, he started walking toward me. The other passengers distanced themselves as he approached. With an ominous expression, he asked for my passport and then ordered me to come with him.

With my heart racing and my knees quivering, I followed him to his desk. I recalled my sister's warnings about going to Iran and began to regret that I didn't heed her advice. I pictured her waving an index finger at my corpse. "Didn't I tell you not to go?"

"What is the purpose of your visit?" the official asked.

I took a deep breath. "I have been away for too long." My hands shook. "It was time for me to come home."

When he was done entering my passport number into his computer, he locked eyes with mine and handed back my passport. Then, he smiled. "Welcome to Iran." In a state of shock, I walked out the door and into the reception area, where a dozen of my relatives and old high school friends swarmed around, hugging me, kissing me on both cheeks and telling me how happy they were to see me.

Every day I was greeted by relatives and old friends who came to welcome me back and to express their desire to host me at their homes. Many of them weren't financially well off, yet they managed to prepare the most scrumptious meals and gave me many generous gifts. I felt guilty, yet out of respect, I couldn't refuse their generosity.

I really liked everyone I met, but there was one person in particular who left a lasting impression. His name was Mohsen, and at sixteen years old, he was the eldest grandchild of one of my hosts. From the moment I arrived at his family's house in the late afternoon, Mohsen kept asking me to go for a walk with him. After dinner, I agreed to go. Mohsen was overjoyed. As we left the house, I noticed a small crowd following us everywhere we went, and I couldn't help but wonder if it was a gang out to rob us. After a couple of blocks, I asked Mohsen, "Have you noticed that we're being followed?"

"They're the neighbor kids who have been waiting outside to see you," he said, blushing as he looked down and kicked a pebble. "I've been bragging about you and they wanted to meet my cousin from America."

So I turned around and said hello. They greeted me with the sweetest and most innocent smiles I'd ever seen. The younger kids giggled and kept saying in English, "Hello," as the older ones welcomed me back to Iran. And then came the questions.

"Have you met Sylvester Stallone?" one kid asked. Then, another asked if I knew Arnold Schwarzenegger. The queries were followed by offers of food and invitations to their homes. I thanked them and asked if they would walk with us instead, a request that they met with exuberance.

Strolling near a barber shop lit up with neon signs, Moshen took my hand and pulled me inside. The neighborhood entourage followed. Moshen told the barber, "Haji Ali, this is Mr. Nikfar. He is my cousin from America." The man had a kind face and offered me a free haircut. "You are my guest," he insisted, a refrain I'd hear often in Iran.

Deeper into the neighborhood, I smelled freshly-baked *naan*. Just as I finished telling the kids that in America I have no access to this kind of bread back home, they turned toward the bakery. I tried to tell them that I was still full from dinner and could not eat another bite, but they were determined to get me the bread. It felt as if I had rubbed a magic lamp and my little genies were trying to fulfill my every wish. But there was a line of about fifteen people in the bakery, so I suggested we turn back. The kids wouldn't give up so easily.

"Move aside, our guest is from America and he wants some bread!" Mohsen said. And just like the parting of the Red Sea, a path appeared for us to walk through to the front of the line. At first I was horrified of having insulted the people in line, but no one seemed to mind. As if I weren't amazed and grateful enough, the bakers gathered around me to shake my hand and offer me their best baked bread. After introducing ourselves, I told them about how as a child I always wondered what it would be like to work in a bakery. Then, before I knew it, one of them took me behind the counter and put an apron on me. Another showed me how to knead the dough and stretch it across my knuckles to make a large disc, much like preparing a pizza. The crowd had tripled by this time and I could hear voices saying that I was from America. Everyone was smiling, not minding the delay, and when I proudly pulled my first baked naan out of the oven, the crowd cheered.

Sometime later we finally left the bakery and headed back to Mohsen's house. But the kids had a hard time letting me go. "Would you come and have dinner with my family tomorrow night?" several asked. One of the older kids invited me to visit him the next time I'm in Iran. "We'll get you some kabobs to go with the bread," he said. I told them I would come back soon, and wondered if I was making a false promise. I simply didn't know how long it would be before I could take this journey again.

On the day of my departure, my flight home was at 3:30 AM, so I decided to take a nap after dinner before having to leave for the airport. But friends and relatives kept dropping by to see me one last time, and they all came bearing gifts. My two bags were already full, and so now I had to come up with an extra suitcase. I was overjoyed by their generosity.

The next surprise was that everyone stayed until midnight and then insisted on going to the airport to see me off, even though it was a one-hour drive each way, and they all had to be at work in the morning. But no matter how hard I tried to dissuade them, many of them came. However, that wasn't the end of the surprises that night.

When we arrived at the airport, I was shocked to see Mohsen and one of the neighborhood kids there with two of the bakers. Like the others, they'd brought gifts, as well as freshly-baked bread, which they'd wrapped in a beautiful cloth. It took all my strength to keep from crying.

Sitting in my window seat staring at the airport lights, all I could think about was my family and friends in Iran. They had helped me reconnect with the place my soul was born. Everyone I had met was warm, beautiful and gentle, and how even going for a walk had become a joyful experience for me. I recalled kids playing on the streets, young couples walking hand-in-hand on the tree-lined sidewalks, and street musicians humbly peddling for a few coins. Contrary to my expectations, nobody resented me or wanted to take me hostage or hurt me. All they wanted was to be friendly and to go about their daily lives as they worked to make ends meet.

As the plane lifted, I started to re-examine my previous feelings for Iran, realizing now what had become lost to me over the past couple of decades: The real Iran was totally different from the images I had formulated in my head with the help of the mainstream media. The events of the past 21 years do not represent what Iran and its people are about. Iran is a land of poetry, compassion, love and respect. It's a place of great generosity.

Catching a whiff of the bread on my lap, I opened the cloth and ripped off a piece. I chewed it slowly, savoring its taste, knowing I would have to go back soon, to feed my soul.

Stones in a New Garden

Aphrodite Désirée Navab

As the Iran Air plane was landing in Tehran's international airport, I began to tremble. Excitement mingled with fear, making my leg shake against my neighbor's seat. "It has been 21 years," I said, attempting to explain the trembling to my neighbor.

It was August 2001. I made my way through the airport, as if I had been there only a month before. I grabbed my suitcase from the conveyer belt and got in line. Once my passport was stamped, I stumbled out of the building, stunned by how easy and uneventful the arrival process was.

The past and present curled themselves into one corner of my mind. I was nine years old, wailing in unison with my three siblings. Each child clutched the other's hand in a line with our mother. A shadow of paper cut-out figures moved along the airport's floor. We kept looking back at our father, who was not allowed to go beyond the security checkpoint. He stared until his entire family disappeared. Two years later, after getting permission to seek medical care abroad for his heart failure, my father joined us. As a family, we never returned to Iran.

A slender woman in a red headscarf and brown raincoat, pulling me out of past recollections, pushed her way through. As she got closer to me, a bigger and older version of my cousin Nooshin appeared:

"Désirée!"

"Nooshin!"

"Désirée!"

"Nooshin!"

We repeated and confirmed each other's call, until recognition was complete.

"Come. First, let's take a taxi to my apartment and stay overnight. Tomorrow you can take a bus to Esfahan," she said, slipping her arm through mine and forcing me to skip as we did when we were children.

"So absolutely wonderful," the tall and talkative taxi driver kept remarking, with typical Persian hyperbole, "that your Esfahani accent is so strong after 21 years of living outside!"

"Thank you so much, I know," I replied, equally sincere and insincere. I looked at Nooshin who rolled her eyes. His statement conveyed both a compliment and a simultaneous insult. "It is so great that you have not forgotten your language," he said, but "the years have not softened your provincial accent," is what he was implying, too.

Once on the highway, I cracked the window open. An enormous sign overhead traveled across the sky. Like a title across a movie screen, I saw my family's name: Navab Highway: *Bozorg rah-e Navab*, written in both English and Persian.

"There is such a thing as this?" I said, looking at Nooshin and then the driver, pointing at the sign. "There is such a highway as this?" My heart pounding with pride.

"Of course, that's the exit for it over there," the driver said. "And not only that, there is a Navab station on the metro, too. It's a very old Esfahani family."

I looked at Nooshin. We squeezed each other's hands, smiling. I closed my eyes. One highway marker wiped away years of shame in the United States: *Go back home Navab! Go back home you dirty Iranian!* Across the sky, I saw my family name. Home is where they know your name.

Distant relatives and food filled Nooshin's apartment. I spent the whole night reconnecting to the family and dishes that I had no access to for 21 years. When I tasted the dried watermelon seeds or *naan-e sangak*, bread baked with stones, I remembered the taste as if it were yesterday. I talked through the night with Roshanak, catching up on experiences we did not share. The time that went away, brought us closer. The next day, I took a bus from Tehran to Esfahan. At the bus stop I caught a taxi. Entering Esfahan at night, I chanted lines I've pondered before: "A stranger to my homeland, even if you should take my hand. Even if we should exchange sand, strangers we will be. The home you were, you are not now. The child I was, I put away inside, all these years and years outside" (Navab, 2009, p. 316).

The closer the taxi got to my childhood home, however, the more the child inside me came out to direct him. I rolled down my window to be led by my senses. The summer air had the same smoky, sweet smell of old. The street names had all changed but the look and feel of my neighborhood had not. The scent of *balal*, barbecue corn, and kabab from street vendors permeated the air, alternating between the scent of roses and cypress trees. Each scent came back to me as though my child and adult selves had become one.

"Over there, near the Khaju bridge, you make a right. My home is in that *koocheh*, alley." I told the driver. I lived near the Zayandeh river, in the center of the city, but I saw no water in it that night.

"Why is there no river?" I asked.

"There has been an awful drought. Mismanagement of water. They say that the water will be redirected in a month," he said.

"Can you stop for one moment?" I asked.

Love and Pomegranates

An urge took over me. I got out of the taxi, walked past the grass, down the steps and onto the dry riverbed. I kneeled down and kissed the sand. Twenty-one years earlier, my three siblings and I kissed the tarmac when we arrived in New York City.

"You have been away a long time, haven't you?" the taxi driver asked me.

"Yes, too long." I climbed back in.

"But not so long that you still don't know your way home, eh?" he winked.

"Twenty-one years is too long," I said, looking out the window. "I wanted to hug my grandparents, Hajkhanom and Baba Navab, like I always could," I adjusted my headscarf, hiding my tears. "I would hear their voices when my father would call them on the phone. But the connection grew weaker and weaker until it stopped altogether."

I heard sniffling that wasn't coming from me. I looked at the driver; tears were flowing down *his* face!

"Honoring your ancestors is a great thing to do. I have to share your story with my wife. Good things can come from America," he said.

"Good things can come from either direction," I responded, thanking him.

A few minutes later, we arrived. Luxury apartment buildings that were not there before, surrounded my childhood home. Even if overshadowed, my former house still held its ground. My father's sister Ameh Meri had moved into this home with her husband and two children, shortly after my father joined us in the United States. She moved my grandparents in, too, and took care of them until they died. She has lived there ever since.

As I walked into the living room, time stood still. The same relatives whom I left, whom I could neither see nor hold for 21 years, were right there—older, more fragile, but sitting right there.

Only my grandparents were not. My heart searched for their faces in the crowd, while my mind saw their images in picture frames. In one month I would visit their graves, resolving heart and mind.

The lights went out and I panicked. It took me back to the revolution when there was martial law, no electricity and we had the gas lamps on.. *No, it can't be!* I thought to myself, shrinking to the terrified child I once was.

Out came my Amoo Reza from the darkness, wrapping me in his arms, reassuring me: "Don't worry, it has something to do with the drought and electricity. It's been going on like this for weeks, but it's random."

Seconds later, the lights came back on, weaving my past memory into a new one, marked by the joy of reunion.

A few days later, I was having dinner with my relatives at an outdoor restaurant. A stranger came up to me, placing a firm hand on my shoulder.

"Do you recognize me?" she asked with confidence.

I had no clue at first, growing uncomfortable. *Who is this woman?* She had a nose job and heavy makeup, veiling herself further.

"I never thought I would see Désirée Navab in Esfahan again! I am Niloofar," she said. "Remember we used to play at our parents' parties? Remember we used to play soccer together and swim in my pool. We used to put…"

"…black pepper in our brothers' sodas. Yes, Niloofar Mohee, I recognize you!" I hugged her. We talked for hours and days thereafter, deafening the years that had gone silent.

Encounters like this would happen every few days, disorienting and reorienting me. A month had passed and the Zayandeh river flowed again. Families celebrated from dawn to dusk by swimming in its waters and picnicking on its banks. It was time to talk to my grandparents.

Ameh Meri, her daughter Nooshin, and I took a car to the cemetery. They taught me what I had to do, Iranian-style. We bought bottled water to wash their graves. We bought flowers. I brought an empty glass jar.

As I walked past rows and rows of stone graves, I noticed that unlike any cemeteries I had seen thus far, no vegetation was allowed to grow on or around the graves. As I looked ahead in the distance, a sight arrested me. From a respectful distance hundreds of Cypress trees stood at attention surrounding the graveyard. I wept at the funeral procession that we never saw.

As I washed my grandparents' graves, writing appeared on the surface: their names engraved in Persian calligraphy. Abol Hassan Navab and Esmat Navab. I knelt and kissed the letters. My grandparents lay side by side.

I then lay down on their graves. Pressing my face against the wet stone, I whispered, "Hajkhanom and Baba Navab, I am here." I could picture them. Memories came to me of gigantic pots of kebab and rice that Hajkhanom made for my family every weekend. I saw a pretty and plump woman in her translucent and flower-patterned chador, smoking tobacco from the hookah. With henna in her nails and her white hair, I would see orange and white shapes bob up and down, as Hajkhanom did her prayers three times a day. Baba Navab would sit in the garden, sipping his tea with a cube of sugar between his teeth, while reading the newspapers in Persian and German. A thin man always in an elegant suit, how wise and peaceful he seemed. Once governor of Esfahan, he was entrusted with the inheritance of orphans.

As I sat back on my heels and looked into the polished stone of my grandparents' graves, a Rumi poem came to me. *Keep polishing and polishing your soul, until it reflects the beauty of the world.* Reflecting on the graves were the cypress trees, the desert sky, and the grieving granddaughter.

I filled a glass jar with the stones and soil that made a home on their graves. I took over a hundred photographs to mark the reunion and bring it back with me. I witnessed that from the deepest sorrow, delight—her sister—can grow. I would replant the stones and soil on a new continent.

As a child in Esfahan I used to stare at the evening sky from a family swing in my courtyard. I was convinced that each time a new star appeared in the sky, one more cricket jumped into my garden. At first solitary and slow, but then crowded and fast, the stars joined the crickets in a symphony that I continue to carry within me.

From my terrace in New York City, I stare at another skyline. As each skyscraper window alights, cars flash in rhythm along the FDR Drive. In my terrace garden, I can't tell anymore which are the stones that were transplanted.

The Fruit of Persian Hospitality

James Opie

James Opie spent years traveling in the Middle East for his Oriental carpet business. He visited Iran over a dozen times, during the "Shah's time" and after the Islamic Revolution. This essay describes his first trip there.

We met Banafsheh not long after we arrived at the bazaar in Tabriz. My wife Patricia and I had been meandering through the crowds, moving from shop to shop, soaking in a sense of *the real Persia* when the young woman approached and asked us if we knew English.

I turned away, hesitant to answer, having previously traveled to other Middle Eastern countries where locals invite unsuspecting tourists to their relative's shops to sell them something. It often begins with them walking up with a seemingly friendly smile and saying they would like to practice their English. I was wise to them; however, Patricia was not.

"Yes, we speak English," she said.

I held my tongue and wandered away, too tired to deal with the situation, the stress of the long day having caught up with me. Patricia and I had spent the morning crossing by land from Turkey into Iran. Although it was exhilarating, making the nearly 200-mile trek from the Turkish border to Tabriz in over 100-degree heat was also exhausting. Thirsty, tired from driving, jangled a bit from "border-crossing nerves," Patricia and I inevitably grew cranky. At some point we had agreed not to speak for a while.

But soon the pungent smells of the spice shops, the tightly woven Tabriz carpets, and the intricately decorated mosaic boxes that filled several shops helped lift our cloud of irritability and soon we were speaking cheerfully to one another again.

And so, as Patricia continued talking with the young woman, I looked at rugs in a nearby shop. Glancing back now and then, I saw that Patricia still had not managed to get free. Eventually I gave up on avoiding the situation and joined them. It was then that I realized that this attractive young woman—dressed in modest Western clothing—was genuine in her eagerness to practice her English, which was already quite good.

"You are from *United States*?!" she said. Her joy was sincere. Her sparking eyes and bubbly tone made it feel truly important to be living, breathing *Americans* here in the

Tabriz bazaar. She opened up to us as if she had been waiting there only for our arrival. It was then that she told us her name was Banafsheh.

The three of us walked together for an hour in the bazaar, where Banafsheh cautioned us against buying from the shadier merchants. Later she surprised us with an invitation to visit a garden in her neighborhood and dinner in her family home. Patricia smiled and answered for us both, saying that we would be delighted.

Admittedly I was still uncertain about just what we were getting into. But driving to the garden, walking among its fragrant roses, and then entering Banafsheh's home, my resistance gradually evaporated as I saw that this young woman represented a side of her country that Americans too rarely see: open, cheerful, inquisitive and respectful. She asked us so many questions—about parents and siblings, nephews and nieces, where we lived and what we did—that we had to keep bending the topic back her way in order to learn anything about her. She told us that she graduated from the University of Tehran recently and would return there soon for more schooling to receive a degree in medicine. She also told us that when she wasn't in school she spent all her free time with her parents, helping her mother. Then she spoke of how sorry she was that her parents could not be there to join us.

"They must meet you," she said. "My mother will love to cook for you." Then she told us to relax and disappeared into the kitchen. She returned a few minutes later with a large plate full of sliced cucumbers. As I bit into one, thinking to myself that it seemed like a strange hors d'oeuvre to serve guests, Banafsheh said that in Iran cucumbers are considered fruit. That's strange too, I thought.

It was while I was eating a second or third slice of cucumber that I suddenly realized that my passport was missing. I always kept it in my shirt pocket, but it wasn't there. Without explaining to either Patricia or Banafsheh, I excused myself to look in the van. But no passport. Thinking about our whereabouts earlier that day, I distinctly remembered having it when we went through customs at the Turkish/Iranian border. I knew that I had to have had it then in order to pass through both the Turkish and Iranian customs. And now it was gone.

Eventually I returned to the house, where Patricia and Banafsheh were huddled together like cousins. Resisting the temptation to tell them about the missing passport, I smiled and pretended to listen to the conversation, all the while racking my brains, struggling to picture the moment when I last saw it.

I visualized the face of the clean-shaven Iranian customs policeman who inspected our visas. He had both of our passports open in front of him and stamped them with rapid gestures that he had surely practiced many times. These clear memories made it certain that he had taken my passport from me. But did he hand it back? The only picture I could bring into clear focus after that encounter was a large stone bowl of pistachios placed at the doorway we passed through to officially enter Iran. Since the bowl was located just after the office of our passport inspector, I reasoned that the passport was in my hand at that point. But then what happened?

I waited until Banafsheh left the room for more tea and then asked Patricia to look for our passports. Only hers was in her purse, so we both went to look for mine in the van. When we went back inside, Patricia explained what had happened, and then—on

Banafsheh's insistence—we all went back outside, and together we scoured every crack and crevice of the van. But still no passport.

When we went back inside, Banafsheh began making preparations for dinner. Patricia followed, while I stewed in the living room alone, fighting the urge to search the van again. Sounds of water running and clanging of pots and pans suggested that dinner was taking shape. A little later appealing smells began wafting into the living room. As I sat there, I glanced over at the plate on the table and noticed that there were still a few slices of cucumber left. I ate one, wondering again why Iranians considered this bland vegetable a *fruit*.

I was still thinking about the passport, when Banafsheh came in and started setting the table. Then we had a lovely Persian meal of *morassa' pollo*, rice with chicken, nuts, raisins, orange peel and barberries. Individual servings of yoghurt, onions and unleavened bread were all quite tasty. Listening to Patricia and Banafsheh talk about the meal, enjoying the food myself, I joined the conversation and finally managed to forget about the passport. But only for a little while.

As we ate our dessert, Banafsheh turned to me. "I see that you are very worried about your passport," she said. "I think you want to go to your van and look some more." Surprised by her comment, I admitted that she was right. She then told us a story about the mythological Middle Eastern sage, Mullah Nasreddin, who once lost the key to his house.

"*One night the Mullah Nasreddin was crawling on his hands and knees near a lamp post located a few yards from his home,*" Banafsheh began. As she continued—with effective voice modulations to represent the two characters—my mind wanted to drift off toward my passport. But I listened. "*A neighbor came by and saw the Mullah on his hands and knees. The neighbor said, 'Have you lost something, Mullah?'*

'Yes. I have lost the key to my house.'

The neighbor was not in a hurry and so he too got on his hands and knees and looked. After a while his knees began to hurt and the neighbor said, 'Mullah, are you really sure that you lost your key here?'

Mullah Nasreddin said, 'No. I think I actually lost it over there, closer to my house.'

'If you lost it close to your house, then why we are looking for it here?!'

The Mullah replied, 'Because it's dark there. The light is so much better here!'"

Banafsheh and Patricia laughed heartedly. I managed to laugh a little too.

"You see how it fits," she said. "You keep looking for your lost passport in your van—the easy place—even though it can not be found there. The *light* is better there! You see. It's just like in the story!"

"I suppose you're right," I said.

That night, having accepted Banafsheh's gracious invitation to stay at her home, I was finally able to put the passport out of my mind. But the problem was waiting for me—for all three of us—first thing in the morning. Without much discussion Patricia and I agreed to return to the border.

"I'll go with you," Banafsheh said as she poured us morning tea.

"No, please," I said. "You've been too kind to us already."

But she insisted. "There could be problems," she pointed out. "You'll need me to translate for you." Then, she made several phone calls to postpone appointments she had scheduled for that day.

The three of us piled into the van and Banafsheh directed me through Tabriz toward the highway leading to the Turkish border. In nearly every village along the way, Banafsheh asked me to stop so that she could treat us to whichever fruit thrived in that particular area. Regarding special apples that she purchased for us in one village, she said, "These are the sweetest in Iran. You will see."

During our third stop—this time to purchase pears—she finally allowed me to pay. Later, back in the van, I looked into the rearview mirror and saw Banafsheh struggling to keep her eyes open. But when we finally reached the border, she insisted she was fine. "I was just relaxing my eyes," she said.

We walked into the customs office, where Banafsheh did all of the talking. After hushed exchanges on the part of the customs employees, it became clear that they indeed had my passport. What was less clear was whether they would return it to me.

The customs officer explained to Banafsheh that the passport had already been reported to Tehran and therefore could only be released if superiors in Tehran approved. He was forbidden, he said, to simply hand it back to me, adding that the law required foreigners to be able to produce passports on demand. Banafsheh insisted on my behalf, then applied charm, and then insisted again. I watched as the officer's resolve weakened. Finally he relented.

Driving back to Tabriz, I wasn't thinking about my passport and how lucky I was to have it back; instead I was thinking about the lengths this young woman had gone to in order to help us, then wondering if I would have done a third as much to help a foreigner in trouble, or if any stranger in the United States would have put themselves out this much to help me.

As we pulled up to her home, Banafsheh said, "Please stay in Tabriz a few more days. My parents will be so unhappy to not have met you."

Unfortunately our plans did not permit it, as we were already days behind schedule. So, Patricia and I made use of all of the Persian and English words we knew in order to express our gratitude. Before we left, however, Banafsheh brewed a final pot of tea and urged us to eat our fill of the fruit of Persian hospitality: *cucumbers*. As I ate a slice—feeling the seeds explode in my mouth—it suddenly occurred to me how sweet it was. A fruit, indeed. Since then any time I eat a cucumber I think of Banafsheh.

Sarah S. Forth

*I*t was already dark when I stepped outside, but I didn't mind. I was thrilled to be out on my own on the streets of historic Esfahan, away from our tour group for the first time in a week, walking amongst the crowds hastening home. The wide sidewalk was filled with men in suit jackets and open-collared dress shirts, and women dressed in calf-length coats and scarves—as I was—or in the more traditional *chador*, a voluminous sweep of dark material held together under the chin.

As I made my way back to the hotel from the Internet café, where I had just spent the last hour answering e-mail from home, I took in as much of the city as I could. I breathed in the dry autumn air, inhaling the smells I was now beginning to associate with Iran: a mix of car exhaust, meat grilling over charcoal, and desert dust blowing in from the vast open spaces beyond the cities. My eyes, meanwhile, drank in the vibrant mix of the familiar—Korean sedans and Japanese motorcycles—with the new—two-feet wide water channels at the edge of every street, and curbs carefully marked with bright blue paint. Walking through the city gave me a rush of discovering things utterly new to me, that is until I realized I might indeed be lost.

I stopped for a moment to take in my surroundings, trying to piece together what I was seeing with the directions our Iranian guide Farzaneh had given me and my two compatriots when she dropped us off at the Internet café.

"This street runs behind Emam Square, where we were this morning," she had said. "Remember?"

Of course I remembered, immediately seeing a picture in my head of the massive rectangular plaza built in the seventeenth century by the visionary Shah Abbas I, with its two blue-domed mosques decorated with ceramic mosaics that were among the very best in the Islamic world.

Farzaneh continued with the directions, instructing us to walk several blocks, turn right and follow the street that ran through the square. Our hotel would be on the other side. It seemed simple enough that I stayed on at the café by myself to finish answering my e-mail when my traveling companions left. No problem, I thought; once I find the square, I'll find the hotel.

But now, here I was, alone with a flicker of fear in my chest, wondering if I would recognize the intersection where I was supposed to turn. The confidence I had on previous excursions in foreign cities quickly diminished. I became more aware of the darkness, as there were few street lamps, illumination coming mainly from the passing cars and neon shop signs. The lack of light made walking along the old and uneven sidewalks difficult. Crossing the street also proved challenging; I had to find the narrow walkway across the water channel and then dodge traffic, which generally obeyed the drivers' inclinations rather than any traffic signal.

Eventually I arrived at what looked like a major intersection and decided this must be where Farzaneh said to turn right. But one block later I came to a two-story wall of centuries-old, sun-dried brick: the backside of the arcade of shops that lined the sides of the great square. There was no through street. I turned around and retraced my steps. As I walked, my stomach started to rumble with hunger. Looking at my watch, I realized I had only fifteen minutes to make it back to the hotel in time to leave for dinner with the tour group. I worried that my being late might inconvenience the tour group and their dinner plans, or cause Farzaneh undue trouble. I picked up my pace.

As if summoned by my Iranian guardian angel, a chador-clad woman pushing a stroller came towards me from a side street. The woman was young and beautiful with classic Persian features: dark eyes, soft cheeks, and high cheekbones. A small girl tramped alongside her, clutching her mother's robes.

"*Bebakhshid, khanoom*," I said, "Excuse me, madam." I was thankful for what little Persian I had learned from my language tapes. "*Meydan-e Emam kojast?* Where is the Emam Square?"

The woman gestured back the way I had come and said something I didn't understand. She read the blank look on my face and her expression grew concerned. And then she asked me where I was from.

"America."

Her face lit up and she smiled that same smile I had been seeing since I stepped off the plane in Tehran. "*Amrika!*" she said. And then she redoubled her efforts to explain where I was to go, gesturing assertively. I caught only some of it, but nodded affirmatively, the way foreigners often do, hoping that in the end everything will turn out right.

"*Moteshakeram*," I thanked her repeatedly before walking back towards the Internet café, which I eventually passed. It was then that I wondered if I had misunderstood Farzaneh, if I was supposed to have turned left when I exited the café.

I looked at my watch again, seeing that I had only ten minutes to get back to the hotel. Farzaneh was very protective of her group members, so if I didn't turn up, she might feel the need to contact the police. I didn't want it to come to that.

Once again I turned off the main street onto an intersecting street in search of the magic pathway through the Emam Square. I walked one block, then another. I spotted a mustachioed merchant lounging in the doorway of his store. I was nervous about approaching a strange man, but hoped that maybe he would know a little English, as many shopkeepers did.

"*Bebakhshid*," I said once again. "*Meydan-e Emam kojast?*"

And once again came the question—in Persian—about my origins, and again, a great smile in response to my reply. The man pointed his arm in the direction from which I had just come and said something unintelligible to me. He then placed his hand on his heart and bowed to me again and again.

I smiled and nodded back. Then I turned around and began walking back the way I had just come, thinking about how ironic it was that everyone wanted to help, but that I had no language with which to take advantage of their generous spirit. I also realized that these strangers expressed a sincere warmth and acceptance of me, an American. Every random person I had met thus far in Iran welcomed me.

But still, I was lost. Anxious perspiration coated my forehead; I reached in my pocket for a tissue and felt a piece of paper. Pulling it out, I found a card from the hotel with its name and address. I had forgotten that Farzaneh had given one to each member of the group before we left the hotel that morning.

With a sudden burst of hope, I looked for a cab. But I was overcome by the reality of the situation: it was rush hour, when all the cabs would be taken, and I wasn't sure I could identify one anyway since not all Iranian cabs were plainly marked. Anyone who owned a car could be a cab driver. I also knew that Iranians tended to share cabs but I didn't know exactly how the system worked. Did I dare to simply flag down *any* driver?

I stood at a curb feeling helpless, somewhat panicked, and shaky with hunger when a small sedan broke free of the jumble of traffic and pulled up to the curb in front of me. It was a wreck of a car, with a well-worn interior and no visible insignia identifying it as a cab. The scruffy-looking driver wore a rumpled shirt and he reached back to open the door for me, less out of courtesy than because the outside handle was missing. I hesitated, unsure if I should trust the man or the car. I had a split-second to make a decision.

I swallowed hard, jumped in, and handed the driver the card. Ten uncertain minutes later, we were outside my hotel. The driver signaled the fare by holding up two of his fingers and one of the green Iranian bills with Ayatollah Khomenei's picture on it—about two dollars. I paid the fair and then held out a third bill for a tip. He waved it away, but I insisted.

I leapt out of the cab and ran up the stairs of the hotel, pushing open the heavy glass door. The clock behind the front desk read 8:10. I spotted members of my tour group seated on couches in the lobby and walked briskly towards them. "I'm so sorry I'm late," I gasped. "I got lost."

Farzaneh looked up at me with surprise. "You're not late," she said.

"We're on Iranian time now," one of the others said, and laughed. "No one leaves for dinner here until at least 8:30 or 9:00."

I took a deep breath and plopped myself down onto one of the overstuffed cushions, exhausted, yet relieved—and grateful for the extraordinary kindness I received on the streets of Iran.

Esfahan with Elnaz

Deniz Azime Aral

*I*t was 2005 and I had a big emergency: the United States was going to bomb Iran, or at least that's what I thought. The tension between the two countries springing from Iran's rejection to suspend its uranium enrichment program was all over the local news in Turkey. In February of that year, the Bush administration was reported by non corporate media of planning an attack on Iran. And then in June Iran elected a more conservative president who apparently was not going to step back from the program. I had to see my neighboring country before anything happened. The US bombed Iraq, I had every reason to believe they might bomb Iran. I'd missed visiting Baghdad before 2003, losing my chances to travel there for an indefinite time. I couldn't fail again. So I joined a group of sixteen people who knew each other through some sort of geography lovers' association in Turkey, and planned to go with them on their overland route from Turkey to Nepal. I would stay in Iran as they crossed into Pakistan.

Normally, I would weave a net of communication with people at my destination prior to my trip so that I could be involved in the locals' lives, absorbing and melting into their culture. But as bombing was weeks, or even days away, I thought there wasn't time for the usual planning. So, in the first days of July, I connected with the group on the Turkish-Iranian border and headed to Iran.

Prior to crossing, I managed to catch some flack from my fellow travelers, school teachers who knew everything a human being could possibly know about traveling, and were all too eager to share their wisdom with me. Apparently, I had the wrong luggage, the wrong headscarf and the wrong shoes. I was without a water bottle, hiking boots, and other vital outdoor accessories.

Once in Tabriz, Iran, the group planned to visit Kandovan for a picnic. Having spent two days with the group I realized that I could not continue with them. They seemed to be interested in getting to know each other more than their host country. What I also realized was that it would be perfectly safe for me to travel in Iran on my own—the whole atmosphere was peaceful. So while the group was boarding their bus for Kandovan, I headed to a travel agency to book myself a seat on the first flight, to any city, so I could restart my Persian journey.

Within the next three days I had crisscrossed Iran's airspace, visiting Mashhad, Shiraz, Persepolis, and Tehran. On board the airport shuttle bus in Esfahan, while waiting to be transported to the terminal, I received a call from Seher, a former fellow traveler from the geography lovers group. She had taken it upon herself to dutifully check in on my well-being. Conversing in Turkish made me uncomfortable. I didn't want to be noticed as a foreigner. While on the phone, I took every opportunity to make eye contact with anyone who might be looking in my direction and nod to greet them. As I hung up, a young woman with whom I had exchanged several smiles approached me and asked, "*Türk müsünüz?*" Are you Turkish?

The next thing I knew, I was in the back seat of a taxi with this woman, Elnaz. Between Elnaz, 26, and me, sat her mother with my duffle bag on her lap. She insisted on making my ride more comfortable and wouldn't let go of my luggage. In vain I tried to pull it from her but she was hugging it with so much determination that I gave up. The taxi's trunk was full with their luggage and she clearly wanted to make my ride more comfortable. In the front passenger seat Elnaz's older brother Ferzad sat with his head turned towards us, quietly listening to the dialogue between his sister and this woman from a neighboring land. I was the object of attention for the entire ride, including the driver's gaze through the rear view mirror.

Elnaz, an ethnic Azeri from Tabriz and a huge fan of Turkey, was the only one in her family to speak Turkish, which she had learned from watching Turkish TV, in particular soap operas and pop songs. She asked me questions about some of the most popular stars of the day, but unfortunately I wasn't the most qualified person to discuss my country's paparazzi scene. Giggling, Elnaz ended up answering her own questions and switched her attention quickly back to me, making me feel like I was the celebrity.

A miniatures artist, Elnaz was taking her mom and brother on a business trip to Esfahan. And now a new member of the family, I would be joining them in their travels. At the four-star hotel where they were staying, Elnaz convinced the receptionist to give me a suite for the price of a single.

Our first night in Esfahan, Elnaz and I went out to meet her friends and have a beer (non-alcoholic, in accordance with the laws of the country). A beige river of cars flowed between our hotel and the Zayandeh River, the life-giving water reflected the orange lights from Si-o-seh Pol, the Thirty-three Arches. We easily jay walked across Mellat Avenue through the thick traffic and got a cab. There was already another man next to the driver so I assumed we were in one of those shared taxis. Yet Elnaz soon whispered to my ear (giggling) that we were in a private person's car.

Would I do this in Turkey? Or anywhere in the world? Would I get into some stranger's car at night? Deprived of any type of defense, without even a properly working cell phone? But Elnaz exuded such a feeling of trust and security that I felt at ease. For the first time in the last five days of non-stop planning and restructuring my trip, I was finally feeling carefree. Great music played on the stereo. The car smelled of cologne, the leather seats were comfortable, the windows wide open. The humming of car engines and the exhaust fumes from idle running, the breeze from the Zayandeh River, the soft chat between Mohammed, the driver, and Elnaz, all contributed to my relaxation. Everything felt so good. Even my inability to comprehend Persian felt good to me.

We soon left the comfort of the leather car seats for wooden chairs in an overly-lit café. But thanks to Elnaz's friendly enthusiasm, her tireless introductions with each new person we met, I became filled with so much joy that the hard chair and bad lighting seemed trivial. The newcomers would usually glue their gazes on me while they listened to Elnaz's intro and would talk back to her without really looking away from me, not wanting to miss any of my reaction. Their questions were mainly about my demographics: age, civil status, ethnicity, etc. The girls would giggle upon hearing my answer "single," and men would look even deeper in my eyes and smile. The absence of a language-based communication forced us to be more expressive with our mimics and gestures.

Almost unmistakably both men and women got visibly energized when they'd hear that I was from Istanbul. Some also sighed and repeated "Istanbul...Istanbul." They too, like Elnaz and her family, asked about Turkish celebrities and beaches on the Turkish Mediterranean Coast.

Thankfully no one asked about my original motive for visiting their country to which the honest answer would be: I came to see your country before it is destroyed by Coalition Forces' missiles. In the company of these generous and kind young people my cruel and superficial rationale embarrassed me.

After a glass of innocent beer my bravery over choosing to travel to Iran became near legendary. I was considered an amazing Turkish woman from Istanbul who came all the way from her home, all by herself, to meet Iranians instead of sipping cocktails at some gorgeous Mediterranean resort. I, too, was feeling proud of myself not because of the risk of finding myself in the middle of a war, but only because of the weather. July is the cruelest month in Iran. In innumerable instants I'd pause and think, "Now?" fully expecting to drop dead of sun stroke. And every time I would become surprised that I'd survived the heat, which had been the only scary thing I faced in Iran.

Next morning, following a ravishing breakfast on the hotel's terrace that offered a clear unlimited sky and in view of the lush plain of Life-giving River, my new family taxied me to Birds Garden. Bagh-e Parandegan is a vast man-made forested park by Zayandeh River, about three miles to the west of the city center. It is home to some 5,000 kinds of birds from all over the world. Not being a fan of birds and residing in one of the greenest quarters of Istanbul, I would never have chosen to go there (nor was it featured in the Lonely Planet). However, I had complete faith in Elnaz's leadership. This was a very popular recreation area for the locals as well as domestic tourists to enjoy the day's hottest hours. We strolled through the moist bushy pathways, ponds, and neatly-kempt bird environments. This turned out to be one of the more serene outings in my life.

Later that evening, Ferzad sweetly objected to our plans to go out again. Elnaz quickly countered, all the while their beloved mother (who would soon propose to me on behalf of her son) watched this rather subtle quarrel with her ever-serene eyes. I knew I would do as Elnaz would, and yet Ferzad's broken heart broke my heart, too. I pretended to be deep inside my Lonely Planet guide until the argument subsided.

Love and Pomegranates

Elnaz easily won the argument, and our brand new friend from the night before, Mohammed, a 21-year-old goldsmith from Esfahan, picked us up from our hotel. In one of the most charming cities on the planet I was being escorted by two angels whose only goal was realizing my wishes. I had one simple wish that night: to visit a hookah café in one of those the alcoves under the Khaju Bridge.

The next day we visited Esfahan's infamous blue-tiled Friday Mosque and after we walked in the traditional bazaar framing the large square. I became an unchained wild thing. I wanted to buy not just one or two things, but a full shelf of handmade items made of marquetry, enamel, copper, wood, blown glass, glazed clay, carpets and kilims, miniatures, and works of calligraphy. Elnaz was splitting her time between helping her mother with her errands and translating for me, making and receiving business calls both for her own business and some for her brother's enterprise. Zigzagging for hours and several kilometers through the alleys made my blood pressure fall and I needed to call the day off before I could buy a single item from the richest bazaar I've ever been to.

I really didn't want to leave Esfahan, but I was pretty worn out by the time I was scheduled to head home. I said my farewells to my Iranian family in their hotel room. My mother-in-law-not-to-be performed a special ritual to protect me on my trip home. Taking a bill from her purse and turning it above my head, she whispered her prayers and then blew on my face. She carefully put the holy bill in a corner of her bag, not inside her wallet, so that she would not mix it with other, unholy bills. She had Elnaz translate that she was going to hand the money to the first beggar she came across. In Islamic tradition, it is believed that giving alms to beggars gives extra protection to loved ones on their journeys. Shielded against all evil, I was now allowed to depart.

Elnaz saw me off at our hotel's gate and entrusted me to Mohammed, who would drive me to the airport for my midnight flight to Tehran. Without Elnaz there to translate, we couldn't really say much to one another along the 20 mile journey. But our silences were filled with the beautiful Persian music coming from the car stereo, a bonus song in Turkish and a rappified Islamic hymn in English. We fell into a comfortable ride without words. I sensed that he understood the joy he gave me with his presence and the gratitude I felt for the time he gave me while in Esfahan.

After he walked me to the terminal, Mohammed and I exchanged quasi-mute goodbyes and checked each other's phone numbers from our cell phone screens one more time before he returned to his car.

During my seven-hour layover in Tehran's Mehrabad Airport, I heard someone call my name. It was Ebru, one of the chattiest members of the geography-lovers I had run away from seven days ago. After I told her about my adventures, she wholeheartedly congratulated me for my decision to disconnect from the group. Apparently, her tour group was unsatisfactory. There were too many conflicts over personal agendas, a small scale scandal involving one good-looking woman in the group and two male members, bus rides were too long and too uncomfortable. Hotels and meals were below average. The weather was too hot. Ebru wished she'd left with me so that we two could have traveled together. I wondered, as her Turkish monologue continued, if I had actually been blessed all along.

Come and See Iran

An Interview with Amir Haeri Mehrizi

Tanya Fekri

Q: Can you please tell me about your work as a tour guide in Iran?

A: Yes of course. I am a tourist guide and I have been dealing with tourists from different countries and different cultures, languages and religions since 2003. I have BA in English translation and I found being a tourist guide is the best and easiest way in Iran to practice and improve my speaking. I passed the courses on tour guiding and I am practicing under the license of the Cultural Heritage Organization of Iran.

A tourist guide is the cultural messenger of his country. I represent my country. My soul crosses the borders of countries and I feel that I am an international guy. I have the opportunity to talk, walk, sit and eat with people of different classes of society—from school children to professors and diplomats, regardless of job title. We chat and express our feelings, our cultures and opinions freely. This exchange of dialogue is neither like a classroom nor an office. Instead, we spend our days and nights together and we become like members of a family during the tour.

This is a job that gives me the chance to learn. Every tour is a new lesson; the classroom is my city and the tourists are my teachers. Every day I go to class eagerly because I know that I will learn some new lessons.

Tourists tell me new stories about the cultures of other nations. I may not have enough time and money to travel around the world, but tourists come and explain to me what they have seen and experienced¬—it's like a virtual tour. It gives me a great joy. It makes me think more seriously about traveling. I have many friends in other countries and it is as if I have many arms and roots spread around the world.

The best lesson I have learnt these past years is that it doesn't matter which country you are from, what your language is and what religion you are, you should always strive to be humane.

Love and Pomegranates

Q: As a tour guide in Iran, what have you observed about American tourists?

A: A good question that I think Iranians have in their mind is the same question I ask my American tourists. Both sides think that inside the other side's life is hard, people are treated badly by their governments, human rights are being violated and people face tough times, but when they travel to each other's countries they see here or there is like any other place on Earth. People have their own family, their own job and life goes on.

There are many similarities between Iranians and Americans, I personally have this feeling. Here Americans are usually treated like VIPs by travel agencies; they always try to give them best services. I was always eager to have an American tour. I had always wanted to talk to an American to discover what they look like and learn about their culture. Moreover, since I had studied English talking to Americans was a good criterion to judge my fluency and my accent.

The first American tourist I met was in 2005. It was a one-day tour of Yazd with a man in his early 40s who was smiling and was very friendly. After one day of talking and walking, I said, "Hey, you Americans are like us Iranians." All day long I thought I was talking with an Iranian friend. He was so warm blooded and this was a wonderful experience for me. He told me that when he was in Tehran once the people came to know that he was American they invited him to their home for lunch, dinner and tea.

This was my first experience, but I know it not enough to judge all Americans!

My next American tour was in 2009. This time it was with an American woman in her early 40s. She was a mother of three children. She already knew Iran; she was a writer and had written some books about Iran and Iranian culture. She loves Iranian carpet and weaving. I learnt from her how precious the Iranian carpet is and she taught me when I step on the Persian hand-woven carpet to remember the delicate hands of the girls and women who had woven it and that every knot is made by their heart. While stepping on a colorful carpet it's as if I am walking on a real flower garden.

My third experience was also, in 2009. A group of four young American footballers, two boys and two girls around 27 years old spent eight days in Tehran and Yazd. They were working on a movie project about the football language among the nations and playing football with Iranian people in the bazaar and the streets. They had traveled to more than twenty countries and Iran was the last piece of the puzzle. They told me before coming to Iran that their parents were worried about their safety and recommended them to travel to Turkey instead, since in their opinion Turkey had a similar culture to Iran. But although there are similarities, there are big differences too. When in the airport waiting to go back to their homes, they said they were happy that they had the chance to see Iran, and they would return back to Iran with their families. They were very nice people and I had wonderful time with them.

Q: What do you believe are the general stereotypes Iranian people may have about Americans? Please be candid.

A: Frankly they don't have a clear image of Americans as Americans do not have a clear image of Iranians. They judge each other from the news they hear from the media and/or TV. Sometimes the image of Iran is so tainted that I am left shocked. An American once asked me, "Do you have paved roads? I thought you rode on camels and I thought Iran was not safe for us and if people knew that I was American, they would shoot me." But when they come and see Iran, they do not believe in such stereotypes.

In Iran, people think that in America everybody is carrying light weapons and it's not safe and children shoot teachers at their schools. Some stories like these are shown on TV. But when they see American tourists they understand that they are like other people, they have their own life, their family, their house.

Q: What aspect of Iranian culture or history do you believe has functioned as an icon for greater peace, human tolerance, and human understanding?

A: In the first hand, I answer you from a historical point of view. The Great Persia is considered to be the cradle of civilizations. We have many documents proving Iranians were kind, generous and merciful to the people of different cultures, religions and nationalities. We have the cylinder of Cyrus the Great. It is the symbol of freedom of speech and human rights. We have poems inspired by Iranian Islamic culture. We have Mowlana known to the English-speaking world simply as Rumi, Hafiz and 'Attar preaching tolerance, love and peace in their poems. Poets like Sa'di, whose most famous poem is a call for breaking down all barriers.

> *Human beings are members of a whole,*
> *In creation of one essence and soul.*
> *If one member is afflicted with pain,*
> *Other members uneasy will remain.*
> *If you've no sympathy for human pain,*
> *The name of human you cannot retain!*

Q: What do you believe to be the most historically significant city in Iran that you would recommend tourists to visit? Are there other cities outside of Iran tourists can visit to gain a better understanding of Iranian culture?

A: It's a really hard question to answer since I believe every city has its own distinct beauty. As a Yazdi that loves his city I would recommend Yazd because it is architecturally unique. It is known as the city of wind towers, the city of mud bricks and I love the archaic part of it, which has an area of more than 700 hectares left untouched.

But honestly I think that since years ago everybody has come to know Iran and the great Persia by the city of Persepolis. It is one of the symbols of the ancient civilization and the ceremonial capital of the Persia and one of the twelve world heritage sites declared by UNESCO.

Today it's easy to copy Yazd buildings somewhere else, as you know, in Dubai they have copied the architecture of many cities, but it's not possible to copy the culture. To gain the real culture of a city or country you have to go to that city. Seeing is believing. It is a common occurrence for tourists to be extremely impressed when they visit Persepolis, old Yazd city and some other historical sites. I have experienced the same kind of feeling—it's as if the walls are talking to you. They want to say something, they want to shout out the old memories they have held on for years. When I walk into the old part of the town, I feel the high mud walls have stories about people born, brought up and who have died there for generations. Then how could Yazd or Persepolis or any other historical sites ever be repeated in another part of the world? The people who lived here made the history of the city their own unique craftsmanship.

Q: What do you like most about your hometown, Yazd? What do you typically do on the weekends with your friends?

A: As a Yazdi person if you had asked me this question about seven years ago I would have had only a few sentences to share, but today I know my city far better and tourists have taught me to look at it from varied angles. I have heard from tourists when in Yazd they feel at home, they feel they have been here before. Even one of those young Americans found the old alleys of Yazd the best place to pop the question to his girlfriend. They said that the old walls of Yazd gave them this feeling of enchantment.

On weekends, my friends and I typically go to a traditional restaurant or café shop for a cup of tea where we sit and chat. In the summer, we go to the countryside in the mountains around Yazd.

Q: Your recent travel to Turkey was with a mix of men and women. Do you often go on trips with both Iranian men and women? Is it typical for most young people in Iran to go out or travel with members of the opposite gender?

A: For me and my family it is normal because since years ago we would go out picnicking with my friends of both genders. My friends and I invite our mothers and fathers to our gatherings and it is great fun and at the same time we enjoy listening to the nice life stories and experiences of our mothers and fathers. It is normal to travel with the opposite gender but mostly inside a group of friends. I mean, if you are a group, you can do it and sometimes some of them even found their match in life and marry each other.

Q: What place in the United States would you like to visit someday?

A: I have met many Iranians living in the United States and heard that most of the Iranians live in California and mainly in Los Angeles. Since a big number of Iranians live there, they call it Tehrangeles. They say you can speak Farsi and buy Persian goods there and that Iranians feel at home. They say the weather and climate in Los Angeles is one of the best in the world. I have also heard about Texas and the big Texan streets and cars. I would like to experience both these places.

Q: How can travel assist Iranians and Americans in acknowledging and celebrating their cultural distinctions and similarities?

A: If they want to discover the realities it is better that Iranians and Americans travel to each other's countries to see and feel the similarities and differences. I know it is difficult for Americans to travel to Iran and more difficult for Iranians to travel to United States, but I invite Americans to take the time and come to Iran.

The Golestan of Sa'di
Chapter 2, Story 26

Sheikh Mosleh al-Din Sa'di
Translated by Richard Francis Burton

I remember having once walked all night with a caravan and then slept on the edge of the desert. A distracted man who had accompanied us on that journey raised a shout, ran towards the desert and took not a moment's rest. When it was daylight, I asked him what state of his that was. He replied: "I saw bulbuls commencing to lament on the trees, the partridges on the mountains, the frogs in the water and the beasts in the desert so I bethought myself that it would not be becoming for me to sleep in carelessness while they all were praising God."

> *Yesterday at dawn a bird lamented,*
> *Depriving me of sense, patience, strength*
> *and consciousness.*
> *One of my intimate friends who*
> *Had perhaps heard my distressed voice*
> *Said: "I could not believe that thou*
> *Wouldst be so dazed by a bird's cry."*
> *I replied: "It is not becoming to humanity*
> *That I should be silent when birds chant praises."*

Persian Lady ~ Rashin Kheiriyeh

Finding Ourselves
in the Other

A Friendship of Words

Susan Fletcher

In the old tales, there is power in words. Words are what you use to summon a jinn, or to open an enchanted door, or to cast a spell. You can do everything else perfectly, but if you don't say the right words, it won't work.

If you know how to use words, you don't have to be strong enough to wield a scimitar or have armies at your command.

Words are how the powerless can have power.

—Shadow Spinner

I met Hussein "Elvand" Ebrahimi, founder of the House of Translation in Tehran, through my young adult novel, *Shadow Spinner.* He discovered it in a publisher's catalog, bought it, read it, translated it, then invited me to a conference in Iran. I think he must have been intrigued by the book's subject matter—the beloved Persian storyteller, Shahrazad. What would an American children's writer have to say about her? he might have wondered. But I like to imagine that what drew him most, in the end, was that *Shadow Spinner* is about the power of words.

Elvand had more faith in the power of words than anyone I've ever known. He staked his career, his hopes for his country, and his dreams for the world on his belief that the printed word can break down barriers, open us up to wisdom, and give power to the powerless. But I didn't realize this about him until much later.

Our friendship began, grew, ended in words. It spanned eight years, from August of 1999 to September of 2007. I didn't meet him in Iran at that conference in 1999 or anywhere else. Ours was a conversation untouched by smile or gesture or tone of voice. There was something old-fashioned about it, like those Victorian letter-writing friendships—pre-telephone, pre-jet travel, pre-Skype. There were only words to shoulder the entire weight of a friendship, with its shared confessions, hopes, and grief.

In the early days, there were faxes, sent and received on our ancient, crotchety machine. I had to time everything for Tehran business hours—eleven and a half hours ahead of Oregon, where I live—and even then the damned machine chronically chewed up paper and spit out stern little admonitions of my "failure to transmit." The early words were stiff and formal. "Mrs. Fletcher." "Mr. Ebrahimi." "I wish you and your honorable family a merry Christmas." "I am still awaiting word from the United States Treasury Department."

Those last words are mine. I had made the mistake of following the State Department's instructions to request permission from Treasury before accepting Elvand's invitation to the conference, because my visit might violate the US trade embargo against Iran. The answer, finally, was that I could go ahead, but it took so long for Treasury to respond—months and months, unconscionably long—that the visa arrived too late. At the last moment, I had to tell him I would not be there.

Elvand's next fax read, "Last night, all the guests were invited to dinner. Believe me, I was thinking of you all the time. My friends (writers, illustrators, and especially translators) asked me, 'Which one is Mrs. Fletcher?' and 'Is she coming later?' But I couldn't answer them. I was sad. What should I tell them? A little later, they read the answer from my face. Many young adults had read *Shadow Spinner* in Persian and had come to see you. They wanted to speak about the book and to thank you! There were other writers from different countries, but nobody had come to see them; nobody had read their books."

I slumped beside the fax machine, head in hands, filled with a strange combination of emotions. Regret, certainly. Why hadn't I just *gone?*, and to hell with Treasury! But there was something else, too. Surprise. Or maybe astonishment is a truer word: the first, glimmering realization that my own words in *Shadow Spinner* had connected me, like it or not, to something extraordinary happening halfway around the world.

For literally years I thought the House of Translation was a publishing house, but actually it was a library. Elvand had begun, in the days when foreign books were not widely available in Iran, by buying old books from people's home libraries and translating them into Persian. Little by little he began to win awards, and government funding followed. Now he could pick and choose. He perused book catalogs and websites, studied lists of international book awards, and traveled each year to the International Children's Book Fair in Bologna, Italy. Over the course of his career he translated over 100 books. He invited other translators to select from and translate the books in his library; he nurtured their careers. He lobbied for Iranian publishers to bring out books from other countries and to honor the copyright laws, even though Iran had not yet joined the copyright convention.

Children's and young adults' books were his passion. There is a vast younger generation in Iran, and Elvand wanted to bring them literature from other cultures so they could see different possibilities for the future.

Elvand wrote: "We writers and translators know that we have a majority of young people here in Iran, and that they need other countries' books. They not only need them for entertainment, but also so that they can learn about the world. We know that no nation can improve in the modern world without reading and using other nations' experiences in literature and in other areas. So when we help this majority, this new generation, to know what is going on in other countries, and how they have come through the difficult ways of new civilizations, we are hoping to have a new society, a society without violence, without superstitions, without war."

Love and Pomegranates

When I read through our early correspondence, I am struck by the confidence of his hope. He wrote me several times of Iranian President Khatami's proposal that prompted The United Nations to declare 2001 as the year of "The Dialogue Among Civilizations." Elvand was pleased with what President Khatami had done, but couldn't help noting that "writers and artists have been carrying on such a discourse since the beginning of civilization... Frankly speaking, this discourse... was commenced by writers, artists, and scientists and then accepted by politicians inevitably."

It's the word "inevitably" that pierces me now, thinking of what happened in September of 2001 and all that has ensued since, and where we are now in our dialogue with Iran. Our non-conversation. Our failure to transmit. Thinking of what has happened, in Iran, to Elvand, himself.

Over the eight years of our friendship, Elvand translated a number of things I wrote: several speeches, an interview, two novels—*Shadow Spinner* and *Alphabet of Dreams*—and the author's notes that I wrote especially for the Persian edition of each novel. He also vetted *Alphabet of Dreams* twice for accuracy, making new suggestions when my first ideas didn't wash and consulting a historian and an archaeologist on my behalf.

We discussed as he translated—first in faxes and later, mercifully, through email. Much of the matter of our dialogue was words.

Elvand wrote: "It might be interesting for you to know that *Shahrazad* is based on two component parts, *shahr* (city) + *azad* (free) and not, as you have written, *shah* (king) as a prefix and *zad* (born) as a suffix."

Ah, Freer-of-the-City. Lovely!

I learned that *Donyazad* (the name of Shahrazad's sister) is composed of *donya* (an Arabic word meaning "the world") and *zad* (born). That *caravanserai* comes from *caravan* (as it looks) plus *sara*, (house, a place to rest). That the first and deepest well in a qanat is called a *madar chah* (mother + well), and the capstan by which a bucket attached to a rope may be lowered into the well is called a *charkh-e chah* (wheel + well).

I learned that, "A 'tar' is not an old instrument. In the time of your book, the most famous instruments were: *tanbor* (a kind of lute), *roud* (a kind of harp), and *chang* (a harp or lyre)." That, "I think one who falls into a shallow well would cry, 'Ahaiii,' instead of what you have written." That, "There is no problem with the name, Aunt Goli. *Goli* means flower, and this name is still used in Iran. But royal families usually used the names of goddesses."

"Sometimes," Elvand wrote, "I think your book needs a small glossary."

We often traded idioms, as well. Once, I asked him if his ears were burning, then told him what the expression means—that I'd been speaking of him. He replied, "A few days ago one of my friends and I were speaking about your book. Maybe it is not just the same as 'burning my ears,' and maybe it is! But in such a case we have an expression in Persian that is more or less like your expression. It is not easy to convey the meaning completely, but it says, 'The friends' hearts are connected to each other.'"

According to my *Webster's Unabridged*, the word "translation" derives from the Middle English *translaten*, which derives from the Latin *translatus*, used as a past participle of *transferre*, whose roots are *trans* (across) and *ferre* (to bear or carry). To translate: To bear across.

I have to admit that I knew woefully little about Iran when I began work on *Shadow Spinner*. And those television images of the hostage crisis of the late 1970s and early 1980s—angry Iranians burning American flags and chanting "Death to America!"—seemed indelibly seared into my mind. So I did lots of book research, and two Iranian-American friends, Dr. Abbas Milani and Zohre Bullock, tutored me with vast patience and generosity of spirit—enlightening me, correcting a multitude of misconceptions. And eventually, I did travel to Iran.

Still, Elvand's words bore across to me a more personal view of Iran, something closer to the heart.

"Yesterday I… began to write to you, but just at that moment the bell of my home rang and a lot of guests (some of my friends and their children), came in, singing and calling out to me. Nothing could be done. I left my PC and joined them. They stayed until midnight. The children call me 'Uncle Hussein.' All of them are my readers. They know that I choose interesting books for translation. They asked me about new books, and I gave them my latest translation, *A Single Shard*, by Linda Sue Park, winner of the 2002 Newbery Medal."

He wrote to me of the remote village in which he had grown up: "Because we had a lot of sheep and goats, we and our herdsmen had to stay in the mountains many days and nights. Most of the time, I lived with my grandmother in big tents in the mountains. She really loved me, and I loved her too. I lived there about seven years. Mostly, I remember the different animals, wild and domestic, from my childhood. There was water in the valleys; there were springs in the foothills; there were wolves, foxes, rabbits, and deer everywhere. Finally, my grandmother died in the sunset of a day that I have never been able to forget."

After we had corresponded for several years, I began to notice that, while Elvand began every letter "Dear Ms. Fletcher," he had begun to sign off as simply "Elvand," instead of "Hussein Ebrahimi (Elvand)." And sometimes, in the middle of a letter, he would address me as "Dear Susan." Hmm. It seemed that we had come to one of those points where, in languages that have formal and informal pronouns, you might segue from the formal to the informal form of address. But I didn't know what to do. I mean, he lived in a country where women had to cover themselves practically head to toe when they met a man who was not a member of their families, didn't he? Well, I knew by now that this was not always the case, but still. Might not first names seem too intimate? I was confused, and I didn't want to make a terrible gaffe. I asked an Iranian-American friend, and she, too, felt that first names would be inappropriate. So I kept up with "Mr. Ebrahimi," but began to feel more and more awkward. Finally, I decided that I had to ask him directly. I kept my friend anonymous, though, saying that the advice had come from some nameless "Iranian friends." Here is how he responded:

"It is a little strange when I read the opinion of some of your Iranian friends. Why would it 'not be appropriate' for a friend to call his/her friend by his/her first name? It seems that some of them have been away from Iran for a very long time. How many years have we been writing to each other? How many letters have we sent to each other? How many times have we been thinking of each other? Isn't it enough to be friends? I prefer Elvand (my pen name) or even my first name."

Okay. Got it. Elvand it is. And Susan!

In 2001, a new word crept into our correspondence: cancer.

Elvand wrote: "I read your interview on the ACHUKA site and hope to translate and publish it soon. But there was something in your interview that shocked me! You told that ten years ago you were diagnosed with cancer. Six months ago, I was diagnosed with cancer, too… I don't know which kind of cancer you were diagnosed with and, though I am willing to know, I think that now you are safe and sound and your body is clear of it completely. Also I would be glad if there is any kind of experience which would be of help to me."

I replied, in part: "I think the thing that helped me most was to think about life after cancer treatment—that I would write again, and see my daughter graduate from high school, and have good times with my husband, my parents, and my friends. All of these things have come true for me—and I am confident that they will come true for you. Many people are so frightened of cancer that they can barely deal with what is happening to the person who is afflicted. However, I was amazed at the kindness that came my way from unexpected sources. When you are suffering, people open up to you and tell you of their own sufferings, and both can be enriched by that."

But cancer took Elvand to places I had never been. After a while, reassurances from my own experience rang hollow. After a while, he was the one reassuring me: "I was hospitalized soon after my last email. Two days ago I came home and now I am resting. I will write you soon. Everything will be OK. Don't worry." And, "I am very well. I read and write and do my job perfectly. No signs of disease are now seen, and I am sure that they will not be seen in the future!" And, "Dear Susan, I thank you again. I know that you worry about me. But don't worry. I will do my best to be healthy and live more! I have a lot of things to do! I will never lose my hope."

For many years, books flew back and forth between Portland and Tehran. I sent him the bound galleys of Donna Jo Napoli's *Beast*, which he eventually translated. He sent me beautiful coffee table books about Esfahan and Persepolis. I sent him Shirley Climo's *The Persian Cinderella* and Aaron Shepherd's *Forty Fortunes*. He sent me Sheikh Mosleh al-Din Sa'di's *The Bustan*. I sent him Terence O'Donnell's *Garden of the Brave in War*. He sent me Mary Boyce's *Zoroastrians: Their Religious Beliefs and Practices* and Richard

N. Frye's *The Heritage of Persia*. I sent him a bibliography of Native American children's literature, in which he'd expressed interest. He sent me two priceless volumes in which Persian text is placed across the page from its English translation: *Gulistan* and *Bustan*, by Sheikh Mosleh al-Din Sa'di, and *Silent Words*, by Rumi.

But one day, when I went to the post office to send the marked-up galleys of my novel *Alphabet of Dreams*, the postal clerk told me that printed matter was no longer allowed to be sent to Iran. Food—yes. Things made of wood and cloth and metal and plastic—yes. Words—no.

"What!" I protested. "But I've been doing it for years."

She shrugged. "I'm just reading what it says here."

"Is it our government doing this, or theirs?" I asked.

"Theirs, apparently," she said. You can try, but they say they won't accept it."

I tried. Twice. Each time, after several weeks, the galleys were returned to me in plastic bags, marked up with Persian handwriting.

Failure to transmit.

Elvand urged me to try a third time. Sometimes things got through, he wrote. When I took the galleys to the print shop to make a clean copy, the clerk said, "Why don't I scan it? Then if you have to copy it again, we can just work from the electronic file."

I blinked at him stupidly. "You can *scan* that?" I asked.

That afternoon, *Alphabet of Dreams* was borne across the world as an email attachment. Elvand translated it, corresponding with me by email all the while, to make sure he captured my intent exactly. The Persian edition came out in December 2006.

But things were falling apart. For so many years, Elvand had connected with the publishing and translation communities at the International Children's Book Fair. But now he wrote: "Unfortunately, because of the new government and the new minister of Islamic culture and guidance, it is not possible for me to travel to Bologna."

Even worse news was to follow: the government had shut down his library. The House of Translation was no more.

Numbers began to enter grimly into our dialogue. "Last night I had a new blood test. My white blood cell count was under 60,000. It was good news for me and my physician because last week it was 105,000. He hopes it will decrease even more." And, "Thank you. Now I am OK. Though the blood test says something else." And, "After six courses of Rituximab we thought my white blood cell count would decrease to normal, but new blood tests show that it's increasing again."

Finally, on September 25, 2007, another friend, Iranian translator Jaleh Novini, wrote:

"I have never thought of being a messenger of bad news, but unfortunately this hard and painful responsibility has been given to me. I am so sorry to inform you that our great friend Mr. Ebrahimi (Elvand) passed away this morning."

Love and Pomegranates

For the longest time, in imagination, I had been writing a different ending to this story. A miracle drug would arrive on the scene in the nick of time, and it would cure Elvand's cancer, or at least give him many, many more years. Both Iran and the United States would elect enlightened new presidents, and the Dialogue Among Civilizations would begin in earnest.

We writers like to believe in the power of words. Or maybe it's just that we need to believe, in order to keep on doing what we do. But in truth, words aren't always enough.

Nonetheless, they can still bring surprises.

In the summer of 2009 on the campus of Lewis & Clark College in Portland, Oregon, the first gathering of the "House of Translators" took place. It was initiated by Dr. Joanne Mulcahy, who heard the story of Elvand and was inspired to name her planned meeting after the institution he founded. Somehow, "Translation" morphed to "Translators" and, Mulcahy says, "what will bloom from this gathering is still uncertain." Yet still. Comparatively few foreign books are translated into English; Mulcahy has opened up an ongoing dialogue among translators—"the unsung heroes of our literary and social worlds," she says. Because people here need other countries' books. They not only need them for entertainment, but also so that they can learn about the world. Because no nation can improve in the modern world without reading and using other nations' experiences in literature and in other areas. Because maybe someday, if we can come to know one another well, we can hope to have a new society, a society without violence, without superstitions, without war.

Well. Maybe that's too much to hope for. Too much, anyway, to heap onto the shoulders of the beleaguered written word.

Still, people will keep on writing. Inevitably! There will be books, newspapers, letters, faxes, emails, blogs, e-zines, text messages, and technologies yet to be conceived. Words will slip between the crevices in borders. They will be smuggled across in suitcases, they will flit across the world wide web. They will be brought to light out of the dusty shelves of old libraries, they will hum across telephone lines. Our words will be borne across the world and bloom in astonishing ways, ways we can't begin to imagine. "What seems like an ending," my protagonist says in *Shadow Spinner*, "is really a beginning in disguise."

Fly, Howl, Love,
A Tribute to the Life of Forugh Farrokhzad

Shideh Etaat

Our house was at the end of an alley,
at the end of all things, it seemed,
when we were little girls living
among the shadows of the walls,
the trees bearing figs, sour cherries.

And Forugh, always with her notebook.
Filling those pages with what?
It seemed so big in her small hands then,
that notebook, as if she herself
could fit inside those pages.

She would climb trees, hop on walls,
howl like a wolf, fight with boys
she would rather have been loving.

She put her arms out one moonless night—
pretending to be an airplane, to be the entire sky,
and I watched from the dull pond,
home to the red goldfish and brown frogs,
because my eyes were stuck on her.
Everyone's eyes were stuck on her.

Love and Pomegranates

At sixteen when she married,
moved to a city named after a song,
she found something like freedom
in plucked eyebrows,
eyes lined thick with black,
in lips painted red
and short, short skirts.

She walked into that editor's office
with her hair disheveled,
her ink-stained hands
as blue as oceans on a map,
taking over the entire earth it would seem
with such small hands as she held a paper
that had been folded
and squeezed between her fingers
for days, years, her entire life.

They would call her a poetess
because poet would mean
being a woman didn't matter.
And it always matters.

And even in such freedom she lost him.
An unfit mother they proclaimed,
a whore making love to all the world
with only words.

I have sinned a rapturous sin
in a warm enflamed embrace.
Sinned in a pair of vindictive hands,
arms violent and ablaze.

When someone wants to reach the heart
of this earth, it becomes impossible
to not always do just this.

I want to hang my heart like
A ripe fruit
On every branch of every tree.

Even in the beginning,
even on that fig tree
at the end of the alley,
at the end of all things,
she hung it there too.
It still sways in the damp air
as if no one is watching.

I will not speak of death,
of cold lips and the movement of machines,
of skin and bone touching concrete
loud enough for all to hear.

But I will say that always, always at the center of it,
even by that dull pond as I watched her write,
fly, howl, it was always love.

I Will Never Wear Her Clothes

Shideh Etaat

In their apartment in Iran
there's a purple painting hanging on their wall,
70s lamps on the side tables.
She's wearing a white satin robe
and is sitting on the couch,
her legs folded to the side
tucked safely underneath her.
And there's something about my mother
here that I've never seen before,
her bare feet young and untouched
by the suddenness of movement.

I can't help but be disappointed that I wasn't there,
that I wasn't a witness to this.
In Iran, in Paris, in Los Angeles
mother looks thin with the perky breasts
that come before children
and oversized sunglasses like a movie star,
elegant blouses, a camel coat, a vintage t-shirt,
an outfit like she's a sailor with her own ship.
She had to leave with only a bag
of diapers for her first born.

I have a dream sometimes
that she never left, that no one ever left.
That there was no revolution, no war,
that I was born in the country
that I have only heard of in stories.
That I buy bread from a man
who bakes it in the oven on the street.
That I am the one who takes trips to Paris
and fills my suitcase with anything I can find that's purple,
that I am the one who dips my feet into the Caspian,
who gets to wear her clothes,
who is thin and hopeful and looks like
a porcelain doll on her wedding day.

In the car the other night we passed by familiar streets
and she began reading the names of them out loud.
Santa Monica Blvd, Maple Drive, Avenue of the Stars.
"What strange names," she said, "in Iran
our streets were the names of kings."

The lights were on in all the buildings we drove by
and she told me that when she first came to America,
and had left the darkness of war behind,
she cried because of this. "Everything was so bright,"
she said. And she had cried when my brother played
in the rainbow balls at Chuck E. Cheese's
because where she came from kids couldn't.
I can see her now inside with him,
taking off her heels and digging her feet deep,
her unveiled body dipping below the surface,
as she floats in that colorful, plastic sea.

Persia/Iran

Jamila Gavin

My parents met in Persia. My mother came from England, my father from India, and both taught in Esfahan. Persia is how Iran was known in the thirties and Persia is how I still think of it: the land of the great poets like Rumi and Omar Khayaam, of heroic stories of Sohrab and Rustum, and the collection of myths, and legends and fabulous tales of the Shahnameh.

This was the heart of the ancient Persian Empire challenged only by the Greeks; the empire which Alexander the Great fought, conquered, devastated, then loved. Like him, my parents fell in love with the country, its landscape, its culture and language. Both learned to speak and read Persian and, by the time we three children were born, my parents felt a sense of loss that we had not experienced Persia, though held a profound hope that one day we would. They spoke so much about their time there, before we were born, that we felt imbued with this country. We knew the names of the cities, of which my parents spoke with such awe—Tehran, Esfahan, Shiraz, and Kerman—and of their beauty, history and culture. Numerous photograph albums still exist filled with tiny sepia pictures of dusty winding Persian roads lined with spindly poplars, of donkey trains, horse rides, picnics in the deserts, distant snowy mountain peaks, minarets and mosques, and Persian gardens.

We grew up and inherited the large highly ornate, carved Qur'an desk, which has moved to and fro, from Persia to India to England; from the Punjab to London, to Cologne, and back to England, where it now stands in a corner of my cottage in the Cotswolds. Likewise, the beautifully woven hangings and carpets, which have decked every room we've ever lived in. Indeed, I thought all carpets *were* Persian! Ours stayed with us wherever we went, till we were grown up and their lovely colors and patterns had long faded, and their pile had worn threadbare.

Thus did we inherit a deep love and respect for Persia, and have learned to call her Iran even though for me it is still the old name Persia, which resonates with history, literature, and romanticism. When I was invited to a children's book festival there in 2005 I almost felt I was going back to some kind of land of my birth—or pre-birth; I felt so strongly connected. I felt greedy to see and experience all the things my parents had, and it was with great joy I visited Esfahan. We walked the bridge I had seen in those photographs, drank tea under the arches, admired the great mosque and the amazing market square. For me, Esfahan would always be the Blue City because of the glorious blue tiled mosques. Most of all, I felt so connected to the people, as if I were one of them, an Iranian. I felt as if I had come home, as though my parents' love for Persia had been passed on to me through their genes.

But I must not to be carried away by some kind of inherited nostalgia. Iran today is not the Persia of my parent's youth. It has been through revolution, change, more revolution and more change. The Shah was deposed decades ago and it is a theocracy. Iran established its independence from foreign influence, especially that of the West, becoming more overtly Islamic. In the nineteen thirties, my mother wore western dress. A tiny photograph shows her sitting by a fountain, her head bare and her arms and legs uncovered in her flowery summer dress. I, however, had to wear a headscarf and conform to the strict dress code for women in Iran, being fully covered except for my face and hands. Indeed, in the 1930s, it was forbidden to wear the veil, and my parents remember the Shah's horsemen riding through villages, and ripping the veil from any woman they saw wearing it. Such brutal measures seem now to be as much an infringement of women's rights, as the strict Islamic dress code imposed on them today.

Yet despite everything, I was still able to recognize the Persia/Iran that they loved: see the cities they loved, the landscape they loved, and the people they loved.

Although this was my first short visit, there was a sense of familiarity and recognition. Whatever happens, Iran will never lose her profound sense and pride of her own history and culture, which will abide and continue to inspire, and I long to return.

So, What Did You Think about Iran?

Nathan Gonzalez

We were sitting in Westwood having coffee, my friend Maryam and I, talking about my recent trip to her homeland of Iran. Maryam had moved to the States with her family several years prior. She was part of the ocean-trotting cadre of Iranian-Americans who loved their adopted homeland but remained steadfastly and passionately connected to their past. But as an Iranian-American, placed in the middle of two nations that profess to hate their enemy but know very little of one another, she quickly changed the subject away from my monologue about Tehran's traffic and Iranian hospitality.

"How did you answer the question?" said Maryam. "You know, the *What do you think about Iran?* question."

I knew Maryam was not referring to the casual, "How was your trip?" She was talking about *the* question, the one every non-Iranian who has ever visited the country has been asked. Maryam, who is married to an American professor of Near Eastern studies, has heard the question countless times from her countrymen as they come to terms with the mind-bending disjunction between the Iran they think exists, and the painful images of hatred and inadequacy the Western media insists are real.

"Oh, *that* question," I said.

For Iranians, Iran is everything, and what one thinks of their country matters a lot. So what Maryam was really trying to find out was, not what I thought of Iran per se, but how I navigated the minefield of conflicting emotions.

"If you say, 'Iran was nice,'" Maryam went on, "Iranians will tell you of all the bad things you might have missed. 'Did you not see the Hezbollahis? Don't you know how they treat their own people?' But if you say you didn't like Iran, they'll think, 'Who the hell are you to talk about my country like that?'"

She was right. When I was on a book tour counseling against a war with Iran, it was Iranian-Americans who were the most unwilling to accept anything that resembled dialogue between our country and the Islamic Republic of Iran. There is a special kind of resentment for the current government that goes well beyond its human rights abuses and aggressive foreign policy. This is because the current leaders are taking part in a long-running clash over what Iran's national image should be: pre-Islamic greatness or Islamic piety. The former represents the Iran many in the diaspora embrace, and the latter is the Islamic political system they abhor.

The last monarchical dynasty of Iran was founded in 1925 by strongman Reza Shah, who took "Pahlavi" as his family name. The name came from the Middle Iranian script used by the Sasanians, the last ethnic Persian dynasty to rule prior to the advent of Islam. To many Iranians, especially Reza Shah and his followers, Iran was greatest before Arab invaders Islamized the country beginning in the seventh century AD. For Reza Shah, Islam represented a backwards system, which was in large part to blame for the lack of development in his country. In 1935, the king went so far as to ban the women's headscarf, along with other forms of traditional dress.

Reza Shah's son and successor, Mohammad Reza, was not anti-Islam per se, but the pageantry of his rule emphasized pre-Islamic greatness, often to the disfavor of the country's conservative majority. Slowly but surely, generations educated under Reza Shah and his son began adopting an outlook that assumed Iran was greatest when ancient Zoroastrianism was the state religion. Islam, to them, represented a foreign Arab culture. In the eyes of many middle- and upper-class Iranians, this makes the Islamic Republic of today the most illegitimate of all forms of government—a slap in the collective "Persian" face of their nation.

"We are not Arabs, we're Indo-Europeans!"

Countless residents of California have heard this phrase from determined immigrants who have established vibrant communities in Westwood, Irvine, the San Fernando Valley, and beyond. For many of these residents of "Tehrangeles," the images of kings Cyrus and Darius are Iran itself, despite the fact that these national heroes lived over two millennia ago. But ask such an Iranian-American about Islam, and you might get a different response. "It's a foreign concept"; "It's Arab"; "We were doing fine before the Arabs came and gave us Islam."

Even in Iran, I managed to upset more than one person when I had the gall to ask about Shi'i religious practices in the country. "That's Arab," said one secular friend from the city of Shiraz. Referring to two foundational figures in Shi'i Islam, he said, "Ali, Hussein, they were Arabs, not Iranians. We are Zoroastrians." That was his way of saying that religion has no place in his country, and it struck me as odd being that we were having the conversation in the *Islamic Republic*. This curious tension between Islam and pre-Islamic "Persia," these competing narratives, are alive today within the borders of Iran as much as they are in the suburbs of Los Angeles.

Today's Iran, which in the Western media invites automatic associations with a turban-donning Ayatollah Khomeini; with images of American hostages being paraded by bearded radicals; this is the Iran that ultra secularists reject. It is the Iran that shattered into millions of frail pieces a picture of Western-leaning, Persian-derived greatness, which the last monarchy had worked so hard to build.

So the question that Iranian-Americans are asking is not, "What did you think about Iran?" The real question, underneath the layers of competing identities, is this one: "Which Iran did you see?" Did you see Cyrus or did you see Imam Hussein? Did you see the miniskirts of North Tehran from the 1970s, or did you see the woman covered from head to toe in a *chador*? Did you see the poverty and chaotic intersections, or did you see Iran's technological ingenuity?

Unlike those who think everyone is suffering under a "foreign" Islamic system, waiting for Americans to somehow come and rescue them from their political misery (yes, many self-exiled Iranians day-dream about this madness), and unlike those politicians who impose a religious order on a people who never asked for it, I happen to be like most non-Iranians: I see *both* sides of Iran. Getting past the cognitive dissonance, I can see what many Iranians, for their own reasons, may be unwilling to accept: that Mohammad Reza Shah, the last king of Iran, and Ayatollah Khomeini, the cleric who toppled him, are two former heads of state who were equally representative of their country. They were both Iran.

Then how do we approach that difficult loaded question that Maryam asked me about? We turn to Maryam's husband Steve for guidance.

"Steve has an interesting way of answering the question," says Maryam. "He says it's deeply rooted in orientalism, as in the sense of Iranians wanting to see themselves from the Other's point of view. Just think about the number of times you've gotten the question of what you thought about Iran, as opposed to Germany. Not that many Germans would ask you what you thought about their country. They don't care. It's the Iranians who are seeking the Other's view."

So we are dealing with "orientalism," as the late Edward Saïd interpreted it. For Saïd, a Palestinian-American, the romanticized and exaggerated visions of the Middle East are what orientalism is all about, a kind of Western "culturism"—being to culture, what racism is to race. Think of a Hollywood movie featuring a dancing cobra or a harem of sexy belly dancers covering their faces with a silk cloth, but baring just about everything else. These would be orientalist images at their most brutish. On a more serious level, orientalism is about a condescending, imperialistic view of the world beyond the West. It's about believing that Western ideas are superior to anything "Eastern," or "Oriental."

US academics have moved away from orientalism, casting it as inappropriate, if not outright racist. Yet rather than reject orientalism, many Iranians have come to embrace it with open arms. It was, after all, orientalism that drove much of the Pahlavi monarchy's efforts to rebrand Iranian identity. It was orientalism that created a story of a progressive, pre-Islamic greatness in Iran; the chariots and fancy balls, and the idea that Iran's Indo-European linguistic roots make the country into some kind of lost tribe of Western Europe. Reverse orientalism in fact seems to have been at work in this Iranian longing for Western acceptance.

But the Pahlavis' orientalism did not reign supreme. It had to compete with other ideas, often within individuals themselves. The resulting dichotomy of identities now lives inside most every single Iranian I've met. It is in the heart of self-proclaimed Muslims who denounce "Arab" influence in their faith; or in openly religious people who recite poems of wine and "lust" as allegories of religious devotion. Iran is Persia. Iran is Islam. Iran is great. Iran is...

Because of the inherent difficulties, Maryam's husband devised a way to avoid answering the question altogether. Whenever he was asked what he thought about Iran, he gave a simple response: "I liked the food." What a perfect answer. The food really *is* great.

While I learned to deflect the question with talk of food, there is something else that I must stop myself from saying every time the question is posed. What I really want to tell my Iranian-American friends is this: Whatever I think of Iran is irrelevant. I want to know what *you* think. Of all the narratives currently floating in the ether, like battling armies on some ancient relief, which one do you accept? Which is *your* Iran? The answer to that question would make for a more lively discussion.

Let Me Tell You Where I've Been

Persis M. Karim

Some have stamps in their passports,
emblems of official entry.
But the places charted
on this invisible map
are etched softly
in the curve of my spine.

Some women go deaf with the sound
of children crying and weep
at the thought of more
togetherness. And I keep looking
for a way to belong.

When you have traveled far
you begin to long for the particular thing:
the sweet mustiness of a childhood room,
the mix of cumin and freshly chopped parsley,
the dull, but knowable color
found in the joining
of four walls.

Conversations about children and debts
have detoured this longing.
Still, I want to speak names
of places with worn roads and blue-domed mosques:
Tehran, Shiraz, Esfahan--
places I want to say I've been.

I keep the box of inlaid enamel and wood--
its pattern of irregular triangles and stars,
the lid that fits a little too tightly--
purchased at a crowded bazaar.
I carry it with me, like a passport
not from this place
where I was born,
but from the other
I think I have been.

Beyond

Beyond this body,
the weathered edges
of the tent we live in
you'll find me.
Not moored to the language
of my father and mother
but creeping,
slipping over,
seeking the blue light
of the spaces between.

Masquerade

Jasmin Darznik

When I was a girl and my grandmother was on one of her longer visits to us here in America, we used to go trick-or-treating together on Halloween. I'd go dressed in the Persian princess costume she had sewn for me and she'd wear her old flower-print veil, the same one she usually kept folded away in the guest room for her daily prayers. Four feet eight inches tall with swaths of fabric trailing behind her, my veiled Iranian grandmother blended easily into the packs of costumed children. Before ringing each doorbell, she would draw the veil around her face, leaving only a small opening for her nose. From under many folds of fabric she'd say "treeeek treeeek," and present her plastic bag to the unsuspecting host.

For my grandmother, America was a very small place, much smaller than Iran. She didn't speak English, didn't know how to drive, and didn't know anyone in the United States whom she could call. She spent her days alone in the house, cooking and puttering, arranging and rearranging the contents of her suitcase. Then she'd tuck her toes under her in an armchair to watch *Days of Our Lives* until I came home in the afternoon, when she'd cook me stews and saffron rice and tell me Persian fairytales.

But once a year on Halloween she stepped out of the house to prowl the streets and re-enact the games she had played with her eight siblings in the alleyways near her childhood home in Tehran. When she was a kid, she and the neighborhood children performed the Persian New Year ritual of pulling sheets over their heads and knocking on their neighbors' doors with wooden spoons and pots. She'd been a girl when the Allies occupied Iran in the forties. Though food was extremely scarce then, children knew they could count on treats at the New Year—a date, a tiny lump of crystallized sugar, or some raisins. Halloween reminded my grandmother of those games, and on Halloween, Americans—of whom she was always shy and a little frightened—would suddenly become unwitting playmates in her game.

By the age of twelve I'd dismissed trick-or-treating as child's play and would have been mortified to be caught out with my veiled grandmother on Halloween night. "But we'll have so much fun!" she would plead.

"No way," I'd say and roll my eyes. From then on my grandmother went out trick-or-treating by herself.

While I stayed home, sprawled out on the couch watching whatever horror flick happened to be on TV, my mother would be out trailing my grandmother in our yellow Cadillac convertible as she made her Halloween rounds. Over the years my grandmother grew savvier, enlisting my mother to drive her out to neighborhoods far beyond our own.

At the end of the night, I might duck into her room to say goodnight and find her spreading out the evening's plunder on her bed, inspecting each piece of candy with her reading glasses balanced at the tip of her nose. She'd laugh as she recounted the details of her night. "Those neighbors in the big blue house gave away full-size chocolate bars!" she'd exclaim, or "Those teenagers with their ugly masks and their toilet paper!" She could easily be cajoled into sharing a miniature Baby Ruth or Almond Joy, and we'd sit side by side on the bed chewing candy until my mother appeared in the doorway to tell me it was time for bed. By the next day the rest of the candy disappeared into the recesses of my grandmother's suitcase.

Some years my grandmother would arrive months after Halloween, so she'd already have missed her opportunity to gather a fresh supply of candy. We'd be sitting together in the backseat of the car on one of our summer road trips to visit relatives in Los Angeles, and my grandmother would nudge me gently and hold out a faded and softly wrinkled packet of M&Ms she'd managed to save from her last Halloween outing— from America to Iran and back, and all the worse for the wear, kept safe in her suitcase through all those long flights.

The Halloween candy would take its place among the toiletries, clothes, and everything else she hoarded to bring back to her friends in Tehran. After a few months here, my grandmother's suitcase would grow so fat that it would not close with ease. Often she and my mom would spend the day of her departure taking turns sitting on the suitcase in an effort to force its metal clasps shut. The Ritual of the Suitcase could go on for hours, and it became my mother and grandmother's way of arguing about my grandmother's insistence on returning to Iran. My grandmother ran a beauty shop called The Lady Diola, a name she'd made up herself. She lived in a small apartment behind the salon. She loved the Lady Diola, and she loved Tehran.

"Why are you dragging all this back again?" my mother would start, bearing down on one corner of the suitcase while snatching vainly at its clasps. "I just don't understand you. What kind of home can you have there when your children have left?"

My grandmother said nothing. She was a quiet woman, who hated arguing.

"What are you going to do when you get really old? What am I supposed to do then?"

At these moments my mother could easily work her into a quivering rage. My grandmother would draw herself up, hands on her hips, and a fierceness would streak through her honey-colored eyes. "I took care of myself all through the Revolution and the war, too!"

To this my mother usually had little to say. My grandmother had survived what my parents and so many had fled, including the Iran-Iraq war, when bombs and air raids rattled the city for weeks on end. Without a husband or children to support her, she had remained in Iran longer than anyone—especially my mother—would have imagined possible. But my mother never gave up trying to make her stay in the United States, and my grandmother never gave up on leaving.

One year we arrived at the airport after a particularly tempestuous exchange. My grandmother hauled her suitcase onto the scale and looked up hopefully at the young male attendant.

"Thirty pounds over," he said, shaking his head.

"What did he say?" my grandmother asked me.

"He says the suitcase is too heavy," I translated. Even I could tell this man would not be won by her usual strategy of flirtatiousness or feigned disability.

"I'm not paying it," said my mother. "I've had it with that suitcase and all the junk you keep dragging around!"

My grandmother didn't respond; instead, she reached into her scuffed handbag and pulled out two crisp one hundred dollar bills to pay the excess baggage fee, enough to buy half a year's groceries in Iran. Nothing in her suitcase was worth that much, but she slid the bills onto the counter without flinching. That was one of the years my mother and grandmother did not say goodbye to each other.

"Please take me with you!" I said, clutching my grandmother's skirt as I cried.

"I'd tuck you into my suitcase, but see how you've grown!" my grandmother said, pinching my sides and then kissing me goodbye.

Eventually my grandmother could no longer make the 24-hour trek to America and her visits stopped altogether. Some years ago she died, alone, in Tehran. None of us ever made the trip back to visit her, and it's ten years ago now that I last saw her. But every year at Halloween I still see her winding her way through the streets in her flower-print veil. She might have looked strange there among the ballerinas and superheroes, pumpkins and ghouls, but that was the beauty of my grandmother's costume—she'd never been wearing one at all.

Movies with My Aunt

Afarin Bellisario

*I*n the early 1960s, Tehran was expanding in almost all directions. New apartment buildings and townhouses provided housing for the emerging middle class in the east and west, while the rich moved into modern villas in the north. Private cars, taxis, motorbikes, and bicycles shared the wide avenues with the newest mode of transportation: the double-decker bus, imported directly from London. Movie houses sprang up in northern Tehran, featuring wide screens, stereo sound systems, and red velvet chairs. They showed dubbed, first-run, American movies—all the films I longed to see. Persian and Indian films were moved to the old theaters on Lale-Zar Avenue, Tehran's former entertainment center, further to the south.

That was when my aunt Manzar and I started going to the movies together. I had always loved movies. As a young child, I looked forward to the annual showing of Jerry Lewis and Norman Wisdom comedies, as well as the occasional Disney film or musical. As I grew out of comedies, I became a fan of historical movies, mostly those with Roman or Christian themes. Later, by the time Manzar and I had begun our cinematic ritual, I had started craving glamour, romance, drama, and action. I sought a new horizon, a glimpse of a world I yearned to explore. Since I was too young to go to the movies with my friends, Manzar's invitation felt like the key to a magical world. We started going to matinées on Thursdays, the start of the weekend in Iran.

Growing up, I had spent little time alone with Manzar aside from when she babysat me. She had finished high school not long after I was born. Like many Iranian girls of the time, she kept busy helping my grandmother around the house, waiting to be married. However, unlike most girls of her age, she was not particularly fond of makeup or gossip. She was quiet and shy, and seemed ambivalent about the prospect of an engagement, expressing little interest in meeting suitors. Instead, when she was about 30 and my grandmother had given up hope for her , she went to work. Within months, she cut her hair short, began wearing makeup and put on the trendy clothes my mother and I made for her. She started to look like a movie star.

This was how I remember her from when we went to the cinema together. American movies were our favorites. We were awed by the desert in *Lawrence of Arabia* and mesmerized by Audrey Hepburn's elegance in *Charade*. We laughed at the follies of *The Pink Panther* and cried at the end of *West Side Story*. After the movies, we would walk home, sometimes stopping for ice cream or pastries, and talk about the film we had just seen. The normally quiet Manzar would become animated, and the age difference between us would disappear. Usually, our conversation was limited to movies and fashion, but one Thursday in the fall, as we walked home after seeing *Charade*, Manzar told me about a new engineer at work named Ali. I still remember the sound of our steps on the carpet of colorful leaves covering the sidewalk as she told me about him. He was shy and worked alongside her, at the next worktable. As she talked, I envisioned a budding romance, and thought, "We are in the movies."

A few months later, in line to get tickets to *From Russia with Love*, she told me more about Ali. The first snow of winter was falling on Tehran and we were trying to stay warm. Manzar said that Ali wasn't handsome like Sean Connery, but was good looking in his own way. They had started talking at work, mostly about the movies she and I had seen the week before. I suggested she invite him to join us, but she said Thursdays were just for us, and what if someone should see?

By the time *Goldfinger* made it to Tehran in the spring, Manzar and Ali were eating lunch together in the park near their office. He seemed to make her less old-fashioned. He would bring sweets for tea and would sometimes walk her to the bus after work. Almost a year and a half after she first talked about Ali, Manzar told me that Ali was going to send his mother to see my grandmother and ask for Manzar's hand. We were walking home after seeing *My Fair Lady*. I could see the red in my aunt's cheeks even in the fading light of the late afternoon sun. The weather was unusually warm and the shade of the poplar trees felt cool. There was excitement in Manzar's voice. Perhaps for the first time in her life she was looking forward to the prospect of marriage. She said Ali would be going to the United States to continue his studies in the fall and that she would wait for him to come back. My mother was excited about the news, but my grandmother insisted the engagement be kept secret until Ali's return from America.

The day after he left Tehran, Manzar and I saw *Doctor Zhivago*. We both cried for the doomed lovers and the choices they had to make, but the warmth of early fall in Tehran was a far cry from the cold of the Siberian steppes, and neither of us took the movie as an omen. Ali wrote letters every week. Manzar shared them with me after the movies as we sat at our favorite pastry shop. To my teenage ears, the letters were a bit drab—no mention of sleepless nights, burning desires, or promises of being together forever. His letters were a simple account of his life in the United States: a new apartment, his roommates, sudden cold weather in Boston, bland food, exams, and his attempt at mastering the subway. Manzar would read each letter over and over with a smile.

By the time we saw *How to Steal a Million Dollars*, almost a year after Ali left, the letters had become less frequent. On that winter day, we went for pastry after the movie. I babbled about the beauty of Peter O'Toole's blue eyes, but Manzar was quiet, not even commenting on the appearance or acting of Audrey Hepburn, her favorite star. Finally she told me that she hadn't heard from Ali for three weeks. I told her he was probably busy with exams and would write her soon.

A few weeks later, a final letter arrived. He had decided to stay in America indefinitely and didn't want her to wait for him and lose opportunities. Manzar was subdued. We continued going to the movies, but she stopped commenting on them. We still chatted afterward, but we never mentioned Ali again. Her story couldn't match the Hollywood endings of all those movies we had seen. I started going to see European films, subtitled, with my friends from Cine-club, discovering Felini, Antonioni, Godard, and Truffaut. I wanted something edgy and different, something dark and realistic. I started spending Thursday afternoons preparing for parties with friends, where we talked politics, smoked and slow danced. Manzar and I stopped going to movies together.

I moved to the United States in 1974, but it wasn't the land I had seen in the movies.

The last time I saw Manzar was just before the Iranian revolution. By then both my grandparents had died, and Manzar was living by herself in their apartment. We sat in the living room by the table, which was covered with a large collection of family pictures she had started to collect. She looked much older than her age and was already growing into the stereotype of the spinster auntie most of our family would remember her as: kind, quiet, and slightly obsessive; the kind who could be counted on as a last minute babysitter, who remembered every birthday and always had a gift ready.

As we sipped our tea, she looked at me with a smile and said, "It was fun going to the movies, wasn't it?"

I looked at her, and although she never got her Hollywood ending, for a brief moment I saw the young woman I knew so many years ago: happy, confident, and in love.

Iranian (-) American

Roger Sedarat

Following the path of contiguous relationships, the realist author metonymically digresses from the plot to the atmosphere and from the characters to the setting in space and time. He is fond of synecdochic details.

— Ramon Jakobson

Never more myself than in metonymy,
the hyphen suspending me in mid-air
on a plane between Iran and America

above the Atlantic as I watch the women
wearing make-up and short skirts disappear
into the lavatory—

Never more occupied with thoughts of existence
than when waiting to piss by the little locked door
as one woman after another enshrouds herself in black.

What a relief to feel such cabin pressure
upon arriving at a place
neither here nor there

with a U.S. passport in one back pocket
and an Islamic Republic of Iran passport in the other.
At last I see the "vacant" sign

and empty my very being
in the toy potty
(so much tea and Diet Coke

imbibed from Paris to Tehran).
On one level I'm just a man
doing his business in business class.

Then the announcement we're making our descent.
Never more myself than approaching
one of two countries from which I came

despite never really being whole—
in Persian they say "nimeh," meaning "two"
instead of "half"—

an apt metaphor for my position in the john,
except I'm only going number one,
(never, as a rule, doing the other in the air).

Nose Jobs

Roger Sedarat

for Stephanie Oppenheim

White strip of significance,
aesthetic band-aid

for twenty-something Persians.
More than an underlying wound,

the post-operation rectangle
transforms the face, framing the question

heretical to ask of art:
did the surgery really happen?

Say Maryam just did it for show;
the veiled mystery endures.

Social psychologists theorize how the law to cover
bodies and hair intensifies the face.

If this were true, how come I stand
in front of my wife's dressing mirror,

facing the fact that in my later thirties
I've come to resemble my Grandma Taj?

Under the knife I could look more
like Clark Kent and less like Ben Kingsley

in the film adaptation
of *House of Sand and Fog*.

Whether real or imagined, the nose job
becomes a post-modern performance.

Follow the appearances of ethnicity long enough
and the individual disappears.

But oh, to cut my own origins
and walk incognito

through the streets of Tehran
like a western superhero!

I can almost smell the new sense of freedom
like Shirazi roses in spring.

Morteza Varzi

Robyn C. Friend, Ph.D.

I nearly met Mr. Varzi during my stay in Iran in 1975, but it happened that our meeting took place in the United States four years later. Neil and I had just married, and we were ready to embark on a joint musical adventure. A musician friend invited Neil to join him in a little concert he was arranging for a classical Persian musician who played the *kemanche,* a small violin-like instrument. I was in graduate school, too busy to continue full-time with the dance company, but liked the idea of cultivating my voice. I got up the courage to ask the kemanche player, Mr. Varzi, if he would teach me classical Persian singing. He agreed, and thus began a musical association between Mr. Varzi, Neil, our friend Peggy, and myself, that lasted two decades and more.

Mr. Varzi told us that he had worked for an oil company in Iran, and later had been the deputy governor of Khorasan province. He had come to America on a business trip in the late 1970s, and decided to stay here and wait out the unrest in Iran from a safe distance. He gained residency as a political refugee—having been part of the shah's government, his return to Iran might have been risky for him—and eventually became an American citizen. As a result, he began life in the States with only his instrument and a suitcase.

We never called him anything but Mr. Varzi, never his first name. Our relationship was somewhat formal, especially by American standards. Our meetings, regardless of where we had them followed a pattern that varied very little over the years. We would arrive, drink some tea, and chat while Mr. Varzi had a cigarette. This small ritual over, the four of us would play music.

It was not always easy to learn from Mr. Varzi. He told us that he had had a sweet voice when he was young, but cigarettes had roughened his voice and age had blunted his hearing, so that it was sometimes difficult to follow him. We did not use music books, but learned in the old way, "at the feet of the master," with the addition of a cassette recorder. He would play whole pieces, seldom breaking out short segments. We were expected to learn by memory—it was a rigorous intellectual activity. Nor was the learning restricted to music; Persian poetry, mysticism, philosophy, history, culture, morality were included. He taught in a holistic style.

Then Mr. Varzi would serve us a dinner that he had cooked himself. He usually refused our offers to pay him for lessons. Our first lessons took place in a condemned apartment building in Westwood, known to locals as "Tehrangeles" for the many Iranians living in the area. The apartment building was owned by a friend of his, and he was allowed to stay there until the demolition began. Over the years, Mr. Varzi moved countless times, from one modest apartment to another. He had a few prized possessions that seemed to make the moves with him, but for the most part, other than his kemanche, he seemed to care little about "things."

Mr. Varzi had not studied at the music conservatory in Tehran, and could barely read music. This caused some derision among the young, conservatory-trained musicians who began showing up in Los Angeles after the 1979 revolution. We liked his delicate improvisations, and his sensitivity to the nuances of setting mystical poetry to music. The young virtuosi were technically brilliant, but could not improvise, and could not evoke the emotional response that Mr. Varzi did. His performances were treasured by the local community. Mr. Varzi had learned music by rote, from some of the masters of Persian classical music in the twentieth century, Bahari and Ney-Davoud. His family were patrons and friends of musicians; he knew the greatest performing artists of that time—Banan, Marzieh, Majd, Payvar, Shajarian, Hussein Tehrani, and many others. Whenever any of them came to Los Angeles, they would always pay him a visit, often on our rehearsal nights.

We soon learned to dress nicely and be prepared for anything at our sessions with him. Sometimes we would arrive to find that some famous composer, singer, or musician would be sitting on Mr. Varzi's couch, and we would be called upon to perform. Often upon arriving at Mr. Varzi's door, he would say, "Let's go to so-and-so's house," where we would find ourselves the main entertainment at an elegant party.

For a time, our rehearsals were held on Saturday mornings at the ocean-view penthouse of one of Mr. Varzi's friends. It seemed like the entire Iranian Diaspora community was either in the apartment, or picnicking and strolling in the park below. Our hosts would have invited a constellation of Iranian and Iranophile stars: a former Miss Iran; a well-known singer; the former poet laureate of Iran; a former US ambassador to Iran. While our own countrymen were sitting in front of a televised basketball game, eating nachos and drinking beer, these party guests took turns reciting poetry, singing, and producing extemporaneous verse. My husband and I felt like small children allowed for once to stay up with the grown-ups.

Love and Pomegranates

At some point, we would be asked to play for the guests. Most people would be very charmed and touched by our obvious enthusiasm and commitment to learning this intricate art. Over the years our knowledge and abilities grew to some level of competence, and under Mr. Varzi's tutelage, we transitioned from a novelty to popular artists. Mr. Varzi also grew in his role as keeper and transmitter of traditional Iranian music. His Iranian students called him *Ostad*, signifying a teacher and "master" of apprentices, art, or craft.

Toward the end of his life, Mr. Varzi and I worked on a project together, just the two of us, translating some books published in Iran on traditional regional music and dance. He began to have coughing spells, and an odd strain appeared in his speaking voice. When asked, he insisted that his doctor could not determine the cause, and dropped the subject.

At our last session together, he gave me the books we had been translating, and said that he was going to Iran for a month and would be back soon. I wanted to believe him, but, however long his visit in Iran might be, I knew that he would not be returning in one month. I spoke with him in Iran about six weeks after he left, by phone; he sounded, if not fine, very much as usual. It was a shock, then, two weeks later when we received a phone call at 4:00 a.m. from Iran saying that he had died, that he had been diagnosed with terminal lung cancer months before and had chosen not to tell us, that he had gone home to Iran to die and be buried there.

How to calculate the debt owed for what was given freely? He never asked for much, and told us little about his personal life and how he managed to support himself here. To others, he referred to us as "my kids." He shared with us his love of the poetry of Mowlana Jalal al-Din Rumi and Hafiz, his philosophy of life, and how to express the intricacies of Persian mystical poetry through music. For this I will always be grateful, and for the gift of music that has given me my own life's work. ▪

Travels with Ramazan

Meghan Nuttall Sayres

From outside my guide Amir and I could hear the *tock* of Ramazan's weaver's shuttle, the loud noise of metal slamming against wood, as we approached his studio in Yazd, Iran. The sound mixed with shouts of glee from the schoolyard beside his workshop, its cheerful gate painted with flowers and stars. On a nearby adobe wall, someone had spray painted in red: "Friendly internet here." I was struck by how the neighborhood, with its mud walls likely dating back some four thousand years, was now wired for web access and adorned with illegal satellite dishes. My guide thought that because I was a weaver, I might enjoy a visit with Ramazan.

"Actually, I love visiting with this man," Amir confessed. "You are a perfect excuse to stop in."

Inside, we found the 90-year-old master weaver perched on a stool in the middle of thousands of blue and orange threads that made up the warp on his loom. He sat knotting split ends together.

"You are very welcome here," he said to me with the help of Amir. The weaver disengaged from his warp threads. He moved very slowly. "You're from America?" His brow lifted, but he smiled.

Fabrics hung on every wall. Ramazan's colors—bright white, yellow, pink, red and orange—I would soon learn reflected his playful inner light. They resembled a hippie-like, striped tie-dye design that is typically found in the Central Asian cities of Samarkand and Bukhara, which were once part of the Persian Empire.

He offered me a chair to sit beside him, explaining that his 65 years of weaving on a fly-shuttle loom left his joints sore. "I hear there is good medicine in America. Do you have something you can give me for my knees?"

While I didn't have a remedy for the weaver's arthritis, I happened to have a skein of my own sheep wool with me. I had been knitting during my travels.

"What am I to do with this?" he said, a grin stealing across his lips. "It's not enough to make a coat." The lines creasing his face hinted at stories of life lived fully. Placing the wool on his nearly hairless head, he said. "Perhaps I'll make a hat."

Ramazan agreed to demonstrate his weaving for me, easing himself upright with the aid of a hand-carved wooden cane. It took some time for him to walk the length of his unusually long warp (at least twelve feet long) and climb into a pit to his bench seat. His 400-year-old loom was made of walnut. Reaching for a rope above his head, he tugged hard, sending the fly shuttle sideways into motion while pumping the wooden foot treadles with his stocking feet. Up and down went his knees. Back and forth went his shuttle. For decades he has come here to work in the heart of the old quarter of Yazd, a maze of adobe homes with domed rooftops.

I told him about a recent tapestry I had woven, confessing how much I disliked warping my little loom. I hadn't the patience to string a mere one hundred threads through the heddle.

"Kheili khoob. Very nice," he said, holding my tapestry depicting a mosque, the Sufi saint Rabi'a, and a poem attributed to her in Arabic script. "Very good." My young guide told Ramazan about my novel in which the protagonist is a nomadic weaver. As Amir translated Ramazan gave me the thumbs up and chuckled. Though Ramazan intended his gesture to be interpreted as it would be in the West, we all knew that in Iran it meant the same as giving someone the middle finger.

That evening at my hotel I sat in the courtyard on a cushioned platform covered with a plush carpet beside a stream of water running through a tiled trench. Sharing this space with me were Iranian families who treated themselves to fruit drinks and late night ice cream while their children ran about. As I sipped freshly-squeezed mango juice, the scent of honeysuckle sweetened the air. While enjoying the outdoors, I knitted a hat I had started on the plane from Tehran to Shiraz, before driving to Yazd. Picturing Ramazan with the skein of yarn on his head, I decided that the colors in this hat would compliment his bright blue eyes. I would give it to him. I knitted until long after the stars crowded the sky.

The next morning Amir and I discussed going to the Zoroastrian shrine located about two hours away at a place in the mountains named Chak Chakoo. For centuries, Yazd has been the home to the majority of Zoroastrians in Iran, and the center of this faith worldwide.

As we left the hotel I showed Amir the tasseled hat that I had finished early that morning.

"You must give Ramazan this gift yourself," he said. So we drove back through the streets of Amir's hometown—a town of about 40, 000 people—and into the maze of adobe-lined alleys in search of the weaver in need of a hat.

When we stepped into his studio, Ramazan smiled and got up from his loom. I gave him the hat and he immediately tried it on. "Kheili khoob! Kheili khoob," he said, nodding. He showed it to his colleague, the merchant who manned the store and sold Ramazan's woven fabrics.

"Thank you," the weaver said in English. Then he spoke to my guide, who explained, "Ramazan says he has nothing to give you, but he would like for us to stay for tea."

The weaver ushered us through his workshop to a bare wooden platform like the carpeted one I had sat upon at my hotel the night before. He lit the flame beneath his two-tiered *samovar*, a teapot for making traditional Iranian *chai*. All the while he wore his knitted hat.

When he heard that we were going to Chak Chakoo he told my guide that as a child he used to travel on horseback with his father to the Zoroastrian cave and that it had been ages since he had gone there. He asked Amir if he could come along and Amir translated. Would I mind?

"I'd love to spend the day with Ramazan!"

The weaver beamed when I gave him both my thumbs up. I showed him how to clink teacups in a toast to the journey we would have together. While my guide retrieved the car so that Ramazan wouldn't have to walk too far, the weaver removed a navy-blue sport jacket and trousers from a peg on the wall. He chatted and laughed with his co-worker as he pulled on his traveling pants over his striped work trousers. I guessed that for modesty's sake he chose to risk feeling hot while on the road rather than change his clothes in front of me.

Before getting into the car, Ramazan enjoyed a cigarette while Amir replenished the thermos of tea that he kept in the trunk. We whizzed through the streets of Yazd—dodging people, motorcycles and cars that seemed unconcerned about traffic rules. Soon the dusty Shirkuh and Karanagh Mountains loomed in the distance. Along the way Ramazan recited the poetry of 'Omar Khayyam from the back seat. Amir translated, "Of eternal secrets, neither you know, nor I. To solve this puzzle, neither you know nor I." We drove past lone tiled mosques, glittering blue jewels in the sand. "The Way is neither that nor this..."

The road to Chak Chakoo resembled some I've driven in the American West, but the desert felt more vast and more sparse. The sand and air parched my skin and throat and I felt in constant need of water. Every so often, Ramazan tapped me on the shoulder and gave me a thumbs up. One time when I returned the gesture he went so far as to squeeze my thumb. I smiled at him, wondering what he might think—a man whose adult life was largely lived before the Islamic Revolution—about some of the more strict traditions of Islam, the rules that would prohibit him from greeting or saying goodbye to me, or any a female guest, with a handshake or a hug. I so appreciated and respected this person who recited "unorthodox" Sufi poetry; who wished to travel miles into the desert to make a pilgrimage to a Zoroastrian temple; and who squeezed the thumb of an American woman, someone from the nation who vilified his people the most.

We made a few more cigarette stops in the blustery expanse of desert. On one occasion we explored a *qanat*, an ancient underground irrigation system that runs from the mountains through the plains, bringing water to cities and villages. Finally, we arrived at the Zoroastrian shrine. At the base of the mountain we found a gravel space, about half a dozen cars, and people picnicking. A concrete building, which sprawled up the side of the mountain, served as a resting place for pilgrims. People camped and barbecued on its open-air porches. Ramazan's legs would not grant him the privilege of the climb, so leaving him with a fresh cup of tea, Amir and I set out together. Lizards scurried out of our way.

Walking up the stony road toward the shrine, Amir told me that guests of all faiths are invited to visit the cave temple to celebrate or to learn about Zarathustra. However, the place is reserved strictly for Zoroastrians during the month of June, when followers of Zarathustra from all over the world come for a pilgrimage. Thousands of years before the Jews settled on worshipping one god, Zarathustra worshipped one God, Ahura Mazda. Amir spoke up when a jeep roared past. "Zarathustra believed that people should strive to harmonize themselves with the rule of justice, and with good thoughts, words and deeds. Such people reflect the qualities of God for the benefit of mankind."

In my hotel in Yazd I had found a book titled *Zarathustra* in English by Jalaleddin Ashtiani. The author compares what all the scholars have concluded or speculated about the origins and practice of Zoroastrianism and he offers new insights of his own. Ashtiani suggests that the prophet Zarathustra settled in this part of Iran much earlier than others believe, sometime between 1500 and 5000 BC.

The road made way to a path and then a set of steep stairs, which led toward the smell of lamb kabob. I recalled reading that most scholars agree that Zarathustra's message was one of free will and choice. Anyone who thinks well and acts well—whether or not they follow a prophet—are dear to God and deserve happiness. Institutionalized practices lose meaning within the framework of Zoroastrianism.

Norooz, the Iranian New Year, a celebration in which Iranians light bonfires, is a ritual grounded in Zoroastrianism. And it was toward a flame that we drove hours into the desert that day with Ramazan. Three small ones, in fact, which we would find glowing from a silver sculpture inside Zarathustra's temple.

The shrine, we learned, after huffing our way up to the cave, was closed. But after hearing that I had travelled all the way from America, the keeper opened it.

The rock inside this cool space hollowed into the mountainside was a deep red-brown, rich in iron. About the size of a high school classroom, I imagined the sanctuary could hold up to 30 people or more. A niche in the wall cradled a silver geometric work of art about shoulder height that supported three small candles, one for each tenet of

Zarathustra: good thoughts, good words, good deeds. The shallow depression in the rock behind the candelabra resembled the arched recess in the wall of a mosque, which aligns the congregation with Mecca.

A waterfall offered a steady trickle of music in the cave while a window punched through the rock wall ushered in a fresh breeze. Earth, air, fire and water, as well as almond incense rising from a lotus-petal-shaped table, awakened all of my senses. The elements contributed to the ambience and perhaps to the meaning of a Zoroastrian pilgrimage. This temple reminded me of the unadorned simplicity of cave churches I visited in Cappadocia, Turkey. Fire, as a symbol of inner light, called to mind my own Celtic roots. Druids lit fires during festivals and considered water to be holy. Surely, my ancestors were from tribes who may have followed Zarathustra somewhere high in the Caucuses before roaming west to Ireland. True or not, the raw nature of this cave temple and the presence of the four elements resonated with me spiritually.

When leaving the shrine a large family of a least a dozen people, who were sitting on carpets under one of the covered porches of the visitors' building, motioned for Amir and me to join them. Women wore in colorful prints that resemble Indian saris. Some of the men dressed in tribal caps and embroidered vests. Learning I was American, they welcomed me to Iran and invited us to eat with them. We would have joined the pic-nickers if Ramazan had not been waiting for us in the car. Surely he had been sweltering in the day's heat in his double layer of wool pants. I felt very warm beneath copious lay-ers of my *hejab*, Islamic wear. We found Ramazan with an empty tea cup chatting with pilgrims who had recognized him from Yazd.

On the way home the master weaver told the legend about a young Zoroastrian princess Shahrbanu (Lady of the Land), likely from Yazdegard III's kingdom near Baghdad, who had fled Muslim Arab armies in Iraq. She rode east through the Persian plains, not stopping until she reached the mountain cave at Chak Chakoo. Here she felt she could live safely and practice her faith. People say that the mountains at Chak Chakoo opened up for the princess. She vanished into the ravines, and the waterfall that trickles into the temple of Zarathustra to this very day is fed by her tears.

In the middle of telling his tale, Ramazan's cell phone rang. "Yes?" he answered. Amir translated what he said next for me. "I'm in Chak Chakoo with an American woman. No. I am not joking." He laughed and hung up the phone. "She doesn't believe me," Ramazan said to us. It had occurred to me that someone might be worried about this man who had left Yazd without notifying anyone.

Smiling, I imagined receiving a phone call just then from my own family members. If I told them where I was, who I was with and what we had just done—maybe they wouldn't believe my story, either. At least twice that day asked myself, *Am I really here?* How had this pilgrimage happened? I wondered if it were Ramazan or myself who was the guest, which of us granted the other this spontaneous gift of a day together in the desert. Or was it the benevolent hand of Ahura Mazda?

Love and Pomegranates

We stopped for lunch at a *caravanserai,* an old camel shelter that served as a rest stop and trading post along the ancient route running between Yazd and Mashhad, in Eastern Iran. Ramazan said that he used to come through here as a boy by camel train on northbound pilgrimages to the Holy Shrine of Imam Reza in Mashhad. The weaver ate very little and gave me the lamb kabob that he didn't want, passing it to me with his fingers. I felt touched that he didn't bother with the formality of utensils. Maybe he felt as comfortable with me as he might with family. I certainly felt that way about him.

Back in Yazd Ramazan told Amir that it was time for "his smoke." Amir and I wondered what he had meant as he'd been smoking every chance he got during the day. When we arrived in the vicinity of his neighborhood in the old part of the city Ramazan confessed that he didn't know his way home. "My grandson drives me to work everyday," Amir translated, then looking into the rear view mirror, he told Ramazan, "I know the neighborhood fairly well. Give me some landmarks to go by and we'll get you home."

Ramazan slid forward on his seat, ducking his head to get a good look out the front windshield. All the while the weaver spewed out a string of mild curses, joking about his recent lack of memory. We drove past a park with plane trees and a colorful plastic jungle gym. Then down a wide street, alleys shooting off in all directions. They all looked the same. It was no wonder Ramazan couldn't recall where he lived.

Amir took a wild guess and turned into an alley where he thought Ramazan might live and something jarred the weaver's memory. He studied every motorbike we passed to see if he could find his grandson's. After passing by a dozen, half-submerged, ancient doors, we came to a dead end. Fastened on the mud wall beside one of these doors was a silver and blue piece of metal that looked much like a license plate on a car. The number matched Ramazan's home address. Ramazan raised his hand. We all slapped our palms together. "High fives!" Amir said, and laughed.

The weaver invited us to dinner, but not wanting him to go to the trouble or the expense we declined. However, we agreed to tea.

Just as Ramazan pushed open the door to the pedestrian alley, his cell phone rang again. "Blast this phone, it's been bothering me all day!" he said. I smiled as I did the math: two calls in roughly eight hours. "Yes. Yes. I'm home now. Where? I've been to London!"

We entered a bare courtyard with stone flooring. The only sign of habitation was the earthen basin beneath a water spigot. A woman wearing a traditional *chador* appeared. Ramazan introduced his granddaughter Nahid to us, and soon after his grandson Mohammad Reza arrived. The two were cousins. We sat on the floor in a cozy, two-room enclave furnished with Ramazan's bed and a carpet.

"I have so enjoyed the time I have spent with your grandfather," I said to Nahid as she set a match to the samovar.

"Would you like to take him home with you?" Amir translated.

"I'd love to," I said, knowing already that this fellow weaver would forever be with me. "But you would miss him."

"You are right," Nahid said and offered us cookies Ramazan kept in a box beside his bed. The grandchildren lived in the adjoining homes and again we were invited to dinner, but politely declined. I felt torn as I would have loved to spend more time with this family, but Amir and I both still felt like we shouldn't accept.

"Then stay for a smoke," Ramazan waved his hand, imploring Amir, myself and his grandson to sit with him around a small brazier in his back room. We all squeezed into the four-by-seven foot space, sitting cross-legged. Ramazan produced a huge, heavy wooden pipe that looked as if it were handed down to him from generations past. Surely it had emitted smoke into the starry nights of desert pilgrims.

Ramazan puffed on his pipe. A thick, pungent, very-not-tobacco scent soon clenched the air. It singed my lungs as it suffused my headscarf, hair and flowing beaded *manteaux*. My intuition suggested that maybe I should excuse myself, that I probably shouldn't pass by the registration desk back at my hotel—located in a tiny alcove—smelling like this. It might raise eyebrows, as it flared nostrils.

I looked at Amir who sat shaking his head and smiling. "That's not tobacco he's smoking."

"I know," I said. "I guess it's the secret to his longevity."

Images of Ramazan's blue, orange, pink, and slightly-fuzzy-to-the-eye, tie-dye colors flashed behind my eyes. The word psychedelic came to mind. Opium-inspired designs?

As we departed, Ramazan put on his hat to show his grandchildren and I wondered would his memory of our day together outlast its knitted threads.

Ramazan and I met in a desert untouched by time or distance, a space devoted to finding gems in the gardens of others where we were told we'd find only stones. An expanse that allowed us to untie the knots that need not bind us.

No Fellow Footfall

Ryszard Antolak

She thought of the narrowness of the limits within which a human soul
might speak and be understood by its nearest of mental kin, and how soon
it reaches that solitary land of the individual experience in which no fellow
footfall is ever heard.

—Olive Schreiner

Thirty miles or so south of Shiraz lies the little village of Qalat, situated among rich orchards of pomegranates and figs. It is a narrow, cramped, Sasanian village constructed on the side of a steep mountain streaked with horizontal lines, as if it had been mauled by a giant lion. It was a place, my traveling companion and I had been told, where nothing remarkable had ever taken place, where poetry had been written and roses had fallen from their stems in silence, a place whose inhabitants had disguised their missions of love and hate behind the privacy of high walls and closed lips for centuries. There was really nothing to interest anyone there.

I tried hard to believe it, but every village has its secrets. We could feel it as we hauled ourselves up the steep lane that twisted between heavy-walled houses washed in faded ochre and terracotta, all of them shuttered and in various stages of dilapidation. We let ourselves believe we could hear voices coming from the thick semi-circular doors built to withstand attack and deter intruders.

Now and again we caught sight of a figure disappearing into an adjoining alleyway. We glimpsed it more than once and presumed it was a dog that had followed us up the steep slope, curious at the presence of strangers.

Finally we reached what we had come to see: an old Armenian church that had been built (so we were told) sometime during the Qajar period. It was magnificently situated on an escarpment of rock near the summit of the village, the best preserved ruin in a town of countless ruins. But when we entered it, we found little more than an empty shell, its walls smothered in graffiti, its floors covered with the stains of countless fires.

Around the church was a crude wall that concealed not so much a large garden as a neglected orchard. We entered through a metal door emblazoned with an Armenian cross. It groaned with gratitude at being opened. The interior was an overgrown paradise of pomegranate and fig trees. The cinnamon of pine needles and the perfumes of various blossoms hung heavy in the air. My imagination flickered to life. This was a space full of expectation, an emptiness that might be peopled with characters from a novel.

Because the faint whisper of trees and the murmuring of birds cast such a spell on us, it was some time before we realized we were not alone. In the far corner beneath the trees was a silent figure in a black chador. She was coming toward us, fingers of shadow caressing her body as she did so.

From a distance she looked young, even girlish. But as she approached she faded visibly. The woman had a face, neither young nor old, unbearably round and regular. She was decidedly matronly, but comfortable and loose within her own body and dressed (as was the custom in those parts) in a many-layered skirt that trailed behind her a little across the ground. The visitor said nothing, but stood observing us intently. She would have cast a shadow in shadowless surroundings. We tried to offer her a few words of traditional greeting. But she didn't reply, and continued staring at us as if searching for the handles of doors to some personal revelation.

Nothing could disguise for us the scent of tobacco and the odor of unwashed laundry that surrounded her. I felt uneasy in her presence and uncomfortable at the disorder of her hair, which could not be contained by her ragged shawl.

My companion made a gesture to leave, and I turned briskly toward the gate. The woman called out to me in a thin grey voice, exposing the ruins of some teeth in the process. I did not understand (or did not wish to) and merely waved my hand at her in dismissal. As we hastened down the cobbled lane of the village, I looked behind me and she was still there, following us with her large dark eyes and the great bulk of the scarred mountain looming behind her.

It was only later, when we entered the local shop and let slip to the owner of our unusual meeting at the church, that parts of a jigsaw began to form around us. The old man came over and seated himself on a crate of bottles beside us. We could see he was kind, and he felt entrusted to tell us something of the woman's history. The stories he told were long and rambling and there seemed no order or logic to them. But we settled down for the next hour or so to listen.

If there had ever been a time when she was genuinely happy (the old man began), the war with Iraq turned everything to ashes. Her husband of only a few months disappeared in the first months of the conflict and his body was never found. No one could tell her what had happened to him, whether he was alive or dead. So she waited for him, mourning her loss. She lived for months and years waiting for a knock, looking for a sign that never materialized, clinging to the hope that one day he would return to her again. But no news arrived. She no longer slept or ate. In the evenings, she would spend her time standing on the veranda of her house, smoking endless cigarettes from a black holder that belonged to her grandmother. With every day that passed, her body became thinner, and her thoughts began to take on an ever more corrosive quality.

I imagined her standing on the road at the bottom of the village waiting for him, the wind blowing her chador this way and that as her eyes swept the horizon. I expected candles to be dashed to the ground when doors were opened, and winds to rush down stone passages, swelling beneath the kilims on the walls around me.

During this time, the man continued, her intermittent headaches became ever more frequent and more severe. She consulted doctors in Shiraz who saw in her sleepless nights, in the shock of separation, in the daily terrors of the war, the root causes of her illness. They prescribed homeopathic medicines and cold water therapies. One of the doctors was blessed with natural healing powers and even offered to treat her for free, but to no avail.

One day, she went into her bedroom and took out the beautiful wooden chest her husband had given her in which she kept her wedding clothes and other items from their life together. She brought them out one by one and laid them on the floor beside her. There they were—the yellow love letters, the locks of hair, the handwritten pages of poetry, the sepia photographs enlarged to ridiculous proportions—and she became overcome with such inconsolable grief that she could not weep enough over the enormity of her loss.

From that day on, she withdrew into the protective walls of her house and emerged only at night. She began haunting the town in her black chador like a living ghost, searching the blizzards of memory for any vestige of him. There followed interminable months of wandering through unremembered villages, sleeping in the ruins of deserted buildings, eating any piece of rancid food she could find to satisfy her hunger. And each time her family found her, they brought her home and nursed her to health. Finally the doctor told them what no longer needed telling, that the woman had broken her mind on the memory of her loss, and retreated into an innocence where no one could reach her.

It was then that the war of the cities began, and the woman found herself caught up in a tide of refugees fleeing to escape the bombing. She found herself in Mashhad where the golden cupola of Imam Reza, the marble courtyards of pilgrims, the mirrored hallways bejeweled with divine art made such an impression that they returned her briefly to life. She spent her days among the pilgrims waiting to enter the tiled halls or wandering through the shaded walkways where the cripples lay outstretched on the floor, chanting their prayers. Each evening she would bring them all home with her in her head, and fall asleep to the music of their rhythms.

In her youth she had written poetry. Now, in the silence of her cramped Mashhad dormitory she found she was writing again, insatiably, on any scrap of paper that presented itself. The process consumed her to such an extent that she wrote for days at a time, hardly pausing for food or sleep. The tidy, minute handwriting of the first pages became gradually larger and ever more chaotic as she struggled to express the immensity of all she had lost. When she was finished, the words were burning on the paper like a lighted torch.

One morning, long before dawn, she made her way to the holy precinct and pushed her way to the front of the assembled crowds. As she drew nearer to the grave of the Imam, she stretched out a hand toward the marble tomb and by some luck or providence, managed to grasp a corner against the seething crowd. She held it tightly with a desperate hand while with the other she searched her pocket and produced the bundles of poems she had written in her room and squeezed them through the railings of the holy tomb. Then she took out her husband's letters, his photographs and everything else that was precious to her and forced them, one by one, into the sepulcher of Imam Reza saying as she did so, "Take this too, and this. Take all of it!"

But they would not fit. An elbow from the crowd nudged her hand, spilling the items like confetti across the marble floor to be churned and trodden under the feet of whirling pilgrims. She lost her grip of the tomb and was carried off on a wave of worshippers out into the adjoining hall where she was left, unceremoniously, against a wall.

It was only then, as she lay on marble floor of the Azadi courtyard before the golden dome and the tiled minarets of the Imam, that something in her lit up, at last, like the striking of a match. She felt a joy running through her like fire in dry straw. She found she was laughing at herself infectiously, loudly, ridiculously, in a way she had never done before.

There was more that the shopkeeper had to tell us. But I didn't want to listen. The room was too confining. I needed to go outside and breathe. I stood in the desolation of the street, thinking about the haunted woman. Her story pursued me as I retraced my steps up the village lane. It laid traps for me in the shadowy doorways that lay on either side. It gave me no rest.

I reached the narrow staircase of the Armenian church and stood once more before the graffiti on its scarred walls. She was like this empty church, burned out, defaced, open to all the winds. What would have become of her, I wondered, if she had married again, raised children, nursed grandchildren? What would have happened if love had touched her once again and opened up the woman in her? Instead, time and circumstance had marooned her among these ruins of Sasanian houses that couldn't be demolished because UNESCO wouldn't allow it, and couldn't be repaired for lack of money: a living ghost.

I set out to look for her in the walled garden, to apologize and ask her forgiveness for my actions. I found her standing where I had left her. Seeing me approach, she turned toward me and opened up the swollen leather of her hand. There, wrapped in the folds of a colored handkerchief were fresh figs, the delicate down still clinging to them like fine dew. I took the fruit, washed them in a nearby stream and returned immediately to share them with her.

We ate greedily, in silence. The woman closed her eyes for a moment and attempted to remove a strand of hair that had lodged on her lips. The operation, delicately performed, allowed me to look at her more properly without being observed. The glow of a distant youth seemed to emanate from her presence. She must have been beautiful once, I thought. There was a great spaciousness of soul in her, a purity of being I could not quite convert into terms of my own reality. But I felt it. The varieties of love are so manifold, I thought, that we do not possess adequate words to define them.

Our eyes met suddenly and we started to laugh, as if we were partakers of some guilty secret. It seemed as if our minds branched out and touched above our heads. At that very moment, something in me shifted and opened like a green metal door in a high wall. I wanted some of that freedom she had: the freedom to expand and burn like a candle flame in straw, to be emptied and vanish into nothing. It was good to be a little mad, I thought.

Madar

Dominic Parviz Brookshaw

In '79 as sisters and daughters began to leave,
predicting chaos, fearing lynching, her hard-earned pension cut,
she too departed.

She came to us in Hong Kong.
I can see her now: swimming fully clothed, half-submerged in the beige water; smiling.
Eldest of the clan, we called her *Madar*—a mother to us all. Her name, Tal'at,
echoed her sublime face, its Arabic roots bearing connotations of the sun on its ascent.

On a German black and white portable she watched:
old John Wayne movies, Snooker, *The Equalizer*;
her three concessions to Western Imperialism.
Before I could speak, she showed me how to write my name.
With tired hands, fingers bent cruelly by arthritis, she wrote
letter after letter after letter, all in a delicate script.
I added the farangi addresses for her and licked the stamps.

Sometimes I brewed her tea (she had her own special teapot and tea glass, of course).
Occasionally I made her popcorn, and she giggled when I called it by its
Persian name.
My working mother, our nighttime interpreter, relayed my questions on
family history. At weekends, I paraded my Persian booty before her, newly liberated
from antique markets.

The shimmer of golden orange rind and pearly almond slivers atop
buttery rice tattooed with Khorasani ink,
the fine balance of herbs in her *ghormeh sabzi*,
baqalaqatoq, a homage to her northern father, laced with garlic and framed in dill,
morgh-e torsh—just sour enough.
I make them all.

She loved my English father's garden and, from her vantage point on the first floor,
directed the planting of orderly geraniums,
and mourned their demise with the first frosts of October.
Indoors, velvety rows of African violets stood water-logged from over-care.

Stretching to encompass her grandsons' Eurasian heights, her well-thumbed
prayer book teetering above our heads to guard our exit through the back door,
and protect us until the hour of return,
Water cast in our wake ensured a white path.

Before leaving for school,
if I found her already knelt at prayer, her back to me, focused in rapture,
she would gracefully raise her right arm,
and bid a silent
farewell.

Return, July 2000

Dominic Parviz Brookshaw

I can only imagine how worried she must have been.
Her younger son off to the land she had left
three decades before, "For better, for worse" – for good.
The same land that had rejected her family a decade later.

Connected via the BBC, images of war, the stamps my parents kept,
cut from the last Nowruz cards of the early 1980s.
A land of tulips in the mind, but not like Holland.
Tulips sprouting from the blood of martyrs;
our martyrs, whether they fell at the frontline or elsewhere.
Connected via colonial narratives (I think we used to call them travelogues).
Connected through my gentle grandmother, a new refugee in her 70s.
She showed us all that is good about back home.

I felt fear, but also uncontrollable excitement.
My first visit to the homeland of the half I identify with best.
I thought I knew what to expect.

The sun still shines bright.
The sky is only grey from the smog.
The young still party, and then they marry.
Children are born. Life goes on and, for some, it is sweet.
Surrounded for the first time by the tongue I had dedicated my intellect to.
But this was a spiritual journey of ear and heart. In the taxis, the banks;
even in the dreaded office of "alien nationals".

In Tehran I visited the Rose-garden.
Not the one destroyed through blind imitation,
but the one where my great-great-great-great-grandmother had penned her poetry
and guarded the key to the royal treasury.
In Shiraz I saw where it all began; a car park now.
I prayed, quickly, in the road: a pilgrim for sure, but not quite a Hajji.
In Shiraz I saw where my *mojtahed* ancestor had preached a new message,
had his beard burnt, and was
whipped in the bazaar.
In Hamadan I saw where he was laid to rest,
nestled in the embrace of the Jewish community that loved him.

Back in Tehran I was enveloped in love; taken in like a long-lost Joseph.
You cannot fault their hospitality.
Do you know, in the right season you can still buy fresh pistachios?
Do you know, they still sell *labou* in Tajrish?
And the *lavashak* of the Shah 'Abdo'l-'Azim bazaar is still the tangiest.
I always felt, and still do, that I was, that I am, returning.

Not everyone shared my sentiments, born from a delicate soul
nurtured in a "multicultural" Britain.
"You're not Iranian!"
"How can you be when your father's not?"
"You haven't lived here like we have!"
(OK, I had an accent back then).
But few realise that belonging follows no territorial logic,
that it has nothing to do with the colour of your eyes.
I wept within, longing for their acceptance,
for the right—my birth right—to self-identification.

Now, after a decade of visits and friendship,
at times they have to rein in my *Iraniyat*.

Not Iranian, Not American, but Definitely a Full-Blooded Granddaughter

Susan Safa

As a child growing up in the low-income southern California neighborhood of Simi Valley, I despised my Iranian background. During the late 70s and early 80s in America, Iran conjured images of an angry ayatollah, hijackers, or women covered in dark veils. Today the name still resonates with memories of the US embassy hostage crisis. Many times in my neighborhood someone in a drunken stupor would drive by our house yelling, "Go back to your own damn country!" Neighbors referred to us as "Eye-rain-ian butt-scratchers," and the local bully called my olive skinned brother "nigger." We were poor and I hated it. I wanted to change everything.

Being the first American-born member of my family instantly made me a fierce leader because I was able to acclimate to our surroundings more quickly than my parents. A Girl Scout and a member of the national honor roll, I ran for the track team and was a teacher's pet. I translated prices of homes that realtors offered my father and bargained down the cost of furniture at yard sales with my mother. An overachiever, I was determined to be seen as a respected member of society. I didn't realize it then, but I had begun to mold my nervous and insatiable personality that would later lead to personal tragedy. Instead of enjoying every moment of life, I ran around feeling pressured. It was a harsh period and I soon realized that I would have to change, since I would not be able to carry on with this painful existence much longer.

The summer of my eighth birthday my grandparents came from Iran to live with us. Never having seen Iran myself, they were the missing link to my history and I instantly adored them—the way they laughed, the way they smelled (a mixture of saffron and burnt toast), and the way they surrounded me with love. My grandmother made tasty Persian tomato rice, dampokhtak, while my grandfather read me excerpts from a variety of philosophical books, including the classical Persian poets Rumi and Hafiz. An instant magnetism drew me to him. By no means wealthy, he took great pride in his appearance, always dressing in stylish white pantsuit outfits and sporting classy, slick-backed hairstyles. A bit of a spendthrift, he managed to save enough money for his travels. He described to me, in great detail, the lovely high teas of England as well as the exotic camel dances in Egypt. He taught me how to think with an open mind. He didn't see color or religion in a person. He saw the inherent goodness of individuals and chose to see all the wonderful opportunities life had to offer. Though I'm sure they existed, I could see no faults. I even enjoyed the scent of his evening cigarette.

One thing he never spoke of was his childhood. My mother later informed me that both his parents had died at an early age, leaving him a young orphan. Never steering off track, he avoided trouble and educated himself by reading books. Our shared thirst for knowledge became our bond. My grandfather became my biggest supporter, and my inspiration.

He was also a devout follower of the poet Rumi. Rumi was an ancient Persian scholar who wrote countless poems on love, integrity and freedom for all. His timeless writings held no cultural or religious boundaries, but rather portrayed life's different periods of sadness, confusion, joy and ecstasy, which everyone encounters. I enjoyed the poems, but it wasn't until later in life that I would reach for them like a lifeline.

I continued my hard work and enrolled at University of Southern California to become an occupational therapist. In the weeks before my graduation grandpa fell ill. I had just interviewed for a job in the elegant neighborhood of Beverly Hills. While I got the job, I felt numb. As I walked down the aisle in the university gymnasium to get my diploma all I could do was imagine my grandfather's kind eyes. Immediately after the ceremony, I drove to seem him. Sitting in the sunlight of the garden in his green bathrobe, his eyes filled with tears of joy as he saw me walk up in my cap and gown. Two weeks later he passed away. I couldn't cry. I tried to tell myself to accept his death as it was all part of the cycle of life, but I just couldn't comprehend losing my kindred spirit. After years of looking to my grandfather for answers, I was now on my own.

Soon afterwards I had to sit for my state board exam to become a licensed therapist—another achievement toward my highly sought-after success. Once the test began, I choked. I thought of the job offer in Beverly Hills. Why did I so desperately want to live in that fancy neighborhood? Was I still ashamed of my past and heritage? That would mean I was ashamed of my dear grandfather. All of the respect and success in the world would never mean as much as my grandfather's love and opinion of me. My chest tightened and I couldn't breathe. I passed out.

I awoke in the hospital. After a thorough exam the doctor announced that I was having an anxiety attack. He gave me a shot of valium and I fell into a deep sleep. When I woke up I saw my mother. I looked at her, and for the first time in many, many years I began to cry. I wept uncontrollably for my grandfather and the confused dark girl in Simi Valley.

Following the anxiety attack, I lost interest in everything. My professional dreams came to a halt. I was unable to leave the house and lost a frightening amount of weight. The energetic young woman I once was had turned into a sad limp figure. Within weeks I had fallen into a deep dark hole without a clue on how to rescue myself.

Weeks passed before two incidents offered me a hold on life. One day a friend came by to show me photos of the orphans she was helping in Nicaragua. I was touched by the images of the innocent expressions of the children. I thought of my gentle, knowledge-loving grandfather who had meant so much to me and had once been a frightened young orphan himself. If I helped this woman with her project, I would be helping kids just like my grandfather. How proud he would be to know what I was doing. Just the thought of helping infused my body with strength.

Soon after my friend's visit, I stumbled across a book that contained a Rumi poem, as translated by Dr. Majid Naini. The kind words filled my heart and soul with joy. It was as though my gentle grandfather was speaking to me all over again.

We should drink the water from the stream like the foal
And do not heed those tempting mockers.
If you are a follower of the prophets, tread the way,
Consider people's sarcasm all as wind.
Those Masters who have traveled far on the path,
When have they ever heeded the dog's barking?
If I become involved in answering the criticism,
How can I give water to the thirsty?

It dawned on me that I no longer needed to run from the mocking dogs of Simi Valley. This poem reminded me of another Sufi saying my grandfather had shared with me: "Sorrow sweeps the heart clean for the next sudden burst of Joy." I realized that this period of grief and depression was a time of reflection, healing and strengthening. Three days later, I retook my exam, and passed.

Having found a much needed sense of peace, the secondhand shopping I hated as a child is now a favorite pastime. The curly hair I once hated now makes up my glorious mane. I also find that I am no longer attached to the notion of having to own things or live in a fancy home. I no longer look to define myself or anyone else by their socio-economic class, ethnicity, religion or educational background. Like Rumi—like my Iranian grandfather—I'm now more inclined to accept and appreciate the moment, rather than want to change everything. ■

Weaving through Generations

Neilufar Naini

*M*y mom and I locked eyes as we folded the Persian carpet. Always the same procedure: thirds the long way, and then a discussion about how many folds it would take to create a compact and square-shaped package. This carpet came from Nain, an Iranian city where traditional carpet weaving was revived in the 1920s, and where my grandmother, Majideh Massumi, had built her thriving rug business. We placed the folded carpet in the car, and I breathed out a sigh of relief knowing I had the one item I could not leave behind. No sum of money could replace it. My grandmother, or *Maman Bozorg*, as I always called her, had produced this carpet.

Maman Bozorg had been the kind of woman who never stopped working, no matter how many times her daughters asked her to rest. The carpet represented the feminine strength in my family and reminded me of the courage I wished to foster as I faced my future as a newly divorced woman.

My husband and I had built the Aikido school in Brooklyn where the carpet used to lie. He'd reap the rewards of the five years we spent establishing this dojo. Leaving my husband, the Aikido school, my students, and my job required all my conviction. Stripping myself away from all my responsibilities, I packed up my necessary belongings and never turned back. The only thread of the past I wanted to weave into my next journey was Maman Bozorg's carpet.

My mother had treated my husband and me to a trip to Iran back when we were newlyweds. At the same time, we were offered a chance to teach Aikido in Kazakhstan. These two opportunities felt like the honeymoon we were looking for before settling down and opening a full-time dojo. My husband, filling the role of interior decorator in our relationship, wanted to bring back artifacts and works of art made by hand. I had always wanted to purchase one of my grandmother's carpets. But I heard from the family that there were no more to be found in Iran.

The three of us arrived at the airport in Tehran and went to my great aunt's home. In the evenings, the women in the family would sit together at the dining room table. One night, when all the women were playing a game of Rummy, my great aunt reminded my mother, "You should call Mr. Mossahebi tomorrow. Sometimes it takes days to get through to him." Mr. Mossahebi was an old family friend who knew my grandmother from when they both lived in Nain. Mr. Mossahebi had always found eager purchasers for the carpets my grandmother produced.

Due to Maman Bozorg's commitment to creating high quality carpets, she gained respect not only from Mr. Mossahebi, but from all her workers too. She balanced a marriage to a wealthy and spoiled husband with the toil of supporting her five children. One day, her husband gambled away one of their carpets. That very day, Maman Bozorg separated her carpet business from her husband's. Because of her honest business practices and willingness to pay a higher percentage of the profits than her husband, the weavers sought positions under her leadership. Eventually, my grandmother orchestrated a thriving carpet business.

My grandmother's responsibilities included hiring weavers and providing the materials. Gathering the wool and dyeing the threads was difficult work. The different colors were made from a variety of natural materials, including walnuts, pomegranates, and grape leaves. Imagining all the painstaking work my grandmother poured into making her carpets reminded me of my Aikido path. For eleven years, I had forged my spirit through a way called Budo. The founder of Aikido, Morihei Ueshiba, spoke of the commitment to working on the self. My mom always told me that Maman Bozorg wanted to better herself through her daily work. The approach correlates with true Budo.

Second to finding one of my grandmother's rugs, we also hoped to buy a *gabbeh* and a pile carpet. Gabbehs are loosely woven rugs made out of thick wool threads, which we thought would work well in the dojo setting. The pile carpet was a more intricately woven rug. But before I could purchase one of these expensive carpets, my decision had to filter through a strict familial hierarchy. My wishes first went to my mom, and she passed them on to my great aunt, who would take over from there. A similar familial pattern came into play for cultural queries. Asking about Aikido dojos, we contacted Keyvon, my first cousin once removed. For buying carpets, we contacted Mr. Mossahebi.

Traveling to the carpet bazaar was a rare occasion since my mom often complained about the heat, especially with the obligatory *chador* covering. Trying to walk through the crowded streets and not lose each other required constant vigilance. My mom frequently stopped to check on prices for gold jewelry. My husband kept peeking into each booth inquiring about tapestries. I tried to keep the group together and move us on more quickly toward the section of the bazaar where we were to find Mr. Mossahebi.

At one point when we had stopped to sample *Naan-e Bastani*, saffron ice cream sandwiched between two square waffle sheets, we saw men passing us carrying multiple carpets on their backs. Some had carts with two wheels to assist in the seemingly ceaseless human-powered carpet shuffle. We hoped to follow them to Mr. Mossahebi's shop.

Once in the carpet bazaar, we found ourselves in a maze of alleys. Stall after stall had their best carpets displayed. My mother asked numerous merchants, "Do you know where we can find Mr. Mossahebi?"

"Is he the short guy that always wears a tie?"

"Yes! Where can we find him?" my mom would reply.

Each carpet dealer would shrug and point his finger in one direction or another, "Maybe he is that way, but come in and have some tea and see this carpet."

While my mom declined, my husband felt obligated to visit several of the merchants. More than once, when they found out we were from America, the conversation soon followed with an invitation to dinner in that person's home.

Realizing I had lost sight of my mother, I urged my husband to finish his tea. "Come," I said with a tilt of the head. We found her talking to a short man wearing a tie. Mr. Mossahebi. Again, we were welcomed with hot tea and a tour of his workshop, where we met the family members who worked with him.

"So what type of carpet are you interested in buying?" He wanted to narrow it down to size and color. I did not know exactly what I wanted, but I told him I wished I could have one of my grandmother's carpets.

"I'm sorry but I have not seen any in years," he informed me as he led us through the storefront to a warehouse stacked shoulder-high with Persian carpets.

We flipped through a mind-boggling array of designs. Mr. Mossahebi kept running back and forth to answer phone calls in the small glass cubicle that held his desk. Meanwhile his relatives showed us more carpets. For hours we shook our heads, "No, not that one." My mom asked her usual list of questions, "Is that a Nain carpet? What is the *la* of threads?" The Naini carpets had different sized thicknesses called *chahar-la*, *shesh-la*, and *noh-la*, representing four, six, and nine strands used to create each thread. We took breaks, drank more tea, and talked. Mr. Mossahebi would ask my mom about the family in America. The hottest topic was my recent marriage.

The next carpet he unfurled caught us all by surprise. Mr. Mossahebi pulled it from the stack and unrolled it in front of everyone. Looking closely, we immediately recognized the design. The carpet had a floral pattern laid on top of a vibrant red background. The border design interlaced with the typical blue, gray, and ivory threads was one of Maman Bozorg's carpets. Even Mr. Mossahebi couldn't believe what he saw. He started blaming himself, "How could I have missed this?" This carpet had silk for highlights even though some Naini carpets were made entirely with silk. Mr. Mossahebi promised to bring the carpet to my great aunt's home the next day.

The next afternoon a knock on the door silenced our clattering of pans and chopping of cucumbers for our midday meal. Mr. Mossahebi brought the carpet, unfurled it for the whole family to see, and finished calculating the price.

Now, I sit on Maman Bozorg's rug in my mother's home in Maryland. Her ability to oversee all the steps of her carpet business: gathering the wool, dyeing the threads, and weaving the design one knot at a time makes a tear come to my eye. Time allowed for artistic creations seems to be less and less frequent in my world. The human integrity my grandmother demonstrated, which is necessary for any art form, continues to bring me to my knees in prayer.

Why I Wrote about an Iranian Heroine

Meghan Nuttall Sayres

Speech delivered at Iran's First International Children's Book Festival, Kerman, Iran, March 2005.

Khanum ha va aghayan, man kheili khosh haalam ke dar in jaa hastam, va baa shomaa sohbat mikonam. Ladies and Gentlemen, I am so very pleased to be here, and to be speaking with you. In many ways I think I have been on a journey to Iran all my life. As Hafiz has written, "Indeed God has written a thousand promises all over your heart." I believe the invitation to join you at this festival was one promise Allah had written on my soul.

I have been asked to tell you why I chose Iran as the setting of my novel *Anahita's Woven Riddle*, and why I chose an Iranian heroine. In this story, sixteen-year-old Anahita, a semi-nomadic Afshar rug weaver, will marry only the man who can solve the riddle she has woven into her wedding carpet.

My inspiration for this tale came from the Afshar tribal rug I have at home in my living room. I found that each day I looked at it, I discovered something new. Its seven borders, its indigo, cochineal and madder root field, its *guls*, trees of life, and bird patterns, all seemed to be telling me a story. My curiosity about the meanings of these motifs led me to books on the symbolism in Oriental rugs. I soon learned that roosters and tassels often represented or acted as talismans against the evil eye, and that the color red stands for happiness while blue represents eternity. The Persian script on my rug was dated to 1925 and says, "Long live the Shah." I imagined the weavers of my carpet to be spiritual women who also took a great interest in the world around them, including the politics of the time that would shape their lives. And thus, like my carpet, Anahita's voice began to whisper to me.

While I had yet to visit Iran, I traveled to Istanbul where I met with carpet dealers, to Konya where I consulted a dye master, and to the village of Sultanhani, where women taught me to weave a pile carpet. From these trips I was given a taste for a Middle Eastern culture and had contemplated setting my story in Turkey. But my Afshar carpet beckoned me to tell *its* story—to set my tale in Iran.

Writing about a place I had never been, in some respects, is contrary to what many American writers are told: "Write about what you know." Yet, with this story, I chose to write toward the unknown—toward discovery.

All I knew about Iranian nomads was what I had read in books and seen in photographs. But I felt that I had much in common with them. I become restless if I stay in one place for too long. I believe that following the grasses and seasons is a more natural way to live in this world, and is friendlier to the earth than a settled lifestyle. My own Irish ancestors, who raised sheep as I do today, practiced transhumanance and migrated until the early twentieth century. They called it *bouleying*, and they moved from winter pastures by the sea, to summer pastures in the mountains. So I suppose, nomadism is a sensibility I have inherited.

Weaving is something else I have in common with the nomads of Iran. From my sheep's wool I spin and dye my own yarn and weave tapestries. Tapestries are much like *gelims* in that the front of the piece mirrors the back. Some of the wildflowers with which I make dyes are the same as those used here in carpet making; for example madder root, cochineal, and dyer's broom. I have spun karakul sheep wool, mohair, and camel down. So I believe I know something about the textures of Iran, as well as the scents and tastes of the herbs and spices favored here for dyes.

I set my story in Iran because I have spent years walking in deserts, and living in the aridity of the American West. I feel at home in barren and mountainous landscapes.

I am also quite taken by the depth and beauty of the work of Jalal al-Din Rumi. I had visited his mausoleum in Konya and knew he was Persian. His poem, *The Great Wagon*, as well as the work of other Sufi poets from Iran whom I admire, such as Ferdowsi and Sa'di, found a place in my novel. Perhaps also, it was the palpable presence I felt when immersed in their poetry, which compelled me to explore Iran's spiritual landscape, and to set this novel in their ancient homeland.

Lastly, I sincerely believe that literature, in particular children's literature, has the power to open new worlds for readers. Fiction set in other lands allows one to travel to that place on their own terms, and hopefully from a position of non judgment as children are so wonderfully receptive and accepting. Literature can transform the strange into the familiar. Familiarity breeds understanding, and understanding leads to friendships across cultures. I have set my story in Iran to contribute to Americans' knowledge and appreciation of the richness of Iranian culture.

Why an Iranian heroine? The most obvious answer is because my story is about an Afshar weaver, so it seemed that the heroine would be Iranian. However, I chose to write about a strong Iranian woman because I know several. But I would like to talk about just one, my friend Mojdeh Khalighi, whose strength of character I tried to replicate in my protagonist Anahita.

Mojdeh immigrated to the United States about twenty years ago, leaving behind her parents and siblings who all live in Tehran. When we met she was a mother of a nine-year-old girl, Farnaz. She held a mechanical engineering degree from Daneshgah-e Elm va Sanat in Tehran, and was pursuing a masters degree in Public Health at the University of Utah in Salt Lake City. I was a new mother in need of childcare for fifteen hours a week while I worked. A friend recommended Mojdeh. She was the first person—a complete stranger from the other side of the world—to whom I entrusted the care of my newborn son. (Many of you may not be able to conceive of leaving your child with anyone outside of your own families. But like many Americans, for better or worse, I live a thousand miles from my sisters and brother and parents.)

Immediately upon meeting Mojdeh, I felt her warmth, and saw the light of intelligence in her eyes. She held and kissed my son behind the neck, just beneath the line of his thick blond curls, pressing her olive-colored skin against his white. It is an image and a moment that I have never forgotten—a revelation for me that the language of motherhood can truly be universal. But when I turned to walk out the door of my home to go to work, despite her kiss, I still felt this was the biggest, most frightening step I would ever take. I remember thinking, *Salt Lake International Airport is only ten minutes from downtown. My child could be on a plane to Iran before I even get to work.* But I shoved the thought aside, scolding myself, *That's ridiculous. Quit being so irrational.* Closing the door behind me, I took the leap of faith.

When I came home from work that day my house smelled like a Middle Eastern restaurant. Mojdeh had made a chicken, rice and saffron dish, which she had pureed in the blender for my son. She had made for me a month's supply of baby food, saving me hours of work. And it was healthy food, unlike the kind sold at the store that was filled with preservatives and sugar that I would have likely resorted to buying. Two years later, I gave birth to twins who also ate this same meal that we call "Mojdeh's Special Recipe," and which we passed on to all of our friends who were having babies at that time. Looking back, I feel silly for the trepidation I had felt upon leaving my son in her care that first day.

Mojdeh came to be my mentor. Watching her thrive in a new culture, far from home, as well as study at the graduate level in a language that was not her own, became my motivation to enroll in graduate school. Her second child, Anahita (the namesake of my protagonist) was born near the time of my twins, and they played together. Although Mojdeh stopped babysitting for me fifteen years ago, and moved to California as my family moved to Washington State, our friendship continues.

Why have I chosen to write about an Iranian heroine? Because I have yet to meet an Iranian woman who is not a heroine. So many Iranian women seem intelligent, resourceful, courageous, gracious and warm, all of which are qualities I attribute to heroines.

I have written a story about an Iranian weaver because in many respects it was scribbled on my heart long ago. I have written a story set in Iran because I believe that in doing so I have tied a knot of understanding between East and West. I have written a story for children that is set in Iran in hopes that my readers will grow into sympathetic adults who will look for common threads with others. I hope they will take steps toward people of other nations, no matter how scary it might feel—a leap that can lead to respect, trust, and lasting friendships.

Man kheili motshakeram az shoma ke be sohbat-e man goosh kardid. Thank you for listening to my talk, and for inviting me to Iran and treating me so well.

A Merging of Three Souls

Mahmood Karimi-Hakak, Bill Wolak and Shams al-Din Mohammad Hafiz

The poems below are from the collection Love Emergencies *in which Bill Wolak and Mahmood Karimi-Hakak translated each other's work. While Mahmood composes in Persian and is a fluent speaker of English, Bill stepped into his heart and mind to interpret the poems according to Bill's own sense of words, syntax and imagery. They anticipated that the result would be more accessible to readers in Western cultures. In turn, Mahmood translated Bill's poems into Persian, a language that Bill studies. Mahmood and Bill met at Rutgers University and have been friends for decades. They have also translated a book of poems by Shams al-Din Mohammad Hafiz. Perhaps in the following excerpts from* Love Emergencies *and* Your Lover's Beloved: 51 Ghazals by Hafiz, *you might detect how the Sufi Master's work may have influenced their own.*

Fountains

Mahmood Karimi-Hakak

How alone
    I feel
           tonight
wandering into
    the city's delirium.
How bitter the confrontation
               awaiting me
                    back home.

How the pounding
        of my heart
            echoes
               your voice.

How far
    I am
      from holding
           you.

And fountains illuminated
the ecstasy of lovers at night.

Song of the Door That Surfaced

Bill Wolak

Between the haphazard penetrations
of your presence and absence,
a door floats to the surface of the water.
On it we have fallen asleep entangled
adrift as if on an iceberg
with every hour a little less domain
and a little more of the sea.

Now as if we were ever nearer,
I'm holding you with the simple grace
of weightlessness.

No dream's triumph of memory could surpass
the feeling of your flesh
vulnerable as the punched face of a sleeper.
No photograph's archeology of light could capture
all the possibilities of balance
you offer me.

With only a door between our embrace and the sea,
we are simply sleeping—
as if we were never farther apart,
as if we were holding each other
in orbit.

The Keeper of Strangeness

Bill Wolak

I am the light's fever in honey.
I am the lullaby heard in a nightmare.

In black-eyed alleys
and along tide calloused wharves,
I am the room where you find what you're missing.

I am the dial tone flesh of frightening energy transfers.
I am the expectant hands hovering over nakedness
and the insomnia of sperm.
My lap is a toolshed reaching dreamward.

I am the scarecrow made of birds.
I am the inexhaustible memory of salt.

Out of anger, I created the wind's solitude;
out of love, the restlessness of the rain's long inhalations.

I am the scream's only bridegroom.

Lost from the Scent of Your Hair

Hafiz
Translated by Bill Wolak and Mahmood Karimi-Hakak

I said, "I'm suffering because of you." You said, "That suffering will pass."
I said, "Be my moon." You said, "If it rises."

I said, "From those who love, learn the customs of faithfulness."
You said, "Seldom is such behavior seen from those with beautiful faces."

I said, "I shut the pathway of my glance to that dream of you."
You said, "It's a thief; It'll break in from another direction."

I said, "I'm lost from the scent of your hair."
You said, "If you understand that, let loss be your guide."

I said, "Morning air feels so invigorating."
You said, "Breezes arising from love's realm bring blessings."

I said, "I've been devastated by my desire to drink from your ruby lips."
You said, "Be satisfied with slavery and devotion, and your thirst will be quenched."

I said, "When will your compassionate heart forgive me?"
You said, "Don't gossip about that to anyone; and we'll make up."

I said, "Look how quickly pleasure passes."
You said, "Be quiet, Hafiz, this suffering will pass too."

Set Fire to the Entire Universe

Hafiz
Translated by Bill Wolak and Mahmood Karimi-Hakak

In the beginning, the glow of your goodness evoked epiphanies.
Love appeared and set fire to the entire universe.

Your form appeared and saw that angels can't imagine love.
Out of rage, it became like fire and ignited Adam.

Logic longed to light a lamp from this flame,
But rage's fire blazed and stirred the whole universe.

A know-it-all wanted to enter the place where secrets are revealed.
But an invisible hand appeared and shoved the stranger out.

From fate's lottery others drew pleasure;
But my suffering heart only won sadness.

My heart desired the height of your cleft chin,
But could only reach the rings of your curling hair.

Hafiz wrote the joyous letter of your love that day
When he dipped his pen into the ink well of his ecstatic heart.

Iason Athanasiadis

Tasting Home

Love and Pomegranates

Dr. Mohammad Abolfazli

The Torah and the Qur'an both call pomegranates the fruit of heaven, and some schol-ars think that it was a pomegranate rather than an apple in the Garden of Eden. There is archeological evidence of pomegranate cultivation in ancient Egypt 4,000 years ago.

The most nutrition can be derived from pomegranates if you juice them whole in the blender including the red outer skin and the white membranes inside, as well as the red fruit. Although the taste is very strong and pungent, this is the way to gain the maximum nutritional benefit. The red skin has lycopene, which is anti-carcinogenic, especially for breast and prostate glands according to a seven-year study completed at Stanford University. The skin is also high in iron, phosphorus, and vitamin C, and has bactericidal properties as well as de-worming and anti-constipational effects.

The seeds sweep the intestines clean. Pomegranates purify the blood and help with fertility for both genders, which is why in Iran bowls of pomegranates are offered as wedding presents.

Pomegranates are good for the heart, they reduce cholesterol and lower blood pressure, and they are also a good antidepressant. One of the reasons Iranians make a paste called fesenjoon served with entrées in winter is to combat depression, because it boosts serotonin. So between helping fertility, acting as an anti-depressant, and rumors that it was the fruit of knowledge in Eden, "Love and Pomegranates" is an appropriate connection.

Tasting Home

Taha Ebrahimi

I went to my first Sufi meditation session when I was 22 years old, the same age my mother was when she left Iran to join my father in Seattle. Both my parents converted to the mystic version of Islam when I was ten, the day my father had gone to an Iranian grocery for a vial of saffron and seen the poster announcing the Order's existence. The Sufi house in Seattle—the *khanikhai*—was located in a quiet, leafy suburb and we attended twice a week in the evenings; I stayed in the basement with the other kids, listening to the chanting and singing from the main floor. Now, at this unfamiliar khanikha in London, I thought about that fateful vial of saffron and how it was no coincidence my father had found Sufism through grocery shopping. I was in London by myself and every time I smelled the waft of steamed rice and chickpeas in this strange new khanikha, all I could do was miss my father's cooking.

Everyone in Iran knew a Sufi or had one in their family. Sufis were not just mystics, but they were poets, philosophers, and wisemen, revered. Many didn't believe in veiling or the other orthodox rules clerics had translated from the Qur'an. It was better to be modest in spirit than to wear a physical veil. Sufis believe in a personal, direct relationship with God, uninterrupted by flawed human interpretation. Depending on which Order one follows, Sufis come into union with God through chanting, mediation, repetitive whirling dances. The best way to know God is through experiences of love. I should have been comfortable at my first session in London, sitting cross-legged in the dark as everyone chanted and clapped a sacred *dhikr*. But I was alone in my travels and without my parents to provide the link to my heritage that I so badly needed. I didn't understand the meditation; I felt like an outsider. For me, "home" had always been a place where people asked me where I was "from" in the very city I was born in. I thought I might find a "home" among the Sufis, but I was disappointed that I didn't fit in here either. After the session was over and the singing had died down, the lights flipped back on, I wondered what had drawn my father and mother to this?

We all sat lining the walls, sitting on the carpeted floor, leaning against *poshti* cushions. People lit cigarettes and the room filled with smoke. I looked around me to identify those I heard crying during the session, only to see them laughing and talking to their neighbors now, seemingly unaffected. The old women were the most animated, having expunged their weekly quotient of tears. They were all large-breasted and many wore thick glasses. Some wore *chadors* or paisley headscarves unlike the younger women who went bare-headed. One whispered *"Allahu Akbar"* as she clicked the numbers on a handheld counter, finally stopping when she reached a hundred repetitions. They talked about how many painkillers they'd had that day, clucking their tongues and shaking their heads, swapping home remedies for the relief of arthritis, constipation, swelling, numbing.

The self-appointed sweets distributor—a young, blonde woman—walked around the circle offering *baklava* on a tray to enjoy with their tea. She wore a large golden pendent necklace with a Sufi symbol carved on it. As she bent over to offer the plate of sweets to the cluster of old women, one exclaimed at the beauty of her necklace. "Look at how beautifully he carved the Sufi symbol!" said one of the women. The blonde smiled and said, *"Kesh-kesh.* It's yours if you want it." This was called *ta'arof,* a tradition of expertly choreographed offering and declining that forms the cornerstone of Iranian etiquette. What had started out as the display of otherwise-worldly jewelry became a contest of generosity.

The older lady chuckled, waving it off, "Oh, no, no, honey. I would never take such a lovely thing from such a darling!"

Suddenly, all the women sitting along one wall shared their Sufi jewelry. "That one is so lovely! So frail! What wonderful handiwork! Who did it?"

"Kesh-kesh, yours." And then the whole routine again. Many wore necklaces, some had rings and bracelets. The subject of Sufi accessories had the corner abuzz with women comparing their things, offering the knowledge of a jeweler they knew who could make one *just* like it. "Here, take it. I'll get him to make me another."

With most of these elders it was hard to imagine them as ever being young girls. In their youth, perhaps all they did was wish and wait for old age so they could fully be themselves. They sighed and complained flamboyantly, comforting each other by placing hands on each others' knees. *"Aye, Allah!* What did we do to deserve such a lot? At least we have each other!"

The disciples stayed long after the meeting, helping to wash the teacups, continuing their conversations in the kitchen late into the night. One woman wearing a leopard-print outfit and thick eye makeup led the washing effort, directing the others as to which cabinet to place the teacups. The head *pir* sat in the main room debating the point of a Hafiz poem with a small group of men.

I washed the dishes with Kaveh, a man wearing a white robe and sporting a long beard. He was a well-known Sufi sitar player and now he dried the cups I handed him.

"Does your father make *kufteh Tabrizi*?" Kaveh asked me.

I was surprised to hear the name of the familiar dish, secretly always thinking it must have only belonged to my father—the giant stuffed meatballs of his hometown were his specialty. "Yes, yes he does!" I replied. Kaveh came from Tabriz, the same city my father was from.

"My mother makes kuftehs this big," he said, stretching his arms as wide as possible to show just how big he meant. "And," he continued, clasping his hands, "in the middle, she puts an *entire bird*."

"A *bird*? Really?" I asked. My father put whole boiled eggs in the center of kuftehs, but never an entire bird. He would sauté chopped tomatoes, onions, dates, and roasted walnuts and mash them together to fill up the center of the gigantic meatballs, placing an entire boiled egg in the middle of each, as a surprise. Maybe people tucked small birds into the Tabrizi dish also and I just didn't know about it? There were lots of things I didn't know about.

"Yes, my mother cooks whole birds into her kufteh," Kaveh replied. "And, when you break the kufteh open," he said, making a ball with his hands and cracking them open, "there is a bird in the middle and it spreads its wings and flies out to freedom." He kept a straight face and made his eyes especially large and tender as he mimed the bird flying away with his hands like a shadow puppeteer. I had believed his joke for a second. He waited for me to smile before continuing, "My mother puts all sorts of things in her kufteh Tabrizi: raisins, walnuts, anything she can stuff in there…" He waited for me to believe him again before he added, "…screws, hammers, nails, anything."

The women in the kitchen exploded in laughter, chiding him, "Anything your dear mother can get her hands on, eh Kaveh?"

"Tabrizis don't waste a thing."

"Did she make *torshi* pickled vegetables also?" asked the oldest woman. "Tabrizis make great torshi. I love torshi."

I remember my family's garage back home, the rows of pickled vegetables in various jars: green tomatoes, mixtures of diced carrot and cauliflower, garlic cloves, celery, shredded apples, miniature cucumbers, anything that could fit in a jar with vinegar. Again, I have thought this was just something my dad did to save uneaten vegetables in our garden—the special afternoons when my mom was shooed out of the kitchen and the jars would be filled with various liquid concoctions, the vegetables chopped laboriously before being put in the jars. I never knew it was something he learned from his hometown, something specific to his culture.

Kaveh answered, "Oh, yes, my mother makes the best torshis and *shurs*. Pickled carrots, pickled garlic, pickled cabbage… mmm…"

I joined in, "Hey… so does my dad! He's a Tabrizi too, maybe that's why."

Love and Pomegranates

"Oh yes, there are a few things that us Azeri Turks know how to do well. Kufteh Tabrizi and torshi."

The fondest times with my father are of when he cooks his famous kuftehs. It only happens on special occasions when more than 30 people are gathered and need something to eat. Everyone sits at the eating *sofreh* and even my otherwise-quiet father joins in the jokes on those meals. "Yes, yes. Turks like to make those things," I tell Kaveh, feeling part of some club I have just discovered.

As distant as I felt from everyone during the meditation session, I felt equally as close as we washed the dishes. This socializing part of the Sufi meditation session I knew well and, to my surprise, having just attended my first formal session, I realized that these moments—more than anything else—were somehow the most true, the most full of holiness. Here, as the teacups were passed from one hand to another, I felt a genuine spirit far from the forced weeping of earlier. Maybe this is why my parents became Sufis—because they wanted to remember their homes, feel like they belonged.

Kaveh dried the last teacup. I was mildly upset the chore was done. The women took their time saying goodbye, kissing each other on the cheeks. I didn't want to be alone again. I was already looking forward to the next session, this familiarity. I, too, found home. God was not American or Iranian, and neither were the Sufis. God was something wholly different—an energy that we shared when we washed dishes and talked about food, intimate moments when one opens up to strangers and realizes that somewhere tangled far back, we are all related. "Home" can be as simple as the smell of saffron.

Shirazi Limes

Farnaz Fatemi

It's 1975 and I am sitting still on the sofa in Mamanjoon's living room in Tehran, family all around, staring at my aunt Farideh across from me in a chair. She is eating a Shirazi *limoo*, a thin-skinned, small fruit whose sour bite is slightly tempered by sweetness—the kind of flavor that one can only find in Iran.

I watch nearly hypnotized as she sticks the half lemon-lime into her mouth and slowly sucks out the juices. She squeezes it into her mouth and then opens it up and folds it the other direction and squeezes it again, making sure there isn't any juice left. I take a deep breath and try not to blink as she puts her fingers on the rim of the lime, her thumbs at the stem, pushing it inward until its turned completely inside out. Her lips pucker in anticipation. I watch the pleasure flush over her face as her teeth grab onto the pulp and steal it into her mouth, leaving only the rind, like a dry bone.

Over the past few days I have watched others in my family suck Shirazi limes, too. I have studied the various techniques and strategies well. But this is the day I will try it myself. I reach into the large fruit bowl and carefully choose a lime, which I then cut in half. I take one of the halves, squeeze the juice eagerly onto my tongue and squeeze it again and again until it's drained enough to turn inside out. As I stick it into my mouth, however, drops of juice drip down my arm. But I'm too excited to care. My girlish impatience gets the better of me, ignoring the tried-and-true methods of extraction, as I bite into the juicy pulp. My tongue recoils from the sour taste. But a moment later it darts back for more, greedy for its tangy, forbidden taste, devouring the fruit. When I eventually take the lime out of my mouth, I look up and see that everyone is watching, both in pride and amusement.

"Oh honey, don't do that," my mother says with a smile and then turns to my aunt.

"Your teeth and gums will rot," Aunt Farideh, says. "Look at mine, I shouldn't do it either."

I look at her mouth as she smiles, but see nothing wrong with her teeth. Then I beg for another. "Please," I say. "I want to see if I can turn it inside out properly this time. Just one more, I promise!"

All these years later as an adult, thousands of miles away, Mamanjoon's living room, Shirazi limoos and Iran in the spring remain strong in me and in my taste for sour things. Some people cringe when I shoot limes into my mouth. Some even try to stop me. But my friend Hussein, who knows the taste well, says, "Aren't these amazing? There isn't anything I have found here in America like this." I nod, sucking hard on the lime, wishing that there were, but happy, too, that there aren't, knowing that they would never taste quite as good.

Exile, Food, and Identity

Angella M. Nazarian

I write in my family memoir, *Life as a Visitor,* "We didn't bring furniture. Not many clothes. No art. If you've never had to leave your homeland forever, the importance of these 'things' might be harder to understand. Most people have family treasures collected over a lifetime of patterned tranquility spent in the same town or the same neighborhood…. They offer their keepers a sense of identity and continuity." The most valued treasure has been the Iranian-Jewish community's love of ritual. Our love for keeping and celebrating our Jewish heritage with its Middle Eastern or Persian flavor has been the glue that has kept us together as community even after more than 30 years of leaving, or rather escaping Iran and setting roots in the US.

Not coincidentally, this love for culture enabled this Jewish community to preserve its unique identity in Iran for centuries. Shabbat dinners are congenial and oftentimes cousins and extended family are invited. It is not unusual for us to host around 40 people for Shabbat. It seems to be the best way to keep our connections to our family and friends—getting together and sharing a meal and catching up with one another.

Persian meals are elaborate. Hosts and guests alike take as a given that many kinds of stews and different rice dishes will be on display at the table, and that a good host will have plenty of leftovers.

Typically, white basmati rice is served with different kinds of stews. Here are two types of stews that are prepared.

Stew
(Serves 6 people)

2 pounds beef stew meat cut into cubes
2 medium onions
2 teaspoons turmeric powder
2 quinces
10 dried apricots
1 large can of stewed tomatoes, puréed
1 cup pomegranate juice
1 tablespoon pomegranate paste
sugar, if needed
salt, pepper

Slice the onions and fry them in a stew pot. Salt and pepper the beef. Add the cubed beef when the onions are translucent. Continue browning the beef until all sides are brown. Then reduce the heat and cover the pot to render the juice of the meat for approximately 20 minutes. Lift the lid and continue cooking on medium heat until all the juices are evaporated. Then add 4 cups of water and 2 teaspoons of turmeric powder to cover the meat and continue cooking until the meat is tender (one hour or more if needed).

Meanwhile, wash and slice the quinces. Remove the seeds and fry the slices in a pan on each side, until golden brown. Set aside.

When the meat is cooked well, add the pureed tomatoes, 1/2 cup of the pomegranate juice, and the tablespoon of pomegranate paste. Add the 10 dried apricots to the pot and mix well and bring to a boil. Then add the quinces and cook on medium to low heat until the quinces are tender.

Taste to see if the stew needs more pomegranate juice (if you want the stew to be more sour). If it does, pour in the rest. It should be tart and a little sweet, depending on the sweetness of the fruit. You may add some sugar if it's not sweet enough.

Adjust with salt and pepper to taste.

Fesenjoon Stew
(Nuts and Pomegranate Stew)

1 onion
2 lbs walnuts, ground
½ lb dates, skinned and pitted
2 bottles pomegranate juice
2 lbs large, seedless raisins
1 whole chicken

Slice onions and fry them in a pot until they are golden brown.

Mix the ground walnuts, with pomegranate juice, the raisins, and dates in a blender.

Boil the chicken until cooked. Once it is cooked, debone the chicken and take the skin off as well and cut the meat into bite size pieces. (Keep the chicken broth.)

Mix 4 cups of chicken broth with the browned onions and the walnut-pomegranate mix, and put on the mixture into a saucepan on medium heat for 2 hours until all ingredients have dissolved. Add 2 teaspoons of salt. The stew takes on a brownish red color.

Add the chicken to the stew, and taste to see if needs more salt or pepper. Again, this is a very popular stew with a sweet and tangy taste.

Basmati Rice with Crispy Outer Shell

Wash and clean 3 cups of white basmati rice. Put rice in a pot with 4 cups of water and 2 teaspoons of salt. Bring the rice to a boil and watch over it until it puffs. Make sure the rice is not fully cooked by sampling a grain to see that it still has retained its firmness. Drain the rice.

Dissolve a pinch of saffron powder in 2 tablespoons of boiling water. Glaze the bottom of a pot (preferably a Teflon pot) with 3-4 tablespoons of oil and add the saffron mixture.

Add the rice to the pot, always checking to see if the rice needs more salt.

Place the pot on the stove with two sheets of paper towels right under the lid to absorb the steam. Rice should cook and the bottom of the rice should become crispy in 1.5 hours on medium heat.

Rice will be ready to serve with the stews. The crispy rice is often the most sought after part of the meal.

Almond Cluster Dessert

1 lb slivered almonds
2 egg whites
1/2 cup sugar

Preheat oven to 350 and grease a cookie sheet. Blend the egg whites with the sugar, then add the almond slivers.

Take a tablespoon of batter and place it on the cookie sheet. Traditionally, this should be a dollar-size mound. Repeat the process until the cookie sheet is full. Place in oven for 10 minutes, until you see the cookies taking a light golden brown color.

Let cool.

The Laughter of Pomegranates

Rumi, *Mathnawi* I, 717-726
Translated by Kabir Helminski and Ahmad Rezwani

If you buy a pomegranate,
buy one whose ripeness
has caused it to cleft open
with a seed-revealing smile.

Its laughter is a blessing,
for through its wide-open mouth
it shows its heart,
like a pearl in the jewel box of Spirit.
The red anemone laughs, too,
but through its mouth you glimpse a blackness.

A laughing pomegranate
brings the whole garden to life.
Keeping the company of the holy
makes you one of them.
Whether you are stone or marble,
you will become a jewel
when you reach a human being of heart.

Plant the love of the holy ones within your spirit;
don't give your heart to anything
but the love of those whose hearts are glad.
Don't go to the neighborhood of despair:
there is hope.
Don't go in the direction of darkness:
suns exists.

The heart guides you to the neighborhood
of the saints;
the body takes you to the prison of water and earth.
Give your heart the food of holy friends;
seek maturity from those who have matured.

Iason Athanasiadis

Arts and Culture

A Journey into Iran's Literary Landscape

Meghan Nuttall Sayres

My plane touched down in Tehran during the same week in February 2005 when American newspaper headlines warned, "Iran Plans for Possible Attack." These were referring to threats of US and Israeli air strikes on Iran's uranium enrichment facilities. I was traveling there to speak at Iran's first International Children's Book Festival—an event sponsored by the Ministry of Culture and Islamic Guidance—because I had written a young-adult novel about nineteenth-century Persian nomads.

I had met no Westerners on my flight between Istanbul and Tehran, except for a German man. My blondish hair, blue eyes and accent must have stood out because he asked me, "Are you American? Aren't you afraid to go to Iran now? Are you alone?"

His questions echoed those from people with whom I had spoken before leaving the United States, as well as others en route, most of whom held images of Iran painted with unrest: martyrs with bombs in backpacks; streets full of bloodied, self-flagellating young men; and women smothered in black cloth. Yet I had been invited to visit a nation of people whom I felt I could trust based on friendships I had made with Iranians at home, on the friendly and professional e-mails I had shared with editors and translators in Iran before going, and on previous experiences I had in the Middle East.

Filled with anticipation, I slid my passport under the glass window to the Iranian customs official, a man in his mid thirties with circles beneath his eyes. He flipped it over, saw the United States emblem on it, and quite literally jumped from his seat. With my passport in hand, he kicked open the door to his cubicle and shouted something at me in Persian, twice, after I apologized for not understanding. He took my passport across the room to a desk full of officials. Meanwhile, someone in the customs line beside mine asked me if I spoke English and kindly translated that the officer wanted me to go sit on the bench behind passport control. I found the bench and sat. I wondered, had the US bombed Iran in the time it took me to fly to Tehran from Istanbul? I watched as the line of tired travelers, it was about 3 am, inched their way through and toward baggage claim and freedom.

An unusual calm spread through me. I sensed I would not be deported or questioned or detained. Too many synchronous events took shape to bring me here. The invitation came as a complete surprise about three months after I had stopped trying to devise ways to go to Iran on my own. It seemed a gift of grace, and something I could trust. After a while an older man with a professorial air walked over to me and asked, "By chance, are you American?" I nodded. "Don't worry," he said, "it's all for show."

A half hour lapsed and the room had emptied before a different young man sporting a tightly trimmed beard approached. "Hi," he said, in his best New York twang. Then he laughed. I could tell he was trying to put me at ease. I followed him to the desk of officials. There seemed to be lots of shy smiles and paper shuffling happening. Then the young fellow led me back to the same customs official who had sprung from his seat an hour earlier. This man ruffled through each page in my passport and found a place to stamp it. "I am very happy to have been invited to your country," I said. This time he welcomed me. As I walked to baggage claim, I wondered how my country would have treated an Iranian who had arrived on our shores during similar threats of war.

As soon as I stepped outside the airport doors I was met by Hussein Elvand Ebrahimi, the gentleman who had invited me to the book festival, who has since passed away. He greeted me with a bouquet of roses. Elvand, who is named after a mountain, is the founder of the House of Translation for Children and Young Adult Books in Tehran. He has received numerous awards for his book translations, including one for the novel *Sees Through Trees* by American author Michael Doris. Elvand later shared his passion for Native American culture with me, noting he especially identified with Native American author Sherman Alexie: "How I enjoyed reading Sherman Alexie's sentences! How I am feeling like his brother those times when I need to go to my birthplace, our garden in Esfahan province to hear the sounds of the birds, the bark of the sheep dogs, and the voice of the wind among the branches of the trees that I planted many years ago."

I realized that Elvand's enthusiasm for Native American culture mirrored my own admiration for the nomadic people of his country. This happy obsession of mine grew out of my appreciation and fascination with Middle Eastern carpets, especially the hand-woven Persian rug that I keep in my living room, which inspired the tale I wrote about a young carpet weaver.

Thus, learning about Elvand's passion helped me to understand that I wasn't alone in my intense fascination—and admittedly possible romanticization—of people from another culture, time, and place. It also taught me about Elvand's perceptive nature; he went out of his way to bring me to Iran so that I could connect with the people and land I so keenly wrote about and longed to visit, even though we both knew this generous gift would be difficult to reciprocate due to US visa constraints. But, he did not give his gift hoping for something in return. His soul was much more polished.

At the Book Festival, I learned that I had something in common with another Iranian whom I will call Shirin, because it means "sweet." While I gave a talk on why I chose to write about an Iranian heroine, Shirin was reminded of and wrote down for me the words of the poem "My Kermani Rug," written by a local poet. I was unavailable to speak with her after she had given me the poem, but she went to great lengths to arrange a moment in which we could connect. Elvand sensed her eagerness and invited her back to the hotel to visit later that evening.

When Shirin arrived, she told Elvand that she had fixed tea and wanted me to go with her to her house so that she could show me one of her rugs. Unfortunately, my schedule wouldn't allow it. "Then I will bring my carpet here," she said and drove home to get it.

Rolling her carpet across the hotel lobby floor, she said, "I wanted you to see the rug I keep in my office that inspires my work. It is like the carpet you mentioned in your talk, which inspired your novel." She smiled and I immediately recognized a kindred spirit. When I looked at her rug I saw a large marine animal with a squid-like eye. I swept my finger along the undulant lines depicting seaweed and waves realizing that the rug's motif was Jonah and the Whale. Aside from the fact that we both found inspiration inside the warp and weft of rugs, Shirin's carpet reminded me of the holy stories many people in both of our cultures hold dear.

I learned much about Iran's literary landscape at this conference. Speakers, including child psychologists, writers, translators, teachers, librarians, television programmers, ministers of education and culture, all seemed concerned with educating children for participation in a progressive and increasingly connected world. They were anything but isolationists. The former President Khatami said in a letter to the conference attendees, "Global borders have dissolved. We must ask ourselves, is our literature sufficient for the needs of our children? Does it show the commonality that our children have with those in the rest of the world? Children's literature should not concern itself with education, but with imagination, creativity, and should question authority."

A mixed crowd of professionals—women in back chadors and bearded men in turbans alongside females sporting lipstick, and clean-shaven men in Western blazers—gathered to openly discuss issues and debate the censorship of literature in Iran. They also talked about the shocking fact that American textbook companies censor books on evolution. They raised the notion of whether stories for youth should address changing family demographics, such as the suitability of traditional arranged marriages, unarranged marriages, and divorce. The Iranians spoke about the necessity of reading—particularly translations of foreign literature—in order to reach out to the world, and they spoke about the new wings for the Tehran library that would house millions of books in translation. I recall having thought at the time, am I really hearing all of this here in Iran? I had presumed such topics would be taboo in a country widely known for its censorship of the press. They also talked about the infringement of video games upon children's reading time, reminding me of similar discussions at American conferences. They discussed the notion of looking to India and China for books to translate, as these are vast markets that share histories and cultures with Iran.

Students of literature carrying notepads, microphones, and tape recorders asked us visiting authors how our feminist views came out in our work, if we considered ourselves religious, and if so, how this influenced our writing. They wanted to know if we knew anything about Islam. I recall thinking that if they knew the skewed version of Islam many Westerners are fed by our mainstream media, these well-educated and spiritual people would be insulted. Faces lit up when I told them that I do, in fact, have characters in my novels who are religious and that all my characters in *Anahita's Woven Riddle* are Muslim.

Apart from the creative stage design for the Book Festival lecture hall in Kerman—one that included a painted mural of the Bam citadel for a backdrop and a stage floor covered with blown glass fountains and a speakers' podium—what I found touching was that each day the event opened with a sung verse of the Qur'an. Although many of the Iranians with whom I spoke would likely consider themselves more secular than religious, they still felt comfortable expressing their sense of the sacred and they began their talks with quotes from the Persian Sufi poet Hafiz. These artful details were a welcome change from most conferences I attend at home, which often take place on bare stages and generally offer a PowerPoint slide screen for a backdrop; where virtually no epitaphs are spoken or sung to remind us of our collective struggle to find understanding or meaning in what we do, much less to celebrate the underlying mysteries of life.

The mood at this conference reminded me of events I had attended in Ireland, in which a local saint or poet might be quoted, or where I might hear the expression, *God willing*, a phrase I heard often in Iran as *Inshallah*. Similarly, the attention to detail of the Iranian stage design recalled a literary event I attended in Sligo, Ireland, which took place in a black room—black everything, including the ceiling and curtains—inside which flames filled two great fireplaces on opposing walls. The effect was both stunning and haunting. Thus, in neither country did the mention or use of religious quotes make me feel as if some "religious regime"—be it Catholic or Muslim—was being forced on me.

Other touching elements of the book festival centered on the Iranians' apparent love and respect for children. One afternoon the masters of ceremonies asked the participants to answer the following prompt on slips of paper and submit them. Although I never did learn how everyone responded, I state the notion here for contemplation: *Explain why the Lord said children are the parents of humanity.*

Similarly, I found it remarkable that 40,000 children's books were given away at Iran's First International Children's Book Festival—distributed among the girls and boys who only months before had survived the earthquakes in Bam, which orphaned most of them and killed more than 25,000 people. Despite this tragedy, the Iranian people's appreciation of children, as well as their love of literature and the arts, compelled them to hold such a celebration amidst the rubble of this immense devastation.

I spent three weeks in the company of a group of writers, poets and translators who shared a passion for children's literature so deep that they devoted their days to translating books from German, French, Russian, English, and other languages into Persian, so that Iranian youth could be exposed to the world's best books. Rarely have I bonded so quickly with anyone, much less a whole group of people.

My Iranian colleagues talked easily about politics, economics, professional interests, and other things on their minds. Often they joked about members of their parliament and "totalitarian" government, much the way my friends at home might talk about politicians. For instance, when I inquired about the blue metal boxes with flowers painted on them called *sadagheh*, which are found along the roadways and look like oversized parking meters, I was told, "They are inoperable, do not put any coins into them." These were state-run charity boxes.

Love and Pomegranates

As we toured Esfahan, Elvand and two other hosts, Javad and Mehdi, suggested that we stop for tea and hookah in a den beneath the bridge called Thirty-Three Arches. We climbed a few stone stairs into a cozy room that seemed built into the underside of the pilings that supported the bridge. A pane glass door and window stood on opposite walls, the window looking out to the buff-colored Zayandeh River, which reflected the color of the mountains beyond. Crimson carpets, two or three layers deep, covered every inch of the floor. We sat with our legs outstretched or cross-legged, and leaned our backs against indigo, purple, and black striped *jajim* pillows and bolsters. Though the February sun shone outside and the weather felt just the right temperature in my knee-length black coat and headscarf, huddling in this tearoom provided a different kind of warmth.

A waiter brought us a *samovar*, glass mugs for tea, and a hookah pipe packed with cherry flavored tobacco. Javad showed us how to draw on the mouthpiece, creating a great cloud of smoke about his head. As each of us took turns, the burbling of the water in the pipe created a soft melody accompanying our quiet conversation.

Several of us women fell into girl talk. A middle-aged mother stated that if she were to get married today, she would choose her present husband, a man who had been chosen for her twenty years ago. This was a response to a question about arranged marriages that I couldn't resist asking as it related to my novel. When I posed it to our small circle of women, it brought smiles to their faces. A young student in her twenties, who had had an arranged marriage and just been divorced, confided, "I've become adjusted to, and relish in, having all of my free time to myself. I've taken up piano and am writing novels." She fiddled with her teacup and continued, "But I'm worried I won't find time for a man in my life. And I don't want to be a spinster!"

Another young woman, who was an engineer by day and tour guide by night for the Ministry of Culture, whispered that she was dating our other tour guide and asked me if I thought he was handsome. She also asked me how I liked her recent cosmetic nose surgery. The women's unabashed disclosures tugged deeply. Our conversations reminded me of those I had with women in a Turkish village who within minutes of meeting me and learning that I had three children, including a set of twins, asked me if I delivered them vaginally or by cesarean section. I reached a level of intimacy with these women that I have not yet reached with women at home that I have known for years. We shared our stories about what it means to be human without veils of vanity or pride getting in the way. These women were so comfortable with who they were, the idea of trying to impress others seemed unrehearsed.

As I sat on the pile carpets with my hosts—feeling a bit like a satiated hookah-smoking troll beneath the bridge—I remember asking myself, What could be better than this very moment? I couldn't think of anywhere else in the world I wished to be or any other activity I would have preferred to do. I felt so completely at peace, empty of wants and worries while in the company of these people, that I believe I experienced a kind of ecstasy about which Persian poets so passionately write. Perhaps it was these Iranians' self-disclosure, their abandonment of affectation or superficiality, that opened a space for trust, engendered a common consciousness that ran through each of us, and made palpable the love within and beyond this universe.

I found peace, friendship, and ecstasy in Iran! I cannot imagine what could be sweeter than to recognize a stranger—a supposed foe—as friend. I recall thinking, if everyone in the West, who has been bombarded with reductionist notions of the people living in Iran and the Middle East, could enjoy even one hour in the company of an Iranian in their homeland, then perhaps they would come back with a better understanding of the culture. Like me, they would ache to cry out to the world, "No, you've got it all wrong! The Iranians I know are compassionate, artistic, and above all, generous people—with their time, with their money, with their hearts."

As I boarded my flight in Tehran for home, I noticed how the flight attendants' uncovered heads looked bare and smiled at the way my perspective had shifted somewhere during my travels. It would take some time to shake off the lightness of being, the vigor that accompanies any experience in which one steps far enough outside of the ordinary to wake up one's senses—including the perceptive abilities of the soul. I was in no hurry to leave Iran and the people whose personal and professional concerns seemed much like my own.

Arriving in Seattle, I was singled out for "further inspection." My luggage and carry-on bags lined up on a long low table. "You traveled to Iran alone? Weren't you afraid?" the customs officer asked, eyeing the knee-length tunic I had bought in Kerman to cover myself—a teal linen outfit that one of the Danish flight attendants complimented and then asked where she could buy one.

No, I wasn't afraid of the people who greeted me with a bouquet of roses or those who sent gifts of oranges, pistachios, or homemade date cookies to my room each day.

After finding nothing of interest in my bags, the officer began searching through the photos on my digital camera. I was too jet lagged to be bothered, and knew my connecting flight wasn't for hours, so I slumped onto the table and put my feet up while the man snooped. I thought back to my arrival in Iran. No one had searched my purse or carry on bags there.

"You went to Iran for a children's book festival?" He crossed his arms and squinted. Then he asked me how I knew enough about Iranian culture to write a novel about it and if met people there with whom I would have further contact.

Dozens, God willing, I thought. *Dozens of friends with whom I hope I will never lose contact.*

Love and Pomegranates

Cultural Exchange through Translation
An Interview with Shaghayeh Ghandehari

Ericka Taylor

Q: You've written that translation is essentially a cultural exchange since it reminds people that humanity shares the same basic anxieties, concerns, hopes, and fears. What is it about Vivien Alcock's *The Cuckoo Sister* that led you to translate it?

A: I was a teenager myself at the time and could therefore clearly sympathize with the main characters, Rosie and Emma, who happened to be about the same age as me. It was very interesting to discover how others feel about sudden changes and how they react in such situations. In this case, there's a huge family secret that changes the direction of life for every family member. Emma, the younger sister, accidentally discovers that she had another sister, who was robbed from her stroller before Emma's birth. Her parents failed to track down the baby snatcher or even the reason behind the abduction. Even though Emma's father is a powerful lawyer, the issue remains unsolved. Since Emma's mother experienced a nervous breakdown after the incident, everyone prefers to pretend that nothing happened at all. All seems normal until the thirteenth birthday of the lost baby, when a teenage young girl appears at the door with a letter. It appears that she possibly could be the lost baby, but they aren't sure if they should trust the woman who made such a claim in a letter.

This was my first experience in translation. I was twelve years old when I read this novel, but it had such an impact on me that I remember wondering, "Why don't I share this pleasure with other readers?" I was inexperienced in translating but wanted to share what I found to be interesting.

As I have said before, in books we are reminded that humanity shares the same feelings all over the world. We realize how man's nature is the same, even though reactions might vary based on cultural situations and traditions. Even now that I have translated over 40 novels for young adults, I still find reading about the passions of mankind and how we cope with life issues to be quite interesting. I just can't get enough. I mean, I am trying to learn as I read between the lines of every single fictional work I encounter.

Q: How did you progress from reading the book in England, as a 12-year-old, and getting it published in Iran? How long did it take?

A: Well, first of all, I have to say that usually no one takes a twelve-year-old girl seriously, especially publishers. Once publishers realized I was so young, they politely excused me and the book, without even bothering to flip over the pages. This happened a few times and with different publishers, so I felt disappointed and I was about to give up publishing my translation of *The Cuckoo Sister*. Then someone introduced me to a great monthly journal for young adults. There, I was encouraged and supported and they published the story as a serial piece. Then again, I waited until I was around eighteen before I tried once more to publish the story I'd adored. So it took about five years to get *The Cuckoo Sister* published in Iran, which was a long time indeed! Then I realized that I needed to be patient to face the challenges of this career if I intended to devote myself to it.

Q: Since then, roughly how many books have you translated?

A: I don't know the precise number, because I am very busy working these days, but I'd guess I have published over 70 books in translation. Counting the titles under development, the figure rises to around 80.

Q: As a child, how much access did you have to literature in translation? What types of books were they?

A: During the 1980s, when I was a child, we didn't have much access because translation was not popular and had not become the common literary activity in the Iranian publishing industry it is today. This was especially true in the field of children's literature.

Still, I remember my mom bought me an anthology of classical fairy tales and stories, which was a translated work and introduced me to classic writers like Hans Christian Anderson, the Brothers Grimm, and many others. It was a great anthology and opened my eyes to a new world of stories.

Q: What were some of your favorite books when you were growing up?

A: I spent part of my childhood in England, where I was fortunate to have access to great libraries and become familiar with authors such as Roald Dahl, who remains one of my favorites, and Judy Blume, whose *Are You There God, It's Me Margaret* and *Tiger Eyes* I especially liked. I also liked some of Enid Blyton's different series that focused on adventures and mysteries. As for Iranian books, I remember reading some stories but I don't remember particular names and titles. I loved the work of famous Iranian poets like Mostafa Rahmandoost, who is still the master of children's poetry.

Q: How has access to children's books in translation changed since your childhood?

A: I must say that the two eras just don't compare. For the last twenty years, at least, Iran has seen very serious and professional translators devoting their time and talent to translation for children and young adults. Because of their active participation, many others have become interested in translation, as well. So now a young reader has enormous access to translated books and can choose from a number of titles.

Q: What are some topics in children's literature that you'd like to see explored?

A: I like this question, even though I had not thought about it this way before. I always love reading about human relationships in literary works. This is also true for children's literature. But I dare say that some of the hidden concerns of children and young adults can be explored more deeply and from new perspectives that take today's world into consideration and respond to the needs and concerns of children and young adults. I mean the complications of human issues and our relationships with ourselves, siblings, family, friends, and society can't be neglected or overlooked.

People can do unexpected things and there are times when they really surprise you, when they give you a terrible shock with their behavior. I am aware that such topics are discussed in children's literature, but I still believe more can be said and depicted about humanity and life.

Q: Hussein Elvand Ebrahimi, the founder of the House of Translation for Children and Young Adults, encouraged your pursuit of translation and your focus on translation of young adult work. How popular are books in translation among adults?

A: As a matter of fact, the history of translation for adults is much older when compared with the history of translation for young adults. In fiction and even other genres, translation for adults has a rich history and is very popular in Iran. Several adult classic titles in fiction were translated long before translation found its way to young adults' fiction. I have recently heard that women are very keen on reading translated works. Serious book readers are interested in reading the most recent titles translated, as they are eager to know all about the latest published books abroad.

Q: Do you expect to continue concentrating on books for young people or do you see yourself also translating books for adults?

A: I have already translated a number of titles for adults, including long and short fiction and psychology, and I intend to do the same in the future. I must admit that now that I am an adult, I'm also drawn to adult books. Translation for me is not all about a career and is connected to my own interests and concerns. I hope that in the near future I get a chance to introduce distinctive authors in adult literature to Iranian readers.

Q: There are libraries for children in every province in Iran. How are Iranian children encouraged to read? Is it common for them to read books in translation?

A: Well, just like in any other country, children are encouraged to read both by their parents and their teachers in school. Also, if they have older siblings who enjoy reading, they might be inspired to read more and learn more. Some excellent state publishers and institutes, such as the Institute for the Cultural and Intellectual Development of Children and Young Adults (known as *Kanoon-e Parvaresh-e Fekri-ye Kodak va Nojavan* in Iran), support authors and readers of children's books by hosting diverse programs. For instance, authors occasionally travel to other cities to read their stories to children. When well-known authors are scheduled for a visit, students are given the chance to prepare questions and are excited to meet a favorite author face to face.

In November, Iranians take part in Book Week, which focuses on reading and supporting authors, translators and illustrators, in addition to the publishers. Usually during Book Week, schools select a particular book and hold competitions in which they quiz the students. Whoever wins is awarded books and other prizes.

Several book exhibitions and book fairs are held throughout Iran during the Book Week too, which helps children find new titles and become more involved with books. Now, a number of children and young adults know Western and other foreign authors and their titles. This is especially true of books written in English.

Q: Multiple interpretations of the same work are permissible in Iran. From a translator's perspective, what are the advantages and disadvantages of this practice?

A: Personally, I am against this. I believe that using copyrights would make this career more professional. When a translator or a publisher has to gain copyright permission, that person will take the work more seriously. In the present situation, one can discover that two or three translators are working on the translation of a book at the same time without even knowing it. Only when their books are published or mentioned in the media do others find out about them. I believe that this arrangement has possibly a sole advantage: a better translation can always be provided in a short time. I have heard that sometimes a professional translator is asked to re-translate a book in order to correct the mistakes made in a previous translation. This could make translators more careful in their work as they know that another version of the original book could be on the way. In other words, you try to do your best.

There is no real copyright law in Iran regarding book translations, and therefore a title could possibly be translated several times. For example, bestsellers are always a risk, because several publishers and translators go for them. In this situation, the reader can select the translation he likes if a few translations are available at the same time.

Q: Since you're pursuing your doctorate, you clearly have a deep appreciation for the field. What do you see as the greatest value of translating literature?

A: I am pursuing my doctorate in English literature because I know that I am going to translate literature and need a rich literary background and insight.

From my experience in the field of literary translation, I think that literature communicates in a unique spiritual language all over the world, even though at the surface level, the languages differ. The concerns of literature are more or less the same and cover similar topics. Yet each time these topics are expressed through a new perspective and from an unexpected point of view, it amazes us and takes us by surprise. I assume that due to these factors, literature will not lose its magic and translation will continue to pave the way for a clear exchange of the concerns of authors worldwide.

Selected Poems

Forugh Farrokhzad
Translated by Sholeh Wolpé

The following three poems are from award-winning book Sin—Selected poems of Forugh Farrokhzad, *edited and translated by Iranian-American poet Sholeh Wolpé. Farrokhzad, who died in a car accident in 1967 at the age 32, was a poet of sensuous extremes. Writing during the 1950s and 60s, her poems were considered unconventional and scandalous, as they very well might have been considered so by Western readers of that era. Today, she is an icon and one of the most beloved and respected poets of twentieth-century Iran. Her work has inspired and continues to inspire many, including the young poet Shideh Etaat, whose poem "Fly, Howl, Love" appears in this anthology.*

On Loving

Tonight from your eyes' sky
stars rain on my poem,
my fingers spark, set ablaze
the muteness of these blank pages.

My fevered, raving poem
shamed by its desires,
hurls itself once again into fire,
the flames' relentless craving.

Yes, so love begins,
and though the road's end is out of sight,
I do not think of the end.
It's the *loving* that I love.

Why shun darkness?
The night abounds with diamond drops.
Later, jasmine's intoxicating scent
lingers on the spent body of night.

Love and Pomegranates

Let me lose myself in you
till no one can find my trace.
Let your dewy sigh's fevered soul
waft over the body of my songs.

Wrapped in sleep's silk
let me grow wings of light,
fly through its open door
beyond the world's fences and walls.

Do you know what I want of life?
That I can be with you, you, all of you,
and if life repeated a thousand times,
still you, you, and again, you.

Concealed in me is a sea:
how could I hide it?
How could I describe
the typhoon inside?

I'm so filled with you
I want to run through meadows,
bash my head against mountain rocks,
give myself to ocean waves.

I'm so filled with you
I want to crumble into myself like a speck of dust,
to gently lay my head at your feet,
cling fast to your weightless shadow.

Yes, so love begins,
and though the road's end is out of sight,
I do not think of the end
for it's the *loving* I so love.

Rebellious God

If I were God, I'd call on the angels one night
to release the round sun into the darkness's furnace,
angrily command the world garden servants
to prune the yellow leaf moon from the night's branch.

At midnight among the curtains of my divine palace,
I'd upturn the world with my furious fingers,
and with my hands, tired of their thousand-year stillness,
I'd stuff the mountains in the seas' open mouths.

I'd unbind the feet of a thousand fevered stars,
scatter fire's blood through the forests' mute veins,
rend the curtains of smoke so that in the wind's roar
fire's daughter can throw herself drunk into the forest's arms.

I'd blow into the night's magic reed
until the rivers rise from their beds like thirsty serpents,
and weary of a lifetime of sliding on a damp chest
pour into the dim marsh of the night sky.

Sweetly I'd call on the winds to release
the flower perfume boats on the rivers of night.
I'd open the graves so that myriad wandering souls
could once again seek life in the confines of the bodies.

If I were God, I'd call on the angels one night
to boil the water of eternal life in Hell's cauldron,
and with a burning torch chase out the virtuous herd
that grazes in the green pastures of an unchaste heaven.

Tired of being a prude, I'd seek Satan's bed at midnight
and find refuge in the declivity of breaking laws.
I'd happily exchange the golden crown of divinity
for the dark, aching embrace of a sin.

Only Voice Remains

Why should I stop, why?

Birds have gone to seek their blue way.
The horizon is horizontal,
movement vertical—a gushing geyser.
Bright stars spin as far as the eye can see.

The Earth repeats itself in space, air tunnels
become connecting canals and day changes
to an entity so vast it cannot be stuffed
into the narrow imaginations of the newspaper worms.

Why should I stop?

The path meanders among life's tiny veins
and the climate of the moon's womb will annihilate
the cancerous cells, and in the chemical aura of after-dawn
there will remain only voice—
                    voice seeping into time.

Why should I stop?

What is a swamp but a spawning ground
for corruption's vermin?
Swelled corpses pen the morgue's thoughts,
the cad hides his yellowness in the dark,
and the cockroach
...ah when the cockroach harangues,
                    why should I stop?

Printer's lead letters line up in vain.
Lead letters in league cannot salvage petty thoughts.
My essence is of trees; breathing stale air depresses me.
A bird long dead counseled me to remember flight.

Fusion creates the greatest force—
fusion with the sun's luminescent soul,
comprehension flooding with light.
Windmills eventually warp and rot.

Why should I stop?
I hold to my breasts sheaves of unripe wheat
and give them milk.

Voice, voice, only voice.
The water's voice, its wish to flow,
the starlight's voice pouring upon the earth's female form,
the voice of the egg in the womb congealing into sense,
the clotting together of love's minds.

Voice, voice, voice, only voice remains.
In a world of runts,
measurements orbit around zero.
Why must I stop?

The four elements alone rule me;
my heart's charter cannot be drafted
by the provincial government of the blind.
What have I to do with the long feral howls
of the beasts' genitals?

What have I to do with the slow progress
of a Maggot through flesh?

It's the flowers' bloodstained history that has committed
          me to life,
the flowers' bloodstained history, you hear?

Bam 6.6, The Movie

Brian H. Appleton

The following is an abridged interview of independent filmmaker Jahangir Golestan-Parast, born in Esfahan, Iran, and now living with his family in California. His film Bam 6.6 *reveals the compassion of the Iranian people in a time of crisis—the 2003 earthquake in Bam, Iran, which killed over 30,000 people. The movie follows the story of two newly-engaged Americans, Tobb Dell'Oro and Adele Freedman, who were victims of the earthquake, the Iranian tour guide who helped rescue them from the rubble, and the surgeon who saved Adele's life.*

Q: Tell me about your family and your early childhood in Esfahan.

A: I was raised in a very loving environment in Esfahan. My father had two wives and two families, one in Tehran and one in Esfahan. We became very close after my father died, when my stepsiblings moved to Esfahan. We now consider ourselves one family. My father was well known in Esfahan and Iran because of his café, a very traditional teahouse he owned for 30 years. Often when we would see a beggar in the street my father would encourage me to take his hand and invite him to our café, where he would give him a free meal and some money. A friend recently asked me now that I am 55 and have traveled the world, if I had to do it again, where would I like to be born and with which citizenship? Without any doubt or hesitation I said Esfahan. I still feel like it's the most fascinating city in the world. It's so beautiful.

Q: What are some of your other memories from childhood?

A: We went to movies all the time—outdoor movie theatres. My father also owned an inn. My brother and I would jump from its roof onto the roof of the theatre, where we could watch for free. Sometimes we brought our friends, too. When we were too young to read, we would sit next to an older person, who would read the Persian subtitles of the foreign films out loud.

Q: When did you decide you wanted to be a filmmaker?

A: I wanted to be a moviemaker from the time I was fifteen. Richard Brooks's adaptation of Truman Capote's *In Cold Blood* made a big impression on me. At that time, I went to live in London with my brother Mohammad. I needed top grades to get into film school there, but I wasn't able to get them, and so I never ended up studying film. Eventually, I went to the United States, where I took several courses on filmmaking at UCLA and made my first film, which was a travelogue about Esfahan.

Q: Tell me about the evolution of *Bam 6.6* and why you chose to make it.

A: Although the devastating tragedy of the earthquake seemed like a grim subject for a film, it really served as a door opening for the American public to see Persian culture. It seems that every filmmaker up until this film has focused on one particular aspect of Iranian culture without looking at the big picture. I was determined to portray the best of Persian culture comprehensively—the essence of its generosity, hospitality, caring, and passion for their fellow human beings. There were many Americans who also believed in my goal, such as Bill Woolery, who edited this film and made a trailer pro bono. The Dell'Oro family, whose son Tobb died from his injuries, greatly supported this film, as did his fiancée's family, the Freedmans.

Q: I know that you wanted to tell the story of Tobb and Adele so Americans would see the compassion and care they received in Iran. How did you connect with them?

A: A Persian student brought me an article about Tobb and Adele. I contacted Tobb's sister who was very receptive and thought both families would want to participate. Both the Dell'Oros and the Freedmans were interested in getting the word out to the American public and the Western world about what kind people Iranians really are and the warm welcome and assistance they received in the hospital in Tehran. When Adele went for a follow-up visit with her doctors in New York, they commented that they could not have done a better job than the Iranian doctors had. When the Iranian surgeon took a look at Adele's crushed foot he had to decide between amputation or reconstructive surgery, which was the difference between a half hour versus five hours of surgery. Despite the thousands of other people in need of medical attention, he elected to undertake the surgery because foreign travelers are guests and guests come first in Iran.

I cannot begin to express how much love I feel for Tobb Dell'Oro, Adele Freedman, and their families. I know it must have been painful for them to revisit the experience, but they agreed to share their story because they shared my mission of peace. Just as a child is born from its mother's pain, so was something born from all the misery and devastation. That something was the opportunity to show the very best qualities that humanity has to offer.

Q: Tell me more about the participation of Dell'Oros and the Freedmans in this film.

A: Adele agreed to the interview in May 2004. I didn't want to overwhelm her, so I filmed the interview myself without a cameraman. I cried throughout the entire session because it was such a moving story. Three years later, I realized I needed more footage, but I was worried that Adele would not agree to further interview. The political climate had changed between our countries and I wondered how they felt about Iran. Also, I didn't know if Adele and the Freedmans wanted to be subjected to more publicity. However, my fears were unfounded. When I finished the film, I went back to New York to show it to her, but she didn't want to see it. Adele's parents watched the finished film with me first. We were all crying. When it ended, Adele's mother said she had learned much about Iranian people and understood now why Tobb had wanted to go to Iran. She thoroughly approved of the film and urged Adele to see it.

During the last three years while making this film, I underwent a transformation. It reconfirmed that the epicenter of my life's motivation is humanity, humanity, humanity. I think many Iranians and other Middle Easterners Anglicize their names and hide their ethnicity for a variety of reasons, including avoidance of persecution and shame of the perceived "backwardness" of their culture. After making this film, I felt even prouder of being Iranian. I want every Iranian, especially expatriates, to feel proud of the good things in Iranian culture.

Q: What's next?

A: I am planning to make a film about my own experience coming to America and the experience of other expat Iranians in the United States. It is my profoundest wish that Iranians find unity amongst themselves and that all the wounds between different factions and political and ethnic groups heal, and that we work to preserve our heritage and our culture. ▪

Persia Primeval

Shervin Hess

Atop a craggy butte in Semnan we posted our elbows in ancient gravel and scanned the surrounding plains through binoculars. Nothing moved across the land aside from our own shadows. Between the nearest village and us lay 70 miles of pink desert. I was slowly yielding to the dead silence of the wilderness when Amir turned and said, "Do you know what happened to Bahram Gur?"

I did, of course. He was the subject of the only Persian poem I'd committed to memory. Bahram was a Sasanid king infamous for turning herds of beasts into hills of bodies. He relished the hunt with such passion that history appended his name with that of his preferred quarry: the *gur*. Bahram always got his gur. But in the end, as 'Omar Khayyam wrote, the gur got Bahram. In Persian, gur has two meanings: one is a type of small, wild horse. The other is the grave. The irony of that homonym was not likely lost on the young king as he pursued his victim into a pool of quicksand. I will never know Bahram V beyond what Khayyam wrote of him, but the gur remains.

The wilderness is the only Persian thing unmoved by the steady march of culture and time. Though greatly reduced, at its heart survives a living link to our mysterious past. It is this aspect of my Persian heritage that I hold dearest. Seeking to experience the fauna and wilderness of my birth land, I visited Iran in April of 2010. I was five months old the last time I'd been there.

For ten days I traversed the country's nature reserves with Amir Hussein Khaleghi, co-founder of the Iranian conservation organization Plan for the Land (P4L). Our journey began in a sprawl of mountains, plains, and desert called Touran National Park. It is home to 200, or roughly a third, of Iran's gur. But in a park the size of Connecticut, the little horses had no trouble hiding from us. Nor did the gazelle, ibex, mountain sheep, or leopard. It occurred to me that Touran, once called the Serengeti of Western Asia, would today be unrecognizable to Bahram V.

The terrible reality is that 80 to 90 percent of Iran's fauna vanished during the past century. Some, like the gur, now cling to a precarious existence. Others, like the tiger, are gone forever. What happened to Iran's wildlife? Their undoing is but a single, short chapter in the story of modern mass extinction. As we did to their kind throughout the world, we killed too many and stole their land. We assumed they'd always be there. Revelation comes at different points for different people, and for Iran it came in 1967, when a group of concerned Iranian sportsmen founded Iran's Game and Fish Department. The Department quickly blossomed into an international model for conservation, establishing by 1977 a network of reserves covering 6.5 percent of the country (today, by comparison, 8.5 percent of the United States, 4.9 percent of India, and 2 percent of Saudi Arabia is protected land). This policy, however, shifted with the current government. Despite a constitutional ban on activities that irreparably harm the environment, little effort was directed toward the restriction of poaching, over-grazing, and deforestation. The situation improved by the 1990s, when Iran's Department of the Environment (DoE) escalated its wildlife defense tactics. But ceaseless damage inflicted by the ever-expanding population continues to stifle their efforts to this day.

Despite the plundering of the past, Iran still possesses the greatest biodiversity in Western Asia. When gur went extinct in Israel, and gazelle all but vanished from Saudi Arabia, Iran provided those countries with a fresh supply. It is a land astride three continents, bringing together cheetah, deer, antelope, wolves, hyenas, bears, and some 900 other mammal, bird, and reptile species. Amir secured permission for me to see some of these closely guarded creatures, one of which my father spent seven years studying in the Dasht-e Naz Wildlife Refuge near Sari. With its gracefully bowed antlers and mantle of white spots, the Persian fallow deer captivated every civilization it encountered. A giant winged figure in the Assyrian Palace of Ashurnasirpal II cradles a Persian fallow buck, and an entire herd is carved into the cliffs of Taq-e Bostan. The oldest known rug, dated to the fifth century BC, is bordered with 24 of these deer. But as this deer, the *gavazn-e zard*, was being immortalized in artwork throughout the Persian Empire, it was quietly vanishing from the wild. By 1923, it was thought to have been hunted to extinction. Three decades later, explorers in a forested pocket of the southwestern Khuzestan province discovered the last remaining herd, and relocated four individuals to Dasht-e Naz to serve as the nucleus of a captive breeding and relocation program. Over 400 gavazn-e zard now roam throughout the protected areas of the country. Their recovery has been called one of the great conservation victories of the twentieth century.

Intervention came too late for other delegates of Iran's wildlife kingdom. "From the dark jungle as a tiger bright, form from the viewless Spirit leaps to light," Rumi wrote of *Panthera tigris* 500 years before William Blake penned his celebrated "Tyger" poem. Once common from Gilan to Khorasan, the Caspian tiger has been missing from Iran since 1958. While I was in Iran, the DoE made headlines by importing a pair of Siberian tigers, which a 2010 study suggested are genetically identical to their extinct Caspian cousins. Some critics question the biological integrity of this endeavor, pointing to a single nucleotide discrepancy between Siberian and Caspian tiger DNA. Others are more troubled by the lingering problems that led to the tiger's extinction in the first place, namely, the conversion of the tigers' habitat into agricultural land. I visited the future home of these tigers in Miankaleh Wildlife Refuge, an undeveloped tract of Caspian coastline alive with jackals, wild boar, and a quarter-million migrating birds.

Miankaleh used to support a thriving tiger population, but it is now surrounded by civilization, ensuring that the transplanted cats will always be restricted to a semi-captive existence. The wild tiger that so inspired Rumi is gone. And today, many Iranians are unaware that those giant striped cats ever lived in their country.

A lack of awareness is at least partially to blame for Iranians' disconnection from their natural heritage. Environmental education is only available at the collegiate level, and public education programs are scant. To aggravate the problem, urban Iranians rarely experience unspoiled wilderness. On a hike up Tochal, the 13,000-foot mountain at the edge of the Tehran, I was shocked to see hundreds of empty water bottles and candy wrappers littering every trail and stream. How a culture steeped in such admiration for beauty could be so negligent of their native soil was difficult to comprehend. The worst insult comes from the myriad mining, industrial, and agricultural activities that pollute the land and exile wildlife to remote sanctuaries.

This wasn't always the case. As recently as the 1960s, leopards were a common sight in the mountains surrounding Tehran. Figuring prominently throughout Iranian culture and folklore, the *palang* particularly interested Ferdowsi, who made hundreds of references to the cat in his epic *Book of Kings*, or *Shahnameh*. Today, Iran's leopard faces the same threats that annihilated the Caspian tiger, including an undeservedly bad reputation in rural areas. Shepherds occasionally shoot or poison leopards out of fear for their flocks. Amir's organization endeavors to counter misconceptions by reaching rural Iranians at an early age. To see his vision in practice I accompanied the P4L staff to the mountain village classrooms surrounding Bamu National Park, near Shiraz. Through demonstrations, art activities, and a creative approach to interactivity, P4L volunteers taught children the basics of leopard biology and the tenets of sound land stewardship. As we left, a troupe of laughing grade-schoolers chased our jeep like fans at a rock concert. If their enthusiasm was any indication of ecological awareness, there may be a glimmer of hope yet for the Persian leopard.

My wilderness journey was ending, and Bahram-e Gur Wildlife Refuge in Fars was my last chance to see a gur before I returned to the US We travelled by jeep from one high point to the next, searching for any sign of the creatures and finding none. By day's end my eyes burned from squinting at the horizon. I had all but conceded when at once, we spotted a herd prancing along a crystalline ridge rising from the plains to the mountains. We carefully darted from rock to rock until we crept within 200 yards of them. Suddenly they stopped to gaze back at us through liquid black eyes. Those eyes had witnessed every transformation of Iran, from the Median Empire to the Mongol invasion to the Islamic Republic. And those same eyes surveyed the plains before the first man arrived, when Iran was one vast, unblemished wilderness. I lowered the camera from my faced and watched them watching me. Like Bahram V, I finally got my gur. But they remained to me as inscrutable as my distant past, and in that moment, I understood they were the same.

When the physical embodiments of our past cease to exist, what becomes of us? I don't know. But I know that much more than biodiversity is at stake should we lose the gur, the leopard, or any of Iran's fauna. A new generation of concerned young Iranians feels the same. They hope to see Iran protect 10 percent of its land by 2020, which will prove critical to the survival of Iran's wildlife. How we treat our native soil will ultimately determine how long we will occupy it. With a wink and a nod, Khayyam may have cautioned us about this over 900 years ago:

aan qasr ke Jamshid dar-oo jam gereft
ahu bache kard-o rubah aram gereft
Bahram ke gur migerefti hame omr
didi ke chegune gur bahram gereft?

In the palace where Jamshid took his cup
The gazelle gives birth and the fox sleeps
Bahram, who took the gur all his life
Do you see how the gur has taken Bahram?

The Oldest Living Iranian

Ryszard Antolak

O n the Silk Road from Yazd to Shiraz, in the desert city of Abarkuh, stands the old-est living being in Iran (perhaps in the whole world). It is at least five thousand years old, and some say eight thousand. Ancient and mysterious even to botanists (who cannot decide on its true age), the Cypress Tree of Abarkuh is shrouded in legend and revered by countless visitors. When it was first mentioned in 1335 AD (by a certain Hamd-Allah Mostofi), the tree was already "famous throughout the world."

To anyone approaching it, the tree appears more mineral than vegetable. You are confronted by a wall of massive trunks—19 meters thick—packed together tightly like the tentacles of a giant squid, each one vying with others for space and sky. High above your head they finally explode, showering a canopy of lingering fragrance and delicious shade down onto the earth 30 meters below. The tree stands next to an old caravanserai, surrounded by a low circular hedge of manicured privet (sometimes also with a small pool of water). Visitors come in their hundreds, their hands immediately drawn to stony surface of the trunk. They feel along it for a time, as if searching for a concealed entrance or a living heart. They circle it in wonder like pilgrims round the Ka'aba, constantly touching and caressing. Some visitors spread out blankets and eat watermelon in the delicious cool of its shade. Others bring colored ribbons to hang on the lower branches as signs of reverence or supplication. At these times the tree resembles a woman in a Qashkai skirt, her hands raised to her hair, ready to perform a dance.

Cypress trees (*Cupressus sempervirens*) are native to Iran. They were carried by travellers to Europe in the distant past, and then spread to other areas of the world. Mediterranean cypresses seldom survive longer than two thousand years. In their home-lands on the plains of Iran, they can grow to many times that age.

Cypresses were once revered all over ancient Iran. Saints and sages were buried in their hollowed-out trunks, the bark carefully replaced so that they would continue to grow.[1] There is a legend that Zoroaster planted two famous cypresses in Khorasan, both of which grew to enormous proportions: the Cypress of Kashmar (near Mashhad) and the Cypress of Faryumaz (near Sabsevar).[2] When the local king Gushtasp accepted the religion of the prophet, Zoroaster ordered the trunk of the former to be inscribed with the words, "Gushtasp accepts the Good Religion." And from that time onwards, cypresses were planted at the doors of many Zoroastrian temples and became a familiar feature of the Iranian landscape. Their slender pyramidal shapes were likened to living flames, burning and transforming the face of the earth. In time, they came to represent the Iranian prophet himself. Islam too, lays claim to this particular tree. A persistent cluster of legends links it to Abraham (who is said to have planted it), and other local traditions and geographical features around Abarkuh are associated with the life of this patriarch. From at least the twelfth century AD, Abarkuh was known as the City of Abraham.[3]

In the pages of the Avesta, the Cypress is listed first among the trees that "give no fruit to man." But anyone who rests for a short time beneath its shade soon discovers the opposite. The water in the pool is brown and warm. Frogs brood nearby and swallows swoop low in the branches. Light yawns its way out of the desert hills and lies smoothly down with the dappled shade. The tree may not feed the body, but it nourishes the spirit and feeds the imagination.

Plans have been drawn up to develop the area around the cypress as a park to protect the tree's future. UNESCO is involved in the planning. A slender young cypress has been planted nearby so that when the old tree sickens or falls, the younger will take its place. There is likely to be a cypress tree at Abarkuh for many centuries to come.

Iran is a country full of remarkable monuments and architectural marvels. But all of them are lifeless. The Cypress Tree of Abarkuh is a living monument, an ancient noble organism well worthy of celebration and protection. ■

'A Bold Hand'
Making a Mark on the Art World

Jeff Baron

Washington, May 21, 2010—Negar Ahkami's canvases are packed with detail, vibrant with color, layered with acrylic, and sometimes accented with glitter to bring out their three-dimensionality. When other artists were making names for themselves with minimalism, Ahkami was unheedingly going for maximalism.

Her artistic influences, drawn from her Iranian roots and American upbringing, are just as rich and complex: Persian miniatures, calligraphy and tiles, plus the work of Ardeshir Mohassess ("I grew up knowing and meeting a lot of Iranian artists," she said), but also expressionism, pop, baroque and fauvism.

In an era of growing attention and prestige for Iranian artists, Ahkami said she understands that people will put her in the Iranian-American category, and she won't complain about that.

"I understand the need to put people in a box. It doesn't upset me. I just hope over time it's not the only box I'm put in," she said. "It's a privilege to be making art at all, and if that means that I'm going to be in a box, that's fine."

But ask her where she puts herself, and she says: "I'm very American. I consider myself an American artist first and foremost."

As for her style, Ahkami said she uses "a bold hand." "I'm not punk rock in appearance or in my daily behavior, but when I'm painting, I have a punk-rock mentality."

At thrity-nine, Ahkami is no rock star, but she has achieved a measure of success in the art world, with solo and group shows at galleries in New York, where she lives, as well as in other US cities and Zurich, Switzerland. She said her career really took off when she was pregnant with her daughter. "I think she's my good-luck charm," Ahkami said.

Ahkami has taken a bit of a roundabout path, artistically and personally, from drawing classes in childhood, to painting in her home studio in Brooklyn. She grew up in the New York City suburb of Clifton, New Jersey, and her father would take her for classes at the Art Students League of New York. She said that even then she grew restless with simply drawing the models in drawing class; she would add ornate backgrounds out of her imagination.

Ahkami studied Middle Eastern languages and cultures in college and soon after went off to law school, but she had not left art behind. "I pretty much went to law school knowing that this was not what I wanted to do," she said. After leaving a job at a large law firm, she worked as a staff attorney for a New York museum and painted in her spare time. But after a couple of years, it was clear that the painting was more important.

"It got to the point where I couldn't do both anymore," Ahkami said. So at about age 30, she switched: She became a full-time artist and practiced law on the side, just enough to pay the bills. She still keeps her law license up to date, but hasn't used it in a few years.

Her artistic journey had taken her away from Iranian art but she has come to embrace elements of it. "It's the aspect of my heritage that I've been most proud of," she said. "I loved the jewel-like qualities."

But she also admired the fierce emotional power of the expressionists. She said she couldn't imagine herself in the role of the classical Persian artist who hides herself in the beautiful details and for whom the work is not primarily a means of self-expression or of showing the anguish of the world.

The more she explored, the more she found that she wanted to form "a messy kind of Persian art that wasn't about beauty and that maybe had some satire in it as well."

According to Ahkami she borrows freely from the Persian tradition ("I seriously love the way rocks are painted in Persian miniatures"), and revels in the connections she can create between Eastern and Western art. Persian paintings might not have had any influence on early American landscape painters such as Thomas Cole, but Ahkami said she loves the way both genres use trees, and she has drawn from both in some of her works.

The subject matter of her art also reflects the links between her two cultures. "I am embracing the absurd aspect of what I've been dealt with my Iranian heritage," what she called the absurdities of Iranian politics and of American perceptions about Iran, in contrast with the glories of its culture that inspire her with pride.

Ahkami said her work is political because she is so deeply pained by the rift between the United States and Iran. "I'd love to create art that didn't have anything political in it," she said.

As for American perceptions, she said, "It used to be that the only images people saw were this 'death to America' thing." Now, she has noticed a hopeful change in that Americans seem to be developing an understanding of Iran's politics and history that they lacked in the decades after the revolution of 1979.

"It's been healing for me that people over here are finally getting what's going on in Iran," she said.

Travels and Wonders in Iran from the Point of View of an American-Greek Woman Musician

Rowan Storm

This is an adapted excerpt from Rowan's blog:
www.iran-rowanstorm.blogspot.com

As a teenager looking for meaning in Los Angeles, my life was transformed at a concert of classical Persian music. As the musicians began to play the *santur* and *tombak* (hammered dulcimer and hand drum), the material environment seemed to dissolve as the sounds and vibrations of this magical music awakened something inside me. Nine years later, my performing career was launched in New York City, singing and playing traditional middle eastern hand drums. After many years of longing to visit Iran, my dream finally came true in 2006.

Monday, April 3, 2006 - Tehran

Dearest Friends!

Arrived, only a few glitches with my visa. I was met by the charming Nima, my guide here, a mightily talented musician and poet. We went to Darband today, a beautiful mountain in the north of Tehran, and walked and climbed and huffed and puffed and found captivating riverside perches to drink tea and escape the fierce sun. Further down the mountain, delicious food and more tea. I quickly learned that drinking tea is a constant theme weaving throughout all aspects of daily Iranian life. Returning to Nima's home, his mother prepared *ghormeh sabzi*, my favorite food. I feel at home here, the people are warm and caring, looking after me so thoughtfully. Nima and I just had a wonderful jam session, with the household parakeets singing along in perfect rhythm!

Love and Pomegranates

Monday, April 2, 2006 - Tehran

Dear All,

Celebrations are just about winding down for Norooz, the ancient Persian New Year. Every home is decked out with representations of nature and renewal, including a clump of earth with new grass. The last day of the two-week celebration is an outdoor fest in the spring air called Norooz Sizdah Bedar, which means "throwing out the thirteen" and is considered a number of misfortune. Families gather, eating and talking and drinking tea, playing backgammon and throwing balls, napping, showing off new clothing, leisurely, jubilantly!

The final cathartic gesture of Sizdah Bedar is to toss the clump of grassy earth into a river, where it is swept into oblivion. Of course in the middle of Tehran or any big city, it is not always easy to find a river, so through the day, these tossed-off green remnants could be found all over—in the water channels that weave through the streets, on top of newspaper stands, car hoods, park benches—a truly lovely sight, and a reaffirmation of the ultimate ground of Nature.

Monday, May 2, 2006 - Mashhad

SALAAM everyone!

Lady T, Lady S and I flew to Mashhad from Tehran, arriving after midnight. The next morning we went to the mountain at the center of Mashhad, and climbed to the top, where we could get a good sense of the surrounding legendary land of Khorasan.

After lunch, we began our preparations for visiting the Haram-e Motahhar (Sacred Precincts) and the tomb of the great Saint, Imam Reza, the most important pilgrimage destination of Iran. As if in counterbalance to the seriousness of our visit, laughter started bubbling up as I began confusing several words. I found my companions doubling up in laughter as I was somberly referring to our destination as the bath (*hamaam*) of Imam Reza, or the forbidden (*haram*), rather than the Haram (Holy Precinct). Woops.

Dressed in full chador, we embarked at dusk towards the magnificent complex of buildings and courtyards—dazzling, otherworldly, and powerful beyond words. The crowd of kneeling worshippers were arrayed across sprawling, patterned carpets in the magnificent courtyard. At the conclusion of the formal prayer, we progressed toward the Shrine. I had been told that it is wild in there, with women struggling forward to touch the tomb to receive healing and blessing. My friends told me it is too dangerous to attempt the approach, since if someone fell down they would be trampled or suffocated. I moved ahead, reassuring them I would be fine.

Focusing on the goal in front of me, I pressed into the churning crowd of hundreds of wailing women. As some were squeezed out of the circle, others pushed in closer towards the center. Bodies were pressed so close it took no effort to remain upright.

Finally I arrived within reaching distance of the Shrine and thrust my hand through heads and clamoring arms, as another surge rolled me away. A woman in front of me, surely an angel, took my hand and pulled it forward towards the Shrine, my arm and body stretched to the limits until I could finally hold onto the bars. Upon making contact, I felt an inexplicable sense of communion with every soul in the space, every spirit and element in Creation. The selfless gesture of my nameless soul-guide in the guise of a woman had enabled me to complete my pilgrimage.

Sunday, May 28, 2006 - Tehran

Greetings again!

When we returned from Mashhad, I fell into a whirlwind of local activities here in Tehran. One day Nima and I went to visit some of his family members for a delicious lunch at their home near the northern edge of Tehran. Enough food was arrayed for an army, and our party of eight barely made a dent!

These outings have taught me unspoken rules in Iranian culture about how to be a well-behaved guest. Even Iranians with modest means will unflinchingly empty their coffers in order to serve their guests a feast worthy of royalty. The most gracious way to show appreciation for such beneficence, naturally, is to consume massive quantities of food, drink, and sweets, not always so easy or comfortable!

Generally when asked where I was from, my answer was Greece, since I have been living there for many years, and I did not want to cause a commotion by broadcasting my American identity. Throughout one particular day of shopping, when I happened to answer that I am American, the shopkeepers became so excited, wanting to drag me down the street to meet their friends, colleagues, and relatives!

In a suitcase shop, I was hounded with questions about life in America, about this musician, that kind of food, film, movie star, etc. The average Iranian is extremely curious about America, and while it isn't politically correct to have such interests, they already know a great deal about American culture, and are eager to learn more.

Sunday, August 6, 2006

Salaam, dear everyone!

As many of you know, a woman traveling alone in this part of the world is most unusual. Nima's family are open-minded and progressive, and even they were having misgivings. I finally managed to persuade them that I would be fine taking off by myself to experience the Holy city of Qom, the heart of Iranian Shiite religious study. I took off after 9:00 pm on a bus from Tehran. I was given a preparatory talk about the seriousness of Qom—no laughter, keep a straight face, don't let any hair show from under the chador, don't look anyone in the eye. Nima's father escorted me to the bus station, requesting the driver and fellow passengers to look out for me. Having braced myself for a somber mood, I was delighted that they were showing a funny movie on the bus! It was a comedy, with two men and a woman with totally correct Islamic attire sporting Superman/Superwoman costumes, flying off into the air for various deeds of bravery. Wild-Western style shootout scenes were complete with lassos, cowboy hats, and boots, with the woman's hair covered properly with bandana under her cowboy hat. I did not quite catch the story line, but that didn't prevent me from getting swept up in the wave of giddiness surging through the bus.

We arrived in Qom around midnight, and as soon as the driver stepped out, he ushered me to a taxi. The next morning I suited myself up in the chador and went to discover Qom. There is something sensual about wearing long flowing cloth from head to toe, and in Qom it was not only the women dressed this way. While men who are not involved with religious pursuits wear standard casual Western men's clothing, the religious scholars wear elegant, long, flowing gowns, reminiscent of the black robes of Greek Orthodox priests.

Finally entering one of several gateways, I was astonished that exactly as I set foot through the door, the *azan* began. Kismet. The azan is the formal call to prayer, a man's voice chanting lines from the Qur'an, broadcast from loudspeakers throughout the Islamic world several times daily from sunrise to sunset. I had not planned to participate in the prayer service, but I could not resist joining the current of women drawing together in silence.

Deeply moved, I stayed for many hours in the women's section of the complex, soaking up the ambience. Various pastimes and pursuits were represented. Many women were intently studying the Qur'an. Several were sprawled out catching a nap, some were sharing a picnic, others seemed to be gossiping, and some were munching on cheese puffs and drinking tea.

My three months in Iran have been magnificent beyond my wildest dreams, and the expiration of my visa is the only reason I am leaving. My gratitude extends to several individuals who opened the world for me here. A professor of Persian language worked overtime to acquire my visa, and introduced me to Nima, who along with his family took me in as one of their own.

If I had not also traveled alone, the simple, precious encounters with nameless human souls would not have happened with the same impact. I realize that everyday encounters form the opportunity for making a difference in this world. I am filled with happiness, gratitude, humility, light, love, and compassion from and for every person with whom I had contact in Iran.

Painting Iran's Secrets
A Profile of Artist Laurie Blum

Laura Ender

*L*aurie Blum is an artist who has traveled on three occasions to Iran to paint within the landscapes and shrines. The Shiraz Cultural Institute gave her the honor of being the first painter to exhibit her work at the Shrine of Hafiz in Shiraz, Iran, in December 2004 and January 2005. In July 2007 the Mission of the Islamic Republic of Iran to the United Nations sponsored an exhibition of her work, titled "Shiraz, The City of Paradise: The Real Dialogue Among Civilizations," in the United Nations Secretariat Lobby.

Her travels in Iran were what she calls "a timeless experience...painting what I felt drawn to in my heart." She was able to paint in the Garden of Paradise—at the shrines of Hafiz and Sa'di—in Shiraz, Iran, over the course of several trips, during which she immersed herself in the culture and hospitality of the city. "I was treated with great respect and welcomed by a very loving people," she says. "In each of the gardens the architects who designed the gardens came forward to meet me. One gardener asked me if I could give him one of my Persian music tapes because he hadn't heard it before. Others presented me with a bottle of poppy seeds from the garden when I finished my painting *Poppies* and asked me why I was painting poppies. Didn't I have poppies in my own country, weren't there more interesting subjects for me to paint in the Garden of Paradise? I told them, I am not painting poppies! I am painting the sublime atmosphere that the poppies imbibe here." While painting in Shiraz she believed that she had found her inner garden.

During her travels, amid Iran's mountains and waterfalls, Laurie Blum was able to experience the tradition of Norooz, the celebration of the New Year and heralding of spring. She witnessed extended families rejoice in nature by camping in gardens, mountains, jungles, and by the sea. During this month-long celebration, Laurie witnessed people picnicking, playing musical instruments, and communing with nature. "There

Love and Pomegranates

is a profound and fundamental connection between the people and their ancient land."

Like the Iranians, Laurie felt respite in the gardens, where she says, "naturalness prevails in an age where modern man has progressed so far that he has misplaced the keys to the door of natural life of beauty and simplicity."

Laurie hopes we all discover "the secret, abundant knowledge, ever-present, which beckons us toward the awakening of the beautiful nobility hidden deep within our souls, and that we may we pierce the illusory veil that separates us from our brothers and sisters around the world."

The Festival of No-Ruz

Abolqasem Ferdowsi
Translated by Dick Davis

*The following is an excerpt from the ancient poet Abolqasem Ferdowsi's
Shahnameh,* The Book of Kings, *written in the late tenth and early eleventh
centuries. It was composed at the request of the princes of Khorasan, who
wished to revive Persian culture after the Arab conquest.*

Although Jamshid had accomplished all these things, he strove to climb even
higher. With his royal *farr* he constructed a throne studded with gems, and had
demons raise him aloft from the earth into the heavens; there he sat on his throne like the
sun shining in the sky. The world's creatures gathered in wonder about him and scattered
jewels on him, and called this day the New Day, or *No-Ruz*. This was the first day of the
month of Farvardin, at the beginning of the year, when Jamshid rested from his labors
and put aside all rancor. His nobles made a great feast, calling for wine and musicians,
and this splendid festival has been passed down to us, as a memorial to Jamshid. Three
hundred years went by, and death was unknown during that time; men knew nothing of
sorrow or evil, and the demons were their slaves. The people obeyed their sovereign, and
the land was filled with music. Years passed, the royal *farr* radiated from the king, and all
the world was his to command.

> Jamshid surveyed the world, and saw none there
> Whose greatness or whose splendor could compare
> With his: and he who had known God became
> Ungrateful, proud, forgetful of God's name.

He summoned his army commanders and aged advisors and said, "I know of no
one in the world who is my equal. It was I who introduced the skills and arts of living
to mankind, and the royal throne has seen no one to compare with me. I arranged the
world as I wished; your food and sleep and security come from me, as do your clothes
and all of your comforts. Greatness, royalty, and the crown are mine; who would dare

say that any man but I was king?" All the elders inclined their heads, since no one dared gainsay anything he said. But

By saying this he lost God's farr, and through
The world men's murmurings of sedition grew.

As a wise and reverent man once remarked, "If you are a king, be as a slave toward God; the heart of any man who is ungrateful to God will be filled with countless fears." Jamshid's days were darkened, and his world-illuminating splendor dimmed.

Norooz

Farnoosh Seifoddini

pari-a geryeh mikardan
mesl-e abr-e bahar geryeh mikardan

Letters soaked and scented
in saffron and rose water—
     in this room we've shredded ourselves
     and pinned the pieces to the walls.

We know what has scattered
     so we gather to die just a little
     and come back later in the Spring. ▪

Welcome, Norooz, Welcome!

Azin Arefi

Hands imitate hands
My hands imitate my mother's
Hers imitate her mother's
and hers before hers
imitating through the years
back to King Jamshid.
Imitating, I lay a feast for Norooz
a *haft-seen* fifteen thousand years in the making,
And I bid Spring welcome.

I lay a feast of *haft-seen*
Worthy of a king
Worthy of a dervish.
In the eyes of Norooz,
they are one and the same thing

Norooz will not come until the blossoms are in bloom,
Until I have swept my room,
Until my *sabzeh* is grown,
And the goldfish swim in their bowl.

Norooz will come with the smell of lilac
With the sounds of "*Eidet Mobarak!*"
With the taste of rice cookies, and almonds dressed as candy.

Norooz comes with news from family and friends,
Some near, some far
Most dear, many far.
With the promise of renewal, rebirth, and new stories.

Norooz comes at the precise second of balance:
Light and dark,
Frost and bloom.
Sometimes Norooz comes with the sun,
Sometimes with the moon.
For fifteen thousand years, Norooz
Has never come too late, or too soon.

No tyrant's word,
No tyrant's sword
Has ever stopped Norooz,
Nor the hands that lay the feast
And bid Spring welcome.

And today I lay my *haft-seen*,
Imitating,
And I say, "Welcome, Norooz! Welcome!" ■

From Tehran to America
A Sketch of Artist Fahimeh Amiri

Rosemarie Brittner Mahyera

Fahimeh Amiri's early years were spent in Tehran. Before the tender age of four, she often sat alone at the *korsi*, a low table with a heater underneath, popularly used by families to keep warm in winter. There were no TVs, toys, or siblings to keep her company, only the korsi, covered with colored pencils and sketchbooks—and this became an important part of her world, where she felt safe and happy. She drew what she saw: details of rooms and their contents. Her future profession was confirmed when at that young age, she drew an entire room and her mother exclaimed, "You are an artist!" From that day on, her mother, an ambitious woman, provided her with the best quality colored pencils and sketchbooks.

Soon thereafter, her mother presented the Minister of Education with one of Fahimeh's drawings, and in return the minister gave her first watercolor paint set. "I remember it vividly, it was a Winsor paint set with 30 shades of color. It was so special to me that I used it ever so sparingly and it lasted through college—nearly fifteen years." As her parents struggled with marriage and divorce, Fahimeh, sitting at the korsi, retreated deeper into her fantasy world where she could create idealized visions of herself living amidst a loving family in settings of comfortable opulence.

When she was about seven years old, a friend of her mother's took some of Fahimeh's drawings to Professor Hussein Behzad (1894-1968), a prominent miniaturist, who was internationally known and considered by many to be the greatest Persian miniaturist of his time. Although Prof. Behzad was not known to have students, he accepted Fahimeh.

Traveling unaccompanied, she took public buses to his studio. Behzad gave her assignments to draw males and females in graceful positions and bring them to him. He would go over each of her figures with his pencil, extending and refining her lines as she watched. She longed to use paints, but Professor Behzad sternly said, "You must first master the art of flowing lines and curlicues with this small brush and only then will you be ready for paints." She worked diligently until one day he said she was ready to use a brush.

Her fine brush was made of a few strands of cat hair, and with it she filled page after page, practicing the flowing lines of curlicues. Fahimeh was never bored. The master Behzad demanded discipline and Fahimeh obliged. When she remembers him, she sees him sitting on his mattress on the carpet, his back supported by a pillow, smoking a long, narrow pipe of opium. "I loved the fragrant smell of opium for it was Behzad I smelled. If I were to smell opium today, I would be flooded with memories of him smoking, stroking the opium with a safety pin; the sizzling sound of the burning coals as he slowly sucked up the wisps of smoke; and the servant bringing charcoal for the pipe and tea in small glasses."

In nearly eight years of studying under Professor Behzad, Fahimeh worked on elaborate scenes and, as before, he would go over each one with his own lines and brush strokes. She received much constructive criticism. "Although I hated it, I accepted it. If Professor Behzad did not get angry, I knew I did okay." She received few compliments and little encouragement. At times her confidence wavered, but she never gave up.

Fahimeh later passed the test to enter a noted high school in Tehran, the School of Fine Arts. She entered an intensive program that provided structure and substance. Her studies included textiles, sculpture, miniatures, and contemporary and classical painting. One of her professors, Mahmoud Farshchian, was considered the second best miniaturist in Tehran. Because of Fahimeh's former training with Behzad, Farshchian appointed her his assistant.

Under Farshchian's training, she began to master the art of Persian miniatures: "This period was the most exciting time of my life—I was the best student and got top prizes. I had not been a great academic student before, but here as I excelled in artistic endeavors, even my academics improved. Art was my portal to understanding and depicting the world." During her studies at the School of Fine Arts she received frequent recognition, including national awards from the Ministry of Education in Iran and from Queen Farah. At the end of three years, Fahimeh became the first woman in the history of the institution to receive the school's coveted top prize in art.

Road to America

Fahimeh's mother was determined that Fahimeh should have access to greater opportunities and top art schools in the United States. In 1968, Fahimeh and her mother went to Boston, where she attended the School Museum of Fine Arts.

Fahimeh's first experiences in an American college were challenging. She was shy and couldn't look at her instructors and struggled learning to draw nude models for the first time. But she eventually opened up to American life, and was joined by and married her Iranian boyfriend who had just graduated from Tehran University.

After graduation, Fahimeh designed posters, children's illustrations, and cloth artwork and sold them to clients such as Bloomingdale's. But now with children she found it increasingly difficult to balance her work and family life. She put her artwork aside.

Finding Her Own Way

Although Fahimeh appreciated Boston's sophistication, she missed Tehran's majestic mountains, and in 1989 she and her family relocated to Salt Lake City, a "city that resembled my birthplace." The landscape and her surroundings inspired her to pick up her brushes and paints. She exhibited in local galleries and was featured in newspapers. One set of her colorful children's illustrations featured a tiger named Babry. (Babry means baby tiger in Persian.) Although she began the project with no story in mind, the illustrations were later turned into a children's book, *Babry*.

By 1994 her marriage of 23 years had fallen apart and two of her children had graduated from high school. She moved back to Boston for a decade, but Salt Lake City lured her back. There, Fahimeh continued giving art lessons to children and kept painting. As Middle East countries were appearing more frequently in the news and Americans showed more interest in those cultures and histories, "It came to me all of a sudden that my cultural background was of interest to others." An art counselor in Boston had once told her to "look back" to her past for direction. "I understood what the counselor tried to tell me. I could look back on what I knew, what I saw, and what I remembered. Whether in miniature or stylized form, I could depict women as their lives unfolded in Iran."

Fahimeh began a new series of paintings focused on traditional women living in Islamic Iran. This work encompasses the early patterns of symmetrical, geometric, and floral motifs found in classical Persian art. Many paintings show a complexity of patterns, precision, and shading. The subject matter becomes a delicate interplay of form and motion.

Her work continues to evolve from her early training in miniature painting and its disciplined techniques. Her stylized form hints at Persian miniatures yet contain bold, fluid strokes, rhythm, and the telling of a story. "For me, my artistic compositions must reflect balance, harmony, and order."

A Conversation with Composer Behzad Ranjbaran

Fariba Amini

You gave me aura, culture and voice
you are my guidance in good and bad
                                    —Ali Akbar Dehkhoda

I knew Behzad from ages ago, when I had met him and his brothers in Washington, D.C. They had composed a song titled "Sar omad zemestoon, shekofteh baharoon" ("Winter Has Passed, Here Comes the Spring"). The melody reminded me of old times when we were student activists. Behzad Ranjbaran has come a long way from being a lover of music at a young age to teaching at the Juilliard School of Music. He is also the recipient of the Rudolf Nissim Award for his violin concerto.

His *Persian Trilogy* album was released on October 26, 2004, on the Delos recording label. It was performed by the London Symphony Orchestra under the direction of JoAnn Falletta. While listening to the music, one is reminded of Gershwin, Wagner, and classical Persian music combined. The trilogy is based on the stories of Ferdowsi's *Shahnameh.*

The *Shahnameh,* Book of Kings is an epic of Iranian history. Written between 980 and 1010 AD by the great Iranian poet Hakim Abo'l-Qasem Ferdowsi, the *Shahnameh* is the tale of kings and commoners, of princes and princesses, of conflicts and battles, peace, love, tragedy, heroism, life and learning. It is the history of urban, sedentary Iran in confrontation with nomadic *Turan* (the Persian name for Turkic Central Asia), written and told in the most beautiful poetry imaginable. It is the story of Rostam and Sohrab, of Bijan and Manijeh, of Afrasiab, Arash and Siavash, of Zal and Simorgh, and Kaveh Ahangar, a total of 98 long and short tales in all. The *Shahnameh* is the essence of Iran, the tale of the mingling and intermarriages of ethnic and religious minorities, of fusion for the sake of uniting Iran.

I asked Dr. Ehsan Yarshater, the renowned scholar and editor of the *Encyclopaedia Iranica,* what he thought of the *Shahnameh.* He said, "Ferdowsi's *Shahnameh* is not only a towering masterpiece of Persian poetry, but also the most important pillar of Iranian national identity. It contains the most engaging rendering of Iranian traditional history with its myths and legends as well as gripping episodes of heroism, warfare, and romance."

In 2008, Behzad Ranjbaran conducted a 75-piece symphony orchestra at the 7th biennial Conference of the International Society for Iranian Studies, which was held in Toronto, Canada.

Here is my interview with Master Behzad Ranjbaran conducted on July 14th of that year.

Q: When did you become interested in music?

A: When we lived in Iran, the late Hassan Shahbaz, the famous journalist and translator, was our tenant. He was a well-known translator of Western classical music texts into Persian. His son played the accordion. Shahbaz had introduced classical music to Iran. My brothers and I became more interested in music due to his influence. It was in the early 1960s.

I attended the conservatory of Tehran at the age of nine, playing the violin. Upon my graduation I came to the United States and attended Indiana University at Bloomington. In the early 1980s I studied at the Juilliard School of Music. After graduating with a doctorate in music composition I was invited to join the faculty. This means that I have been at Juilliard for 23 years now.

Some of my pieces deal with Persian literature and Iranian history. For example, "Songs of Eternity" for soprano and orchestra, based on the Rubáiyát of 'Omar Khayyam, was premiered by Renée Fleming and the Seattle Symphony Orchestra conducted by Gerard Schwarz. My violin concerto was in part inspired by Kamancheh (a Persian musical instrument), premiered with Joshua Bell as soloist with the Royal Liverpool Philharmonic, also conducted by Gerard Schwarz.

Q: When did you start working on the Trilogy and how long have you been working on this piece?

A: From a young age, I was truly mesmerized by the stories of *Shahnameh*. I began to write the Trilogy about twenty years ago. It took about eleven years to finish. Although I wrote many other orchestral and chamber pieces in between, the Trilogy has a special place in my heart. The piece called "Simorgh" premiered with the Long Beach Symphony Orchestra in California in 1993. The second piece was "The Blood of Seyavash," a ballet in seven scenes that was premiered by the Nashville Ballet in 1994. The last piece, titled "Seven Passages," from the Seven Stages of Rostam (*Haft khan-e Rostam*), was first performed by the Long Beach Symphony Orchestra in 2000. JoAnn Falletta, who premiered "Simorgh" and "Seven Passages," eventually recorded the whole Trilogy with the London Symphony Orchestra on the Delos label in 2003.

The ballet production was quite attractive with Old Persian costumes and Persian sets. The dancers' costumes were hand-painted individually on silk, with vibrant colors inspired by sixteenth-century Persian miniatures. The costumes were original and beautiful. I had given the team of designers books about Persian art and copies of the

Shahnameh in preparation for the ballet. It took almost eighteenth months to write the music and prepare for the production.

Q: I hear you are going to Iran on a trip and you are to meet Morshed Torabi and work together on the program for the upcoming concert in Toronto.

A: I am going to Iran to meet Morshed Torabi and work with him in preparation of the Toronto concert, which is the first time a fusion of symphony orchestra and *pardeh khani* and *naghali* (Persian scene-narrating) is presented. It is going to be a 75-member symphony orchestra with the Toronto symphony and Morshed on stage and 80 minutes of music. Naghali (stories from the *Shahnameh* told by a dervish recited in a special rhythm) is eleven movements of the Persian Trilogy. Each episode is preceded by a short narration, while themes of the "Haft Khan" and "Simorgh" are projected on a large screen.

This is the first time such a concert will be performed anywhere in the world. It brings together aspects of traditional Iranian culture with symphonic music inspired by the *Shahnameh*. It is a fusion between tradition and innovation, between old and new.

Q: What have been your recent concerts in the US and in which cities have you had performances?

A: My most recent piece is a piano concerto, which was commissioned by the Atlanta Symphony Orchestra with the fantastic Jean-Yves Thibaudet as the soloist and Robert Spano as the conductor in June 2008. In this piano concerto I was inspired by *deraz nay* a musical instrument used in ceremonies in Persepolis. Its sound is also reminiscent of the traditional *taziyeh* (Persian/Islamic mourning rituals commemorating Imam Husain's martyrdom). I used the *daf*, a traditional drum-like instrument, in the all-American orchestra. The Atlanta Symphony purchased a daf, and one of the orchestra's percussionists practiced it intensively to prepare for the concert.

Q: You work mainly on classical music. How have you combined Iranian classical music with Western music?

A: Classical music is no longer associated with European countries. It has been embraced by many countries, including Russia, Latin America, China and Japan. It is widely accepted as a truly international classical music versus national forms of classical music. In my music, I use many Iranian motifs, rhythms and figurations. I also use instrumental colors and characters to emulate Iranian instruments. For example, in "Fountain of Fin" celebrating *Bagh-e Feen* (a famous garden in Kashan), I use the flute in such way that at times it emulates the sound of the *ney* (Middle Eastern flute).

Written in honor of Amir Kabir, a nineteenth-century Iranian grand vizier who was murdered in this garden, the music of "Bahgh-e Fin" premiered in February 2008 in New York. Barge Music commissioned the piece for their 30th anniversary and will perform it in late August in New York.

Q: Are your students interested in Iranian classical music?

A: Yes, among my music courses at Juilliard I also teach a graduate course in world music. As part of this class, I teach Iranian music. I have invited leading Iranian musicians such as Kayhan Kalhor and Kazem Davoudian to perform and give lectures in my classes. My students are very interested.

Q: Have you ever played in Iran?

A: My string quartet had played as part of a music festival in Niavaran palace in Tehran several years ago. The musicians had come from Armenia. Unfortunately I was not there to hear it.

Q: How has your work been received?

A: I always enjoy meeting people who come to hear my music in concert halls. It is fascinating to hear their comments and their reaction to my work. Last month, I had three concerts in Atlanta, where my piano concerto was performed with great success. They commented on the freshness of its musical language.

It seems to me that the audience and the musicians enjoy listening or playing my music as they find elements of Persian music and culture in my overall musical style and language.

Last March, "Seven Passages" was performed several times by the Philadelphia Orchestra in their educational concerts. In preparation, thousands of students in Philadelphia learned about the *Shahnameh* and my music. In the concert, a narrator described the story, while Persian miniatures, depicting scenes of the *Shahnameh*, were projected on a large screen. In fact, the Philadelphia performances were a precursor to the Toronto concert.

Q: What was the message?

A: The goal and the message is that the *Shahnameh* is a literary masterpiece. There is no comparable work ever written before or after. We should take advantage of the millennium of the *Shahnameh*, sharing it with people around the world. The Toronto concert, with its unique mix of music, narration and multimedia, could reach out to a larger audience. We are hoping to enrich humanity and send a message that this belongs to the whole world and not just Iran.

Iran's Literary Giantess is Defiant in Exile, But Missing Home

Mohammed Al-Urdun

Shahrnush Parsipur was jailed in Iran for her writing during the time of the Shah and in the 1990s, chosing exile in America over another term in prison. Her bestselling masterpiece Touba and the Meaning of Night *was published in the UK. This is an adapted excerpt from Mohammed Al-Urdun's essay about Shahrnush, which can be read on her website at: www.shahrnushparsipur.com/wp/press/*

Ts been almost twenty years since Shahrnush Parsipur published her bestselling masterpiece *Touba and the Meaning of Night*, sparking a storm in Iran and wooing European critics. Now with the first British edition published, we are at last properly introduced to one of the giants of Iranian literature and to a book that took two decades to arrive.

Touba is a masterful curate's egg of a novel, mixing mysticism, history, philosophy, and personal tragedy. Set against the backdrop of occupation, war, revolution, and social transformation in Iran, it depicts the last century with more pathos and insight than any mere history book. It is the story of a girl who begins wanting to marry God; searches for the meaning of life but encounters death; marries a royal but falls on hard times; and in her last moments has the meaning of womanhood revealed to her.

It was an instant hit in Iran and Europe, but when in the early 1990s she faced another prison spell for her next novel, *Women without Men*, she chose self-exile in America.

Parsipur has a complex relationship with America. It has been a safe haven, she admits, but has never been a home-away-from-home. In fact she confesses to feeling unsettled—a feeling made worse by the recent war hysteria. A "wanderer by nature," she says the only place she's ever likely to feel at home is back in Iran with her son.

She also finds herself instinctively swimming against the political tide. There is a new interest in Iranian women writers, in particular those who condemn Iran, but Parsipur voices ambivalence and unfashionable ideas that have brought howls from the politically correct. Femininity is her central theme but, while exiled Iranian writers like Azar Nafisi (*Reading Lolita in Tehran*) have made a name for themselves as feminist opponents of the Islamic state, Parsipur scornfully declares: "I am not a feminist!"

Love and Pomegranates

But neither is she a stick in the mud—far from it. Her views, she says, are shaped by her study of ancient philosophies. Toying with her elegant Ying-Yang ring, she explained there's a bit of femininity and masculinity in all of us. The problem is that we're too often ruled by our masculine side, she says. Technology, war, and social upheaval are symptomatic of our masculine urge to rip things up and start again. Whereas we need to get in touch with our feminine side, the creative instinct in tune with our environment.

Jinn Struck

Javad Mohsenian, M.D.

Karbelai Sid Hussein lived not long ago in the small but ancient city of Jahrom, in southern Iran. Well-known as the town's barber, Karbelai was also the dentist and general surgeon. But he was most famous for being the only *jinn geer* in the city—the only man fearless and knowledgeable enough to catch ghosts and free the souls of the possessed.

Karbelai believed he attained special powers as a jinn geer because he had achieved so much else. During his lengthy career he had extracted at least one tooth from most of the city's adults, including himself, and circumcised the entire male population within a radius of 50 kilometers.

When confronted with an excruciating toothache in his cluttered barber shop, Karbelai simply reached for his pliers and relieved the pain for good. There was no need to make an appointment and one would never receive a bill; one simply paid as one could. Some patients enjoyed a haircut at the same time, and a cup of hot black tea was routine.

The beneficiaries boasted about the ceremonial circumcisions performed by Karbelai. Proud parents threw elaborate parties on such festive occasions, offering expensive gifts to the honored surgeon who practiced ingenious tactics. "Look up at the pretty bird in the sky! What kind of bird is it?" he'd say to his patients as he performed his surgeries. When complications arose during his many years of practice, he refused to take the blame. "I am only a therapist; the cure is up to God," he said.

Karbelai's surgical fame spread across the region. Nana Ghassem, the town's well-regarded midwife, delivered every child around, but would always consult Karbelai Sid Hussein when there was a difficult birth. In addition to all these responsibilities, he also managed two public baths in his neighborhood. But still, he took most pride in his status as a jinn geer.

Love and Pomegranates

There came a time in Karbelai's town when many claimed to have encountered ghosts. The shifting sands outside the city had covered many a graveyard during the long centuries, and ghosts were believed to lose their way when searching for their sepulchral homes. Citizens blamed the malevolent spirits for any serious illnesses that wouldn't respond to herbs or home remedies. These spirits were the jinn, the lower-ranking beings who nonetheless had a place in the holy Qur'an. They could not only possess humans, but could appear in animal form. When traditional cure-alls such as sacrifices, vows, and donations to holy sites failed, sufferers turned to Karbelai. In the case of animals, he recommended they be slaughtered. If their meat was halal, they would distribute it outside the immediate neighborhood. He claimed that the ghost vacates the animal once the butcher knife touches its throat.

Over the years Karbelai developed specific methods of catching haunts. He would hang a colorful Persian carpet covered with a long white curtain in a hallway or side yard of his home. The patient would sit on one side of the curtain, within a circle of long sewing needles embedded in the rug. Karbelai would chant and weave his spells on the other side. His paraphernalia included a whip, a pair of scissors, and a whistle. Of course, he also had a long tongue with an elaborate vocabulary and many ancient magical tomes.

Karbelai would begin with a prayer in Arabic and then, with his eyes full of tears, he would ask the Prophet and his grandson, the slain Imam Hussein, not to let him down. He was *Ostad* Karbelain Sid Hussein, he reminded the spirits.

"Remember you devilish creatures; I am a *Sayyed*, descendant of Prophet Mohammad, and a Karbelai. I went on pilgrimage to the holy burial site of the third Imam in Karbela, Iraq. I received my title and therapeutic skills by praying on the Imam's grave, touching its elaborate *maajer* covering. I didn't get my titles for free."

If this did not impress the ghosts, it certainly impressed the subjects. He was a maestro, an expert and spiritualist, which was very important in influencing and hypnotizing his patients.

After his ceremonies, he would blow a special wooden whistle and call on the wraiths. "This is a warning, the first one. I only warn you twice. If you don't leave I am going to clip your wings with these scissors." He made snipping motions in the air. Then he stated his biggest weapon. "I have hidden notes with *B'esm Allah* written on them throughout the house and you know that jinn cannot survive wherever the name of God and special prayers are buried."

Invariably the patient's head would begin to feel lighter and lighter. "Come on, you are doing beautifully. Once you feel stronger, you will jump out of the circle of needles and curse the devil. Go and thank Allah and the good old Karbelai for freeing your soul."

Indeed, Karbelai's fame spread so far that one day he was called to the estate of Hajji Ali, where an infestation of ghosts plagued the inhabitants. Hajji owned so many properties, farms and orchards that he could not keep track of them. Many of the villagers owed their livelihood to him. His residence was more a mansion than a house.

Karbelai knocked on the massive wooden doors, decorated with metalwork. A servant opened the portal for him. Bearing a satchel of accouterments he walked grandly in through a stable, a courtyard, and a smaller pair of doors, into the main part of the house. Here was a large living room and an adjacent dining area in the midst of an elaborate garden. Several man-made waterfalls surrounded the rooms, splashing into elongated pools full of fish. Karbelai climbed many steps to an open foyer and then to an elaborate living room. Antique china teapots decorated the shelves.

Here, on many silk cushions, sat Hajji Ali, a portly man whose normally merry face was creased with care, with deep circles under his eyes. He smoked a crystalline water pipe, as if he were doing the designer a favor.

"Magnificent," Karbelai breathed to his host. "A superb dwelling! They don't build them like this anymore. It has to be the workmanship of master builders of the past."

Hajji waved a dismissive hand. "Yes, but the problem is that no one dares come in here after dark because of the ghosts!"

Frowning, Karbelai sat down beside his host to listen.

"Anything we leave out," said Hajji. "Bread, food, fruit, pastries—anything—simply disappears. The greedy ghosts soak the dates in sesame paste and throw the pits all over the floor! Thursday nights, just before the weekend, are the worst. Orange peels everywhere! Even pastries contaminated with rat poison didn't affect them."

Karbelai clucked in sympathy.

"Mind you, I've not seen any spirits myself, but my servants and maids swear they have, and heard them, too. My wife simply won't come in here alone without a guard and a large hand lamp. I've had to put the place off limits after sunset. I tell you, I've even had the wind catchers on the roof blocked, because my chief servant says he's sensed ghosts flocking toward my lovely house from every direction." He leaned toward Karbelai. "You have got to do something!"

"Well, of course I will try, Honored One."

"You must do better than that. I promise you not only a year's supply of rice and wheat, but also ten gold coins from the Qajar Dynasty, embossed with the image of their founder, Agha Mohammad Khan-e Qajar." He ordered two cups of tea by clapping his hands, and sat back.

Karbelai drew in his breath. Such riches! He met Hajji's eyes. "I will not fail, you can be sure."

When Karbelai set foot on Hajji's estate next, he had made all the necessary preparations. Among his equipment were several large burlap bags in which he intended to capture the ghosts and prevent their escape. He also brought his oft-blessed copy of the Qur'an and a number of other prayer books, along with a few hand-written, worm-eaten, and moldy manuscripts. It was a Thursday night, the eve of the customary Muslim day of rest, the day people visited their ancestors in cemeteries. It was widely believed that the ghosts had more freedom on Thursday evenings and traveled in groups.

Karbelai spent all night praying and reciting many blessings and benedictions, focusing on those specifically designed for the purpose of getting rid of jinn. He puffed his words and blew his breath to every corner of the halls, and hid his written prayers and incantations in secret spots.

In the early hours of the morning, he wrestled some of the opponents who were trying to get out of the burlap sacks and tied them in. Confident that all of the surrounding spirits had been swept up, he thanked God and asked for his blessings.

Summoning Hajji Ali, Karbelai said, "All the evil shadows have been trapped. Those roaming free will never dare to show themselves in the future."

"But the bags look empty," Hajji said while lifting one. "Nothing!"

"Ghosts have no weight, no volume!"

Karbelai took the gold coins and left the mansion. It was nearly time to oversee the daily opening of the public baths.

The men's public bath sat close to the entrance of the city's roof-covered bazaar. The streets were not lit, and most citizens shunned the place at night for fear of drifting demons. Shadows moved around Karbelai's antique oil lamp like a flickering army of phantasms. Karbelai met no one on his way, but had no fear. He had walked this route at this hour for years. In fact, he liked the privacy and quiet.

On reaching a ramshackle bridge over a rivulet, he untied his burlap bags and shook their evil contents into the dark, sluggish water. "God never gave you the ability to swim; you are all going to drown," he said with a mix of pleasure and hatred.

When Karbelai reached the bathhouse, he inserted an old brass key into the heavy lock, evoking as he did the name of God in both Arabic and Persian. He also breathed a protective incantation against the machinations of Satan, who was always hanging around for sabotage.

The screech of the door opening into the dark hall was usually disconcerting and creepy, but tonight Karbelai had the heart of a lion. He lit the wall candles. At the end of the hall he entered a circular cloakroom that was divided into different sections. Cold and silent now, the room would not see the morning's first guests for hours yet. He decided to freshen up and wash away the long night's fatigue. After removing his clothes, he wrapped himself in the customary red garment and then opened the door to the interior of the bath, a large rectangular chamber surrounded by showers and a heated pool.

He lit all the lights and added oil to a few lamps that burned low. After trying all the showers he decided they were all hot enough and ready for the day's bathers. He stood under one and allowed the water to cascade over him. Exorcising ghosts wasn't easy for a man of his age. He washed his sparse white hair with a paste of ground lotus tree leaf, and then stepped into the heated pool. He had barely settled when he heard a splash.

He was flabbergasted to see another man in the steaming pool, a stranger. The light was dim, but he didn't understand how he could have missed this fellow.

Smiling, the man addressed him. "Salam, Karbelai. How are you today?"

"I salam you as well, friend. I am quite well. I don't believe I have the pleasure of knowing you."

"But I know you. You are a famous man. Everyone in the area knows you. You cut everyone's hair and are a doctor and surgeon. You also treat the jinn-struck, do you not?"

Karbelai smiled in a self-deprecating manner. "I try to be useful to God's subjects. I see you are an early riser, too, Mister."

"I decided to keep you company today. I didn't want you to be alone in the early hours after your efforts at Hajji Ali's home."

"How in the name of the Prophet do you know where I have been?"

The stranger laughed.

"Well, thank you, but solitude doesn't bother me," Karbelai said, hoping the other man would take the hint.

He didn't budge. "But you are looking very tired," said the stranger, shifting his position in the pool.

"Yes," said Karbelai, noticing the oddly scaly skin of his companion with a medical man's curiosity. "I had a busy night."

"My dear Karbelai, you are no longer young. You should get your sleep. You shouldn't place your feet in everyone's shoes."

Karbelai licked his lips. Was this person threatening him? Rather than responding, he plugged both ears with his fingers and submerged his entire body in the water three times. Now he was *taher*—fully clean—and ready for the morning observances.

As if reading his thoughts, the stranger said, "I guess you still haven't had your morning prayer?"

"No, I'd better rush." Karbelai leapt out of the pool.

He was taken aback when the man followed him making strange clock-clock sound as he walked.

Karbelai turned around and opened his mouth to speak. His words caught in his throat. The man, naked, had hooves instead of feet.

"Karbelai, I need a kiseh kesh to help me wash up, but I guess your workers don't start until later."

Karbelai stared at the hooves, frozen for a moment. "I'll see if the workers have arrived," he said, and asked the man to wait where he was.

In front of the bathhouse, he saw a worker preparing for his daily chores. This must have been someone his son had hired, because Karbelai couldn't place him.

"You won't believe what I saw inside!" he said, wiping perspiration from his brow. "A man with hooves. As God is my witness!"

The man frowned. He lifted his right leg, pulling back his pantaloons. "Was it like this?"

Goggling, Karbelai saw that the man's leg ended in a massive, black hoof instead of five human toes. He bolted, with the laborer's laughter echoing behind him.

Heart pounding and drenched in sweat, Karbelai ducked into the maze of alleys, soon becoming disoriented but not daring to stop. Stones cut his feet but he ran toward his barber shop. Abruptly, a figure on a donkey materialized out of the gloom. It was his next-door neighbor, headed for the market.

"You don't know how happy I am to see you! I think the Almighty wants to punish me. I am dying." He rested his head on his neighbor's lap.

"My dear Karbelai, what is the matter?"

Karbelai gulped for breath and told his neighbor about the men with hooves like the ones on his neighbor's donkey.

"I believe you," his neighbor said, stroking Karbelai's head. "You know too much about spirits for me not to believe you."

Karbelai raised his head, but wished he hadn't. His neighbor of many years had hooves where his shoes should be.

Karbelai fled before his neighbor could step down.

Clock, clock.

Karbelai ran for his life. *My incantations are useless*, he thought. *Am I a fake?* He stumbled and fell on his face. His lamp broke into pieces and he was completely in the dark. He found himself in a roof-covered cul-de-sac, with no way out.

Clock-clock. Clock-clock.

The next morning, Karbelai's son found his father dead in front of the shop, branded with hoof-marks.

Quatrains from Rubáiyát

'Omar Khayyam
Translated by Talie Parhizgar

Of eternal secrets, neither you know nor I,
To solve this puzzle, neither you know nor I:
There's a talk of you and I behind the curtain,
But when the curtain falls not will you be or I.

*

Some think of religion as their life's bliss,
Others fall into the Doubt and Reality Abyss;
I fear that from far beyond will come a cry,
Ignorants! The Way is neither that nor this.

Quatrains from Rubáiyát

'Omar Khayyam
Translated by Edward Fitzgerald

For in and out, above, about, below,
'Tis nothing but a Magic Shadow-show
Played in a Box whose Candle is the Sun
Round which we Phantom Figures come and go.

XLVI

*

For let the Philosopher and Doctor preach
Of what they will, and what they will not—each
Is but one Link in an eternal Chain
That none can slip, nor break, nor over-reach.

LXXVII

Iason Athanasiadis

Islam and Other Faiths

We Are All Pilgrims
Exploring Spirits and Selves with Iranian Women in a Damascus Shrine

Karen G. Ruffle

*I*n July 2004, I spent four months in Iran studying Persian and conducting doctoral dissertation research on a Shi'i devotional text about the Shi'i Imams, who trace their lineage through the Prophet Muhammad and his daughter Fatimah al-Zahra. As part of a research fellowship that I had been awarded, I traveled to the Shi'i shrines of Damascus, Syria, following the completion of my research and studies in Iran in mid-November. My goal was to participate and observe the rituals of Iranian Shi'i women who were on pilgrimage to the shrine of Imam Husain's sister Sayyidah Zainab, and Husain's daughter Hazrat-e Roqayya—both of whom are a significant part of the religious life of the residents of Damascus and its pilgrims who travel here from throughout the Muslim world.

In this essay, I reflect on my own experience interacting with Iranian women pilgrims to the shrine of Imam Husain's young daughter Roqayya, who died of grief while imprisoned in Damascus. The two weeks that I spent in Damascus were transformative for me because I, too, was on pilgrimage and seeking the healing and saintly powers of the family of the Prophet Muhammad. I entered into the world of Iranian Shi'i women pilgrims and learned more about my own spirit and faith—these women became conduits for helping me to learn more about myself. This essay is based upon fieldnotes from November 24, 2004, when I made my second visit to the tomb of Hazrat-e Roqayya.

Yesterday was an exciting day at the Hazrat-e Roqayya shrine in the Old City of Damascus. At first glance this Shi'i shrine dedicated to the martyred three- or four-year-old daughter of the third Imam, Husain, seems plain in appearance and unimportant, as it is tucked away in a quiet neighborhood in the Old City. Entering into the shrine dedicated to this child, who suffered at the battle of Karbala, Iraq, in 680 AD, and died from her grief here in Damascus while imprisoned, an entirely different world engulfs the pilgrim. The interior of the shrine is decorated with brilliant mirror work that catches the light of the chandeliers refracting the movements of Shi'i pilgrims into a million pieces. The latticework of the grille (*zarih*) surrounding Roqayya's tomb is pure silver, reflecting the effulgence of Roqayya's grace (*barakat*) that emanates throughout this sacred space.

I arrive at the shrine just after three o'clock in the afternoon and I remain here until the dusk prayer. The late-November weather in Damascus is rainy and cold, yet the interior of the shrine radiates warmth from the devotional activities and spiritual fervor of the pilgrims who hail from every part of the Shi'i Muslim world. The majority of the pilgrims are Iranian, and they hold a special place in their hearts for the daughter of the martyred seventh-century leader of the minority Shi'i community, Imam Husain.

The shrine has an atmosphere that is part carnival, part funeral—perhaps these are not always two different phenomena. I enter the sacred precinct (*haram*) and offer my greetings to Hazrat-e Roqayya. I kiss the silver grille surrounding her grave, whisper some prayers, and incline my forehead in her direction to express my respect and dedication. After completing my salutations, I take a place on the Persian carpet not far from the tomb's grille. This time I want to be closer to the ritual action, rather than off to one side and observing.

Sitting several feet in front of me are two women wearing the all-encompassing chador. I hear the keening of one of the women as she was laments the suffering of Imam Husain and his daughter Roqayya. For this pilgrim, the battle of Karbala and its aftermath is not located in the distant historical past. The filial relationship between Imam Husain and Roqayya is alive and real—they have the kind of relationship that all fathers and daughters ideally should have, which is based on love, sacrifice, and respect. This woman sways back and forth and she punctuates her weeping litany with loud wails, especially when she mentions the names of the *Ahl-e Bait* (the family members of the Prophet Muhammad and his grandson Imam Husain). Her companion, who is partly turned in my direction, is trying to console her, but tears are running down her face, too. This weeping continues, and it becomes progressively louder and more passionate. Finally, it seems that the woman's grief and crying has reached some tacitly acknowledged threshold of acceptability, for one of the shrine attendants comes up to her and says, "*Yallah*. It's time to go." The shrine attendant says this several times, and at first the woman ignores her, but the attendant is insistent, and the mourning woman gets up to leave. I then see the woman's face. She is older than I initially thought—perhaps she is in her 50s. I suspect that her sorrow is not only for Imam Husain and his daughter Roqayya. After she walks away, I continue to observe the devotional activities of the pilgrims.

This afternoon there is a steady flow of women coming into the shrine. As I sit and read the *ziyarat*, or prayers, recited in Arabic to individual Shi'i saints, a woman walks through the sacred precinct passing out pieces of bread (*tabarruk*) in fulfillment of a vow made when a request or wish has been granted by the Shi'i saints. I tuck my 'gift' aside and I continue to sit on the floor with the women. One approaches and takes a seat on the floor next to me. She is wearing an inexpensive navy and white printed chador, and she has arranged all of her bags near me. We sit next to one another for a while, before she strikes up a conversation.

As a prelude to so many conversations that I have had with pilgrims in Iran and Syria, there is a tentativeness and furtiveness that eventually gives way to the commencement of the conversation. Another group of Iranian women came into the shrine. Fayza is the matriarch of the group, an elderly woman with failing eyesight and no teeth. There is Zainab who is accompanied by her two daughters Masumeh and Maryam. Masumeh is twenty years old and has been married for two years. Her sister Maryam is seventeen years old and is no longer in school. These women are as curious about me as I am of them. We want to discuss matters of faith, love of the family of Imam Husain, and our own families.

Fayza asks Zainab a question about me, "What does she study?" Zainab turns to me and asks me what I study and I tell her. My response generates a ripple of approval and happiness. I shift into the center of the group so that I can speak with everyone. Masumeh asks me if I am Muslim, and I reply, "No, I am Catholic. I have been studying Islam for the past twelve years, and I love the family of Imam Husain very much. I feel sadness for their sufferings and appreciate their virtues." I tell the women I have been to many other important Shi'i shrines in Iran, Syria, India, and Pakistan. Masumeh asks me if I keep the fast during the Muslim month of Ramadan. "Yes, when I was in Mashhad last month, I kept the fast." I sense that Masumeh is not entirely content with my response, and she asks, "Do you pray?" I smile and reply, "Yes." I ask Masumeh, who seems to be the most interested and opinionated of the women in the group on religious matters, how she feels about being in the sacred presence of Hazrat-e Roqayya, to which she replies at length. She loves Roqayya because she was young and she suffered so much at Karbala and afterward. "She suffered for her faith and her father," Masumeh says, "When I come to the shrine I feel close to her."

At the end of this conversation, many of the women in the group prepare for the dusk prayer, and Masumeh tells me that she must go. I sit down again, and within five or ten minutes, Masumeh returns to retrieve me. The women invite me to sit in the women's section of the mosque and I feel flattered. I feel that some sort of connection has been established between these women pilgrims and myself. We are all here in Damascus to experience Roqayya's spirit. I have experienced a deep change within myself after having spent four months in Iran, where the spiritual power of Imam Husain's family permeates so many aspects of life. I no longer feel like a scholar, an outsider, who merely observes and scribbles notes in my field book. I, too, am a pilgrim seeking succor and asking Roqayya for her help in solving my problems. These women and I are not so different from one another in our lives and in our problems and desires. We all share a bit of Roqayya's spirit of love for our families, faith, and a desire for a better world for all of us.

Ripened Fruit

Rumi, *Mathnawi* III, 1289-1303
Translated by Kabir Helminski and Ahmad Rezwani

Do you remember how you came into existence?
You may not remember
because you arrived a little drunk.
Let me give you a hint:
Let go of your mind and then be mindful.
Close your ears and listen!

It is difficult to speak to your unripeness.
You may still be in your springtime,
unaware autumn exists.
This world is a tree to which we cling—
we, the half-ripe fruit upon it.

The immature fruit clings tightly to the branch
because, not yet ripe, it's unfit for the palace.
When fruit becomes ripe, sweet, and juicy,
then, biting their lips,
they loosen their hold.

When the mouth has been sweetened by felicity,
the kingdom of the world loses its appeal.
To be tightly attached to the world is immaturity.
As long as you are an embryo,
all you think about is sipping blood.

There is more to be said,
but let the Holy Spirit tell it.
You may even tell it to your own ear.
Neither I, nor some other "I," needs to tell you,
you who are also I.

Just as when you fall asleep,
you leave the presence of yourself
to enter another presence of yourself.
You hear something from yourself
and imagine that someone else
has directly spoken to you in a dream.

But, you are not a single "you,"
my friend—you are the wide sky and the deep sea.
Your awesome "You," which is nine hundredfold,
is where a hundred of your you's will drown.

Forest Fire

Manijeh Nasrabadi

*T*wilight, like a giant eraser, attacks the edges first. Cars, trees, people smudge and bleed into the encroaching darkness until they're blurred beyond recognition, slipping from their solid forms. I squint into the distance, try to get my bearings as the light fades across the winter countryside, the snow packed hard under our thin city-people shoes. A stranger and a cousin, I'm a contradiction walking down a snow-covered road, searching for a trail that will connect me to my father, to myself. My family and I have left Tehran behind for a special occasion, one they've celebrated every year stretching back for generations, only still a mystery to me.

I came here alone, on a one-way ticket, hoping to remedy a situation that had changed in my estimation from normal to dire. Growing up in the United States with my Iranian Zoroastrian father and Ashkenazi Jewish American mother, it seemed natural that I should only speak English and only know her family, since they were also in the US. I never questioned the fact that I knew nothing about my father's family, that I'd never seen their faces in photographs or heard their names; they were all faraway in Iran, a place that was as unpopular as it was inaccessible to me. After September 11, 2001, when Iran was included on the "Axis of Evil" and threatened with war by the US, I suddenly felt the shame of my ignorance and the fear that my Iranian features would make me a target of hatred in the charged anti-Muslim atmosphere. Knowing nothing about Iran, how could I defend myself, my father, his family, against the demands for revenge?

Now, in the dead of winter 2004, I'm living with my relatives, who are among the fewer than 30,000 Zoroastrians remaining in Iran. Long before I was born, my father gave up practicing his religion and taught me almost nothing of its history or beliefs. I had to find the basic facts in books and on websites, as if I were a researcher with no personal ties to this faith. I read about the prophet, Zoroaster (ca. 550 BC), whose teachings became the official religion of the Persian Empire for over 2,500 years. Zoroastrians have survived waves of repression, forced conversion and expulsion ever since the seventh century AD and do not have equal rights with Muslims today in the Islamic Republic of Iran.

Religious ceremonies always make me feel like an imposter, and this is a feeling I'm trying to shake altogether. With little more than a week in this country, in this family, my footsteps are tentative, each one resonating against the noisy questions in my own mind. *Will I ever feel at home here? Is there space in this culture or in this household for me an atheist, a leftist, a single woman fast approaching 30?* At any moment I might slip on a patch of ice and land hard on the unforgiving ground.

"Jashne Sade was the first celebration in the history of the world," my uncle explained earlier this evening, before we left his house in the polluted labyrinth of central Tehran and drove out to where the ground is frozen and the air is clean. He told me this day commemorates the invention of fire. Just like my father, I thought. He was always making claims like this, insisting that everything from pajamas to chess to civil engineering was the invention of enlightened Iranians during the Persian Empire. As a child, I never knew whether or not to believe him. If the Persian Empire was so great, I reasoned, then how come no one else ever talked about it? How come it was never mentioned in any of my public school history classes? I've since learned that the Persian Empire spanned such a sprawling territory that Indians, Pakistanis, Turks, Greeks, Afghanis and Iraqis can all make similar assertions. So history's first celebration happened in ancient Persia? Why not? How much celebrating could there really have been before the discovery of fire anyway?

Tonight we could use some fire out here, a torch, a flashlight even, to help us see where we're going. The clumps of families moving alongside us grow denser as we approach a large brick wall interrupted by a wooden door. It's crowded when we step inside so I stay close to Raha, my uncle's daughter who's three years older than me. She's married with two children, lives with her parents and has never left Iran, while I've lived away from home since I was seventeen, traveled abroad and have only myself to look after. Nonetheless, our connection was almost instantaneous. Something sparked from the moment I landed in the Mehrabad Airport and she recognized me with her tea-colored eyes.

"I've seen your picture since I was young but I never thought you'd come to Iran," she'd said. And sure enough, there was a picture of me as a toddler on the top half of a page in the family photo album, with a picture of her at a similar age on the bottom half, as if our photographs had been waiting patiently until I would find my way to her in person. I didn't tell her that there were no pictures of her or her parents in our family albums back in America.

Now I let Raha lead me into a pool of light emanating from inside a large white tent and illuminating the faces of several women she knows who've gathered out front. "Salam, *khanum.* How's your health? Your mother, your father, your husband, your children, everyone's good *alhamdulellah?*" She deposits kisses on rosy cold cheeks, radiates sincerity even in the most perfunctory greetings. When she introduces me as her uncle's daughter from America, the women look surprised, switch instinctively from Persian to Dari, the Zoroastrian language I can't understand.

Inside the tent, bright lights shine on an audience of at least a thousand people, some alert, some dozing in rows of folding metal chairs. A man speaks from a podium on a stage, his scholarly vocabulary soaring to heights far above my comprehension. A large banner hangs above him with an image of what appears to be a man riding a giant headless bird. Or it could be that the creature is itself half-human, half-bird, the beard of a wise man and the wings of an eagle its anatomy was never explained to me so I can't be sure. This symbol repeats like a motif around my uncle's house, filling the centers of multiple frames, guarding doorways, even gracing the top of the television. It rests against Raha's skin too, strung on a thin chain in bright gold miniature. She's grown up with this man, this bird, this faith, all of which mean nothing to me. For the first time since I've been here, I feel like a tourist. "Good thoughts, good words, good deeds," the banner says with a flourish of white calligraphy. This mantra is one of the only things my father taught me about the religion he grew up with, which he'd fused with Marxism as an adult and turned into his moral guide for clean living in a corrupt world.

We squeeze through a packed row to some empty seats at the far side of the tent, creating a chorus of whispered requests to be pardoned as we go. "*Bebakhshid, bebakh-shid*." Once we're seated, Raha whispers in my ear that the women outside were surprised I would want to come to Iran and learn Persian. "All of their children who haven't already want to learn English and go abroad," she says. "They used to want to go to America but now people are saying Canada and Australia are better."

"Yes, they're better," I agree. I don't yet know what Raha thinks of when she thinks of America, how the patchwork of black market Hollywood movies and government reports on the "Great Satan" fits together in her mind. As the months go by, we'll spend many hours comparing our countries, our lives. She'll be shocked that I have no health insurance, that my college education cost more than a house while hers was free. Much later, she'll ask me if she should leave Iran, what I'd do if I were her, and I'll feel the weight of inflation, of sanctions, of her daughters' uncertain futures, pressing down on her.

When the speakers finish, people begin to rise and move towards the exits on one side of the tent. Raha gets up with some effort, clasping her hands underneath her infant daughter Hediyeh, who's sleeping nestled against her breast. Her seven-year old daughter Golnar and I follow them out into the night.

The dim moonlight hides more than it reveals. Shadows fan out and rush past us across what seems to be a wide plane. "Do you want to go with them?" Raha asks Golnar and me, the brightness of her eyes indicating her preference.

"*Baleh*," we say. Our breaths linger in the winter air and then quickly disappear.

"Then hold hands tightly so no one gets lost," she says.

We wade into the streaming crowd and soon we're keeping pace with its brisk current. There's the thrill of holding Raha's hand, of our voluntary binding, of our bodies in sync. Lucky Golnar, I think, to be able to cling without reserve to her mother like this, to be led on a big adventure by the woman she loves most in the world.

Love and Pomegranates

A slim tree trunk appears in front of me and Raha pulls me out of the way. Our eyes reflect what light there is, flash a message back and forth: I'm OK. Are you OK? I'm OK, too. We don't slow down and the recklessness of our journey distracts me. *If Raha were to fall with Hediyeh, with the rest of us in tow...* It becomes my job to make sure this doesn't happen, to peer as far off into the distance as I can and anticipate any potential disaster. I peek at Raha sideways. Her face open to the wind, she breathes the night air in, smiling. My eyes dart back to the threatening ground beneath our feet. But we don't bump into trees or catch on rocks. We're forest nymphs, flitting among the barren branches, striking out across the land, bursts of snow flying upward in our wake. And I feel I could run like this, with Raha and her children, for a long time.

An orange glow ignites the horizon. I start backwards, a flicker of hesitation, and almost upset our precarious balance. Fire. In a forest. A menacing combination, or so I'd been taught throughout my childhood by a campaign of public safety announcements. But no one around me betrays any sense of alarm. In a clearing in the forest, the glow deepens and the people ahead of us swell into an enormous circle. At the center of the mass of bodies, a bonfire crackles and spits, licks the night, pushes us back even as it draws us closer.

A procession in white threads its way like a ribbon through the crowd to form the innermost ring of the circle. The priest, who wears a white cap like a yarmulke only with an extra band around the circumference and a long white robe, leads the train of luminous men and, to my surprise, women. One behind the other, sometimes a few across, they dance, slapping and shaking their *dafs*, banging their *tonbaks*, blowing their *neylabaks*, pounding out the rhythm of their steps. Men and woman draped in white from head to toe with fire in their eyes a wildly un-Islamic scene.

I can only wonder what it might feel like for the men and women who've grown up here to dance together under the night sky. If special permission hadn't been granted, this celebration would've been illegal under the laws that ban socializing by unrelated members of the opposite sex. Raha told me once that in the early, stricter years of the Islamic Republic, no one was supposed to show joy in public. The whole country was instructed to wear black and mourn as much for the teenagers killed in the war with Iraq as for the Prophet's grandson Hussein, who was martyred in the seventh century. Now the Zoroastrian dancers shimmer in their white costumes, smile but don't exactly let loose; their movements are controlled, concentrated in their feet and in their hands thwacking against the skins of their instruments. The priest sings out a prayer that mingles with the sounds of fire conquering wood, rouses the clamoring drums and raises the spirits of the hand-clapping, foot-stomping faithful.

We want to get closer so we squeeze each other's hands and knit ourselves more deeply into the fabric of the circle. The flames are near enough to warm us now, to mark our faces with campfire ghoulishness, to melt away self-consciousness until we too are clapping and thumping our feet to the contagious beats of our ghostly drummers. I wondered, what was this like a hundred years ago? A thousand? How big was the party in those days?

Only then do I see the film crew. Consciousness of their presence spreads like wildfire through the crowd. Europeans, someone explains, here to film an ancient rite of a dwindling people. I imagine myself behind the camera, capturing these relics, anachronisms, a mystical spectacle for modern folk to marvel at on television. *They still exist?* the viewers might say. Or, *never heard of them before.* But this is almost how removed I, too, have been from my Iranian family, living my life as an atheist in America, and I know that their rituals, their faith, will never be mine. At the same time, a protective impulse rises inside me. When the footage is uploaded into a computer, digitized into that international language of zeros and ones, when it's edited and voiced-over and sent into living rooms, will people learn that Zoroastrians are fire-worshippers, a common misconception, or monotheists? Will they be able to feel the energy of this crowd, to see that people in Iran are bursting with life and not always dour and serious like their politicians?

The young men near us can't resist the camera's gaze. They kick their festivity up a notch, grab hold of each other across the shoulders and trace the line of the circle, faster and faster, hotter and hotter, kicking their legs towards the orange and smoke. Raha, Golnar and I step back to give them room. Our hands drop; no chance of getting lost now that we're standing still. Again the familiar nudges me gently. Except for the leaping fire at the center, this whirling circle of men could just as well be celebrating a bar mitzvah, dancing the Horah. Folk music, peasant dances, same God, different prophet. I can't feel the presence of this God like Raha does, but in the ecstatic pounding of the drummers, in the cries of the dancers as they fly passed us, I hear the call of my ancestors. Jews and Zoroastrians, persisting through centuries of persecution, dancing as much in tribute to their faith as to tell themselves, "We are still here." Gripping each other by the shoulders, they found the solid reassurance they needed that there was joy and purpose in life here on earth. That will to survive, I feel it in the mixture of blood that travels through my veins. I feel it as I stand in a place and among a people who may soon be threatened by American bombs. It links the past to the future, gives me reason to think I belong here.

My face warms enough to heat my whole body. Zoroastrians snug around me, I forget the camera crew and see nothing but the glowing crowd in motion, hear nothing but the drums. My hand finds Raha's and they weave together.

Ghazal 374, Hafiz

Translated by Shahriar Shahriari
Contributed by Jaleh Novini

I met Jaleh Novini at Iran's First International Children's Book Festival. She has translated many books from English into Persian. She writes, "Hafiz is my favorite poet. You may not believe me, but I speak with him though his poems, I ask him questions and he answers me. But he answers others, too—everyone in Iran turns to Hafiz for advice. After these many years since his death, he is still alive."

Rose petals let us scatter
And fill the cup with red wine
The firmaments let us shatter
And come with a new design

If sorrow's soldiers incite
To shed lovers' blood tonight
With beloved I will unite
And his foundations malign

Pour the red wine with control
Like rose-water into the bowl
While fragrant breeze will roll
And sweet incense refine

With a harp on display
We ask the players to play
While clapping we sing and say
And dancing, our heads decline

Blow our dust O gentle breeze
And throw at the Master's knees
The Good King has the keys
While we glance at the sign

One boasts & brags with his mind
One weaves talks of idle kind
All the judgment that we find
Let the Judge weigh and define

If Eden is what you need
To the tavern let us speed
The jug of wine let us heed
And Paradise will be thine

Merry songs and fair speech
In Shiraz they do not teach
Another land let us reach
Hafiz, and then we shine.

Bagh-e Eram

Aidin Massoudi

*Aidin says this poem is about lacking a fear of death, which is a typical Sufi
ideal. A Sufi will achieve two deaths: one being the denial of the simulacrum
(material/ego/identity), which ignites paradise on earth (Bagh-e Eram) and a
union with the Beloved; the second death, of course, is biological.*

a chauffer of confession
the end   a canal

to depart from nothing
Lazarus

a map of existence
a tail of opium

thaw and radiance
an atom's flare

paradise

there is none in death
that truth conceals

I am the way, the leper
what navigates

the eye of Ibrahim
come   rest in me

What Iran's Jews Say

Roger Cohen
Reporting for *New York Times* from Tehran,
February 22, 2009

*A*t Palestine Square, opposite a mosque called Al-Aqsa, is a synagogue where Jews of this ancient city gather at dawn. Over the entrance is a banner saying: "Congratulations on the 30th anniversary of the Islamic Revolution from the Jewish community of Esfahan."

The Jews of Iran remove their shoes, wind leather straps around their arms to attach phylacteries and take their places. Soon the sinuous murmur of Hebrew prayer courses through the cluttered synagogue with its lovely rugs and unhappy plants. Soleiman Sedighpoor, an antiques dealer with a store full of treasures, leads the service from a podium under a chandelier.

I'd visited the bright-eyed Sedighpoor, 61, the previous day at his dusty little shop. He'd sold me, with some reluctance, a bracelet of mother-of-pearl adorned with Persian miniatures. "The father buys, the son sells," he muttered, before inviting me to the service.

Accepting, I inquired how he felt about the chants of "Death to Israel"—"*Marg bar Esraeel*"—that punctuate life in Iran.

"Let them say 'Death to Israel,'" he said. "I've been in this store 43 years and never had a problem. I've visited my relatives in Israel, but when I see something like the attack on Gaza, I demonstrate, too, as an Iranian."

The Middle East is an uncomfortable neighborhood for minorities, people whose very existence rebukes warring labels of religious and national identity. Yet perhaps 25,000 Jews live on in Iran, the largest such community, along with Turkey's, in the Muslim Middle East. There are more than a dozen synagogues in Tehran; here in Esfahan a handful caters to about 1,200 Jews, descendants of an almost 3,000-year-old community.

Over the decades since Israel's creation in 1948, and the Islamic Revolution of 1979, the number of Iranian Jews has dwindled from about 100,000. But the exodus has been far less complete than from Arab countries, where some 800,000 Jews resided when modern Israel came into being.

In Algeria, Tunisia, Libya, Egypt and Iraq—countries where more than 485,000 Jews lived before 1948—fewer than 2,000 remain. The Arab Jew has perished. The Persian Jew has fared better.

Of course, Israel's unfinished cycle of wars has been with Arabs, not Persians, a fact that explains some of the discrepancy. Still, a mystery hovers over Iran's Jews. It's important to decide what's more significant: the annihilationist anti-Israel ranting, the Holocaust denial and other Iranian provocations—or the fact of a Jewish community living, working and worshipping in relative tranquility.

Perhaps I have a bias toward facts over words, but I say the reality of Iranian civility toward Jews tells us more about Iran—its sophistication and culture—than all the inflammatory rhetoric.

That may be because I'm a Jew and have seldom been treated with such consistent warmth as in Iran. Or perhaps I was impressed that the fury over Gaza, trumpeted on posters and Iranian TV, never spilled over into insults or violence toward Jews. Or perhaps it's because I'm convinced the "Mad Mullah" caricature of Iran and likening of any compromise with it to Munich 1938—a position popular in some American Jewish circles—is misleading and dangerous.

I know, if many Jews left Iran, it was for a reason. Hostility exists. The trumped-up charges of spying for Israel against a group of Shiraz Jews in 1999 showed the regime at its worst. Jews elect one representative to Parliament, but can vote for a Muslim if they prefer. A Muslim, however, cannot vote for a Jew.

Among minorities, the Bahai — seven of whom were arrested recently on charges of spying for Israel — have suffered brutally harsh treatment.

I asked Morris Motamed, once the Jewish member of the Majlis, if he felt he was used, an Iranian quisling. "I don't," he replied. "In fact I feel deep tolerance here toward Jews." He said "Death to Israel" chants bother him, but went on to criticize the "double standards" that allow Israel, Pakistan and India to have a nuclear bomb, but not Iran.

Double standards don't work anymore; the Middle East has become too sophisticated. One way to look at Iran's scurrilous anti-Israel tirades is as a provocation to focus people on Israel's bomb, its 41-year occupation of the West Bank, its Hamas denial, its repetitive use of overwhelming force. Iranian language can be vile, but any Middle East peace—and engagement with Tehran—will have to take account of these points.

Green Zoneism—the basing of Middle Eastern policy on the construction of imaginary worlds—has led nowhere.

Realism about Iran should take account of Esfehan's ecumenical Palestine Square. At the synagogue, Benhur Shemian, 22, told me Gaza showed Israel's government was "criminal," but still he hoped for peace. At the Al-Aqsa mosque, Monteza Foroughi, 72, pointed to the synagogue and said: "They have their prophet; we have ours. And that's fine." ■

Sohrab Sepehri at 80

Ryszard Antolak

There is a city somewhere beyond the seas
Where windows open on illumination...
Where the earth listens
To the music of your heart
And the wind carries sounds
Of the fluttering of mythical birds...

October 7, 2008, marked the 80th anniversary of the birth of one of Iran's most celebrated modern poets, Sohrab Sepehri. On that day, hundreds of people made their way to the lonely, remote mosque of Mashhad Ardehal on the desert road between Kashan and Dilijan to pay their respects, recite poetry, and lay flowers on the grave of this much-loved poet.

Awaiting them was no grand memorial tomb such as that of Hafiz or Sa'di: no pavilion with fragrant gardens, no trees to adorn and give shade. All they saw was a marble flagstone in the courtyard of the mosque, sometimes trodden below the feet of visitors on their way to prayer. The inscription on the stone reads:

If you come to visit me
Tread softly,
Lest you break the fragile shell
Of my loneliness

It is a modest and humble grave, one eminently in keeping with the character of the poet. His was a truly singular voice in twentieth-century Iranian literature: fresh and natural, almost childlike sometimes in its directness. At a time when other poets were wrestling with complex social and political concerns in their works, Sohrab Sepehri was an advocate of all that was small and personal, intimate and homely. He was a friend of roadside flowers, of people walking home from work, of goldfinches and swaying poplars. For him, the most familiar objects—a willow, a red rose—could open suddenly to reveal an aspect of the divine hitherto concealed. He explained in his poem "Water's Footfall" that the poet need not go beyond his own immediate environment to discover the wondrous and the divine. Transcendence was perception, seeing through the everyday details of life to the empowered presence beyond.

I am a Muslim.
And my direction of prayer is the red rose,
My prayer rug is... the fountain,
My prayer stone is... light,
The meadows are my prayer hall.
And I kneel down when the muezzin wind
Calls out the time of prayer
From the cypress tree.

The words sound almost like a paraphrase of Ibn Arabi's famous profession of faith. Born in Kashan in 1928, Sepehri's imagination was dominated by the Dasht-e Kavir, the desert that stretches before the city like a grey nothingness for a thousand miles. Something of that emptiness, that loneliness, filtered into his bones and sank deeply into his heart.

Come to me and I will tell you
How colossal my loneliness is.

It was as if the desert called out to him in an almost religious voice, just as it has called many prophets and mystics in the past, and Sepehri responded to it both physically and metaphorically:

Tonight I must go
I must take my suitcase
Large enough to hold the garments of my loneliness
And go to the place where trees sing out in epic song
And where the vast wordless expanse
Calls out to me: "Sohrab!..."
Listen! There it is again!
I must find my shoes quickly..."

He became a restless spirit, unable to settle, traveling the world in search of something he could never quite define, which lay just beyond the horizon, just out of sight. During his wanderings, he encountered a variety of different literary styles, some of which found their way into his poetry enriching the language in ways that bore the indelible seal of his genius. Through his writing and his painting, he created a home for himself "on the far side of the night," one that could not be taken away from him by force or by distance.

It does not matter where I am
Because the sky is always mine
And the windows, ideas, fresh air, love...

Love and Pomegranates

In the end, his body "descended from a piece of pottery on the Sialk Hills," longing for the soil of its birth. He discovered at the age of 50 that he was suffering from leukemia and that the illness was incurable. In 1980, the poet made his final journey home to his beloved Kashan to be buried in the grounds of Mashhad Ardehal.

When I visited his grave recently during the baking heat of a torrid summer, the place was almost deserted. There was only a family of dark-skinned gypsies from Khuzestan taking advantage of the shade and the water. Their many children splashed around in the fountain and chased each other amid great bouts of laughter. None of them ventured out of the shade of the central courtyard. The poet remained alone in his element.

Until a frail old man arrived asking for the grave, dressed in a smart, black business suit despite the searing heat. He was supported on a walking stick and was evidently in great pain. I led him around the side of the building to the poet's marble flagstone, and he stood over it for some time, seemingly in deep thought. Then he put his stick between his legs and slipped abruptly to the ground. I rushed to assist him, thinking he was falling, but he thrust an open palm out at me to stop. This was evidently something he needed to do for himself. Holding his stick firmly in his left hand, he got down painfully on one knee and reached out an exploratory hand to the gravestone, tracing his finger lovingly over the inscription. I could see by his face that he had reached his destination. He was home.

I was deeply moved. I remembered the words of another poet, one from my own country, who had written

> If you want to drink from a carafe
> You can grip its neck and press it to your lips.
> But if you want to drink from a spring
> You have to get down on your knees and bow your head.

Over the next few months, many more pilgrims will come to this isolated place to drink from the spring. For the works of Sohrab Sepehri are a breath of fresh air, full of the sights and sounds of nature, redolent with the joys of being alive, of being a human being with a face and a name.

Sohrab Sepehri, poet and painter, October 7, 1928 – April 21, 1980

The Reapers of Dawn

Sohrab Sepehri
Translated by Mehdi Afshar

I open the window to the expanse of the world,
the road is empty, the tree is pregnant with night.
You aren't there and there is no oscillation, the
stem is shaking, the brook is tired from flowing.
When you aren't, the heart beats like the whirlpool.
When you aren't, the roaring of rivers are not
perceptible and valleys cannot be read.
When you come and night moves away from faces,
mystery flies away from existence.
The moment you go the lawn grows dark, and the
spring ceases to gush.
Vagueness spreads over the glass when you shut
your eyes.
When your image trembles, the water awakes.
When you pass the mirror breathes.
The road is empty, you won't return and I don't
expect your return.
The reapers will arrive from the opposite road at
dawn, they have observed the ripeness of my
clusters in their dream.

Baba Kuhi and Hafiz of Shiraz

Damon Lynch

Shiraz, Iran's cultural capital, is home to the tomb of Hafiz, whose poetry is revered the world over. Every day, masses of visitors and locals flock to his magnificent tomb, touching his grave and reciting his poetry.

Baba Kuhi, who died approximately 1050 AD, is far less known. In fact, many Iranians know little about him, if they have heard of him at all. Unlike Hafiz's tomb, which is prominently located in the city, Baba Kuhi's is perched on the side of a small mountain. There are no signposts pointing the way to his tomb, nor is it found on most tourist maps.

After making my way up the mountainside under the heat of the mid-afternoon sun, I discovered that it was being reconstructed. The grave itself was tiny and nondescript. The entire site was covered in dust. Rickety old chairs stood to one side. I looked up and admired the handsomely painted ceiling. Only after clambering up the scaffolding using a makeshift ladder did I realize that the ceiling work was lovingly constructed from countless colorful ceramic tiles cut into pieces and neatly arranged, including detailed geometric designs.

Hamid, the man undertaking the work, proudly showed me his handiwork. I thought to myself that one day his children will come and tell their children that it was their grandfather who built the ceiling, piece by piece.

When Hamid left, I meditated using Baba Kuhi's poem, "Only God I Saw," as my passage:

In the market, in the cloister—only God I saw.
In the valley and on the mountain—only God I saw.

Him I have seen beside me oft in tribulation;
In favor and in fortune—only God I saw.

In prayer and fasting, in praise and contemplation,
In the religion of the Prophet—only God I saw.

Neither soul nor body, accident nor substance,
Qualities nor causes—only God I saw.

I opened mine eyes and by the light of his face around me
In all the eye discovered—only God I saw.

Like a candle I was melting in his fire:
Amidst the flames outflashing—only God I saw.

Myself with mine own eyes I saw most clearly,
But when I looked with God's eyes—only God I saw.

I passed away into nothingness, I vanished,
And lo, I was the All-living—only God I saw.[1]

When I finished, I reflected on the story linking the lives of Hafiz and Baba Kuhi. It begins when Hafiz is a young man, madly in love with a beautiful woman, Shakh-e Nabat. It was a hopeless love, as she was due to marry a local prince. In desperation Hafiz remembered the legend that if he were to stay awake for 40 nights at Baba Kuhi's tomb, he would be granted immortality, the gift of poetry and whatever his heart wished for. Determined, Hafiz undertook a lonely vigil at the tomb. By the end of the 40 nights, his most fervent wish had changed. His longing for Shakh-e Nabat was supplanted by a longing to achieve union with God, which he achieved 40 years later.

I found myself dazzled by the symbolism of the two tombs. Hafiz, poet of the masses, awaits his many visitors in a manner befitting his role as a great troubadour of love. Meanwhile Baba Kuhi, his spiritual father, quietly looks down from the mountain, seeing God in everyone and everything. I did not know then that some Iranian scholars believe the poem was written by a namesake of Baba Kuhi who lived more recently. Given both Baba Kuhis were mystics it may not matter much. Just like Baba Kuhi's reconstructed tomb, true love is something that always requires work. Perhaps in the future more visitors will come to his tomb, finding what they may. ∎

I Have Learned So Much

Hafiz
A rendering by Daniel Ladinsky

I
Have
Learned
So much from God
That I can no longer
Call
Myself

A Christian, a Hindu, a Muslim,
A Buddhist, a Jew.

The Truth has shared so much of Itself
With me

That I can no longer call myself
A man, a woman, an angel,
Or even pure
Soul.

Love has
Befriended Hafiz so completely
It has turned to ash
And freed
Me

Of every concept and image
My mind has ever known.

In the Reed Bed 2 ~ Judith Ernst

A New Path Forward

A Gentle Breeze Once Briefly Blew

Nancy Matthews

In the summer of 1980, my husband Free and I were preparing to leave Cairo after nearly five years at the American embassy where Free had served as Deputy Chief of Mission. Many things had changed since our arrival. Egypt was still recovering from a series of Arab-Israeli Wars, and daily life was still challenging. The long negotiations that led to the historic Camp David Accords (1978) and the Egyptian Israeli Peace Treaty (1979) had made those years particularly exciting. But simultaneously there were also dramatic changes happening around us that were of great concern. These events would ultimately have a direct impact on my life.

In July 1980, the deposed shah of Iran lay dying in a hospital near Cairo, less than two miles from our house. The turmoil created by the Iranian Revolution and the hostage-taking were dominant issues that alarmed and confused Americans and Egyptians alike. We had known the last ambassador to Tehran well and many of the hostages were friends and colleagues. Egyptian president Anwar Sadat had allowed the shah to come to Cairo in his dying days. The atmosphere was charged and the outcome unknown as we sailed from Alexandria that summer on the long journey home to Washington. Once in the States, we were suddenly aware of the influx of Iranians who had fled their country and were appearing in Washington and elsewhere. Although the hostages, who were held for 444 days, were finally released on the day of Ronald Reagan's inauguration, the crisis endured. The events of those days created an atmosphere of suspicion, fear, and enmity between the United States and Iran that still lingers.

I could not then have known that at the end of November 1999, I would board a plane in London bound for Tehran on a cultural mission designed to open a window that had been closed for twenty years.

In 1999, few Americans went to Iran, but with the election of Mohammad Khatami, a more moderate Iranian President, there seemed to be a chance for a dialogue that had hitherto been impossible. After testing the waters in Washington with influential Iranians produced positive signals, Meridian International Center, a leader in the field of cultural diplomacy, decided to act. I was to travel to Iran to seek Iranian partners to initiate a cultural exchange in the form of a major exhibition of traditional Iranian art to be circulated around the United States. Though I had worked in many countries on joint cultural exchange exhibitions, I had never done so under such circumstances. There was no American embassy in Tehran. I was on my own and tensions still existed. I was unsure of what to expect as I boarded what would be the first of many fights between London and Tehran.

I need not have worried. From the moment I landed at the airport, in the early hours of the morning, having donned my Islamic dress for the first time, I was assured of my welcome. I was met by a polite and friendly delegation from the hosting organization, and given a headscarf as a gift (just in case I had not known it was needed), and taken to my hotel in central Tehran. My work began the next morning as I followed a schedule of visits that introduced me to an Iran I did not know. There was real enthusiasm for the art project. An early meeting was with Hojatoleslam Zam, who headed the Islamic Institute, host of this first trip. The Institute's primary concern was to revitalize the strong cultural wealth of Iran. He expressed his enthusiasm for the proposed project when he said, "Art speaks a golden language.

Over the next year and a half I made many trips back and forth, working along with Iranian artists, experts, and the Contemporary Museum of Art, to create the exhibition *A Breeze from the Gardens of Persia* the name of which would reflect the opportunity we all saw for the beginnings of a new relationship between the two countries. What also began for me was a new and very deep appreciation of the Iranian people and their rich culture, which I have never lost. I made deep and solid friendships that I hold dear to this day.

I worked closely with the artistic community, but I also visited schools, universities, mosques, think tanks, and museums and monuments in Tehran and other cities. I met university and religious leaders, as well as artists, musicians, officials and ordinary Iranians. I shopped in local stores, ate in restaurants and private homes, attended art openings and parties and a beautiful Persian wedding; drank numerous cups of tea and was offered wonderful fruits and sweets at every stop.

I joined in the daily routine as I worked at the Museum's curatorial office, used their telephone and one computer, and had free access to store rooms and conservation spaces. Dressed in my manteau and headscarf, I was welcomed each day by the security guards as the front gate. I joined in the habit of drinking tea, brought at regular intervals during the long days to give strength to these busy people. The planning work, our conversations, meetings, visits to artists in their homes and studios, and travels to other cities to complete our selections, gave me a real insight into daily life. Many of my working colleagues were women and I came to have an enormous admiration for them.

Prominent in every field, women also made up a significant percentage of university students. Whatever their profession or position, they were attractive, intelligent, well educated and respected by their male colleagues. They were elegant in their hijab, often ordering their stylish manteaus and headscarves from Paris.

What I learned in my days among Iranians and my travels about the country seeking representative art was that Iranians in general are warm and lovely people who are very friendly toward Americans and proud of their rich and ancient heritage. Famous and revered poets like Hafiz, Rumi and 'Omar Khayyam are listened to on car radios and read at dinner tables. Even contemporary artists often make reference to the past in their paintings. An entire museum is devoted to Persian musical instruments. Traditional feasts and wedding ceremonies have ancient and beautiful meanings. Poetry, art, philosophy, spirituality, order, hospitality to all, extreme courtesy and refinement are a part of everyday life. Long philosophical discussions on almost any topic, such as aesthetics in the way a fruit bowl is arranged, or vegetables stacked in the market, the beautiful symmetry of the Persian garden, and the delicate architecture of ancient buildings are all outward signs of a refined and beautiful culture.

The Breeze exhibition was financially supported by several prominent American corporations who sensed a possible opening of dialogue, as well as by the Tehran Museum of Contemporary Art. Once completed, it was shipped to Washington, D.C., where it officially began a tour of thirteen American venues. It opened in New York, just one week after 9/11. The attendance was extraordinary. Two large notebooks were filled with appreciative comments, as candle light vigils were held in Tehran. Throughout the tour visitors flocked to get this glimpse of a country little known to Americans since the hostage crisis.

Participating artists traveled from Iran to most venues and were warmly received as both artists and human beings. The success of the collaborative project was greeted with enthusiasm by both countries and a detailed report was sent to the Ministry of Culture at the conclusion of the two-year tour.

Not long afterwards, a large banner hung outside the Museum of Contemporary Art in Tehran announcing an exhibition of photographs by National Geographic photographers—the first American exhibit in over twenty years to be officially held in Iran. It was packed with viewers, many of them students and young people. It was an exciting moment that completed this exchange. But the air was beginning to chill with elections coming for a new Iranian president.

More than three years later, in December of 2006, I was welcomed back by my Iranian friends and colleagues to work on a new exhibition that focused on Iran's dynamic young artists. No one was happier to see me than the smiling hotel staff. There had been changes in many directions under new Iranian President Mahmoud Almadinejad, but we worked as we had before, with no interference.

I now met an entirely different segment of Iranians, members of the new generation, some born after the revolution. They had new ideas and were a little less conservative in their dress, while basically keeping up required standards. They were excited, creative and bold as they looked to their future. The name of the new exhibition, *Wishes and Dreams*, expressed these youthful feelings. On one visit I was given a massive birthday party, attended by both generations of artists and friends. It touched me deeply.

Again, the resulting exhibition, which was totally new and charming, was sent on tour. One of the most successful venues was Washington's National Cathedral, where it was installed in the Tower overlooking the city. Some of the artists came to the Washington opening and others visited several other American cities. They enchanted all those they met. But Tehran's new government was less pleased by this exchange, suspicious of the motivation of the project, as an official chill continued to descend upon hopes for new dialogue.

Although the official climate has changed today, and the breeze that started to blow so sweetly has subsided, the Iranian people are the same. They are warm toward Americans and will say they have learned from their long history that change comes gradually. Artists easily speak for this new generation of dynamic young people, bright, positive in outlook, and hoping for a new future. It is to them that it may eventually fall to bring about new opportunities for dialogue and cultural exchange. They seem willing to let it come in due course, as it always has, but they push the envelope when they can. Their way has not been violence, rather working within the system, and continuing to look for ways that will allow the window to open once more.

The fact that we once tried together will not be forgotten.

Your Mother and My Mother

Hafiz
A rendering by Daniel Ladinsky

Fear is the cheapest room in the house.
I would like to see you living
In better conditions,

For your mother and my mother
Were friends.

I know the Innkeeper
In this part of the universe.
Get some rest tonight,
Come to my verse again tomorrow.
We'll go speak to the Friend together.

I should not make any promises right now,
But I know if you
Pray
Somewhere in this world—
Something good will happen.

God wants to see
More love and playfulness in your eyes
For that is your greatest witness to Him.

Your soul and my soul
Once sat together in the Beloved's womb
Playing footsie.

Your heart and my heart
Are very, very old
Friends.

Travel as a Politcal Act

Rick Steves

Rick Steves recently produced a PBS documentary about Iran. The following is excerpted from a blog post on April 19, 2010. Read more of Rick Steves's posts at: www.ricksteves.com/tapa_blog/

Returning home from Iran to the US, I faced a barrage of questions—mainly, "Why did you go to Iran?" Some were skeptical of my motives, accusing me of just trying to make a buck. (As a businessman, I can assure you there was no risk of a profit in this venture.) Reading the comments readers shared on my blog—some of whom railed against me for "naively" acting as a Jane Fonda-type mouthpiece for an enemy that has allegedly bankrolled terrorists—was also thought-provoking. The whole experience made me want to hug people and scream at the same time. It was intensely human.

I didn't go to Iran as a businessman or as a politician. I went as what I am—a travel writer. I went for the same reasons I travel anywhere: to get out of my own culture and learn, to go to a scary place and find it's not so scary, and to bring distant places to people who've yet to go there. To me, understanding people and their lives is what travel is about, no matter where you go.

I have long held that travel can be a powerful force for peace. Travel promotes understanding at the expense of fear. And understanding bridges conflicts between nations. As Americans, we've endured the economic and human cost of war engulfing Iran's neighbor, Iraq. Seeing Iraq's cultural sites destroyed and its kind people being dragged through the ugliness of that war, I wished I'd been able to go to Baghdad before the war to preserve images of a peacetime Iraq. As our leaders' rhetoric ramped up the possibility of another war—with Iran—I didn't want to miss that chance again. It's human nature to not want to know the people on the receiving end of your "shock and awe"—but to dehumanize these people is wrong. I wanted to put a human face on "collateral damage."

I left Iran struck more by what we have in common than by our differences. Most Iranians, like most Americans, simply want a good life and a safe homeland for their loved ones. Just like my country, Iran has one dominant ethnic group and religion that's struggling with issues of diversity and change—liberal versus conservative, modern versus traditional, secular versus religious. As in my own hometown, people of great faith are suspicious of people of no faith or a different faith. Both societies seek a defense against the onslaught of modern materialism that threatens their traditional "family values." Both societies are suspicious of each other, and both are especially suspicious of each other's government.

When we travel—whether to the "Axis of Evil," or just to a place where people yodel when they're happy, or fight bulls to impress the girls, or can't serve breakfast until today's croissants arrive—we enrich our lives and better understand our place on this planet. We undercut groups that sow fear, hatred, and mistrust. People-to-people connections help us learn that we can disagree and still coexist peacefully.

Granted, there's no easy solution, but surely getting to know Iranian culture is a step in the right direction. Hopefully, even the most skeptical will appreciate the humanity of 70 million Iranian people. Our political leaders sometimes make us forget that all of us on this small planet are equally precious children of God. Having been to Iran and meeting its people face to face, I feel this more strongly than ever.

Iranian Cure for the Delta's Blues

Joel K. Bourne, Jr.

Baptist Town, with its tumbledown clapboard shacks on the wrong side of the tracks in Greenwood, Miss., seems an unlikely spot for any kind of revolution, especially one inspired by the Islamic Republic of Iran. But soon, that Mississippi neighborhood and others like it in the Deep South may see some startling changes.

While political leaders in the United States and Iran are practicing boisterous brinkmanship over nuclear proliferation, a small group of health care professionals from both countries are quietly working together to practice a new type of medicine, beginning in Mississippi, a state that has been mired at the bottom of nearly every health index for decades. Their primary focus is the storied Mississippi Delta. The flat, hot, rural landscape that gave birth to the blues—the quintessential American art form that put suffering to song—now suffers a host of health woes, with some of the highest rates of diabetes, obesity, hypertension and infant mortality in the nation.

Despite hundreds of millions of dollars spent over the last decade to improve residents' health there, the disparities between the Delta and the rest of the state have only widened.

"I've been in and out of the Delta for 40 years and nothing much has changed," says Aaron Shirley, a 77-year-old pediatrician who pioneered public health care in the Delta. "I was wringing my hands and crying about it one day when he said, 'Why don't you come to my country and learn how to do it?' And so I did."

"He" is Mohammad Shahbazi, M.D., chair of the Department of Behavioral and Environmental Health at Jackson State University, who was born in southern Iran.

Despite its reputation in America as an international pariah with an infamous human rights record—part of former President George W. Bush's "Axis of Evil"—Iran has won kudos from the World Health Organization for its innovative primary health care

system. That system has eliminated health disparities between rural and urban popula-
tions over the last 30 years, reducing infant mortality in rural areas by tenfold.

Back in 2009, as the United States was gearing up for its political slugfest over health
care reform, Shahbazi—with the tacit approval of the National Institutes of Health and
Iran's ministry of health—organized a tour of the Iranian health system for Shirley and
James Miller, a health care consultant from Oxford, Miss. They met with the doctors
and public health officials who built the Iranian system, visited rural "health houses"
and hospitals, and returned home convinced that the Iranian model could be just the
cure for what ails the perpetually ailing Delta, and perhaps even the nation.

"The health house system in Iran is like the German VW Beetle," says Miller, of the
Oxford International Development Group. "It's simple and it works. It was developed
by a country that wasn't too popular at the time, but it solved a basic transportation
problem." Yes, he says, Iran is a rogue nation. But "if the Iranians came up with a cure
for cancer, would we not use it just because we dislike their leaders? This has nothing to
do with politics," he says.

In Iran's health care system, remote village health houses are the first line of defense, staffed by villagers known as *behvarzes*. The behvarzes are trained to provide basic
health services for villages of up to 1,500 people. Male behvarzes take care of sanitation,
water testing and environmental projects. The women concentrate on child and mater-
nal health, family planning, vaccinations and tracking each family's births, deaths and
medical histories.

Iran, a country roughly twice the size of Texas, now has more than 17,000 health
houses and more than 30,000 behvarzes who cover more than 90 percent of the rural
population—about a quarter of the country's 72 million people. Recently Iran began
creating health posts in city neighborhoods to perform the same functions for its growing urban population.

But it's not the health house alone that makes the system work; it's integration with
more advanced care. The health house is the first stop, says Shahbazi. It's supervised by
doctors at a regional health center, which takes the cases the health house can't handle.
Together, the health houses and regional centers handle about 80% of all cases. Larger
hospitals care for the patients who need treatment the regional centers can't provide.
Iranians can go to whatever health facility they choose—but if patients are referred
through the health house their costs are lower.

"I think they'll have to tailor it to the culture here," says Zahra Sarraf, M.D., from
Shiraz University in Iran, who recently visited a clinic in Belzoni, Miss., to talk to residents and local medical staff about the health house concept. "It's very different from
Iran." But in both cases the aim is "to make the health houses teach preventive care. So
people who have diseases but don't know it can be made aware of it."

Shirley hopes to transform a donated Baptist Town shack into a clean, well-
lit place—a welcoming, primary care clinic where screenings and immunizations

will be free and local families will feel at ease being treated by people from their neighborhood.

Iran's health house system was established with the full support of the Iranian government, which provides inexpensive health insurance for all its citizens. But in places like Baptist Town, health insurance is a luxury most people simply can't afford. According to longtime resident Sylvester Hoover, who owns and runs the only business in Baptist Town—a convenience store and laundromat—little has changed in the former sharecropper community since blues legend Robert Johnson sat on a street corner in the 1930s singing "Hell Hound on My Trail."

"I don't have insurance," says Hoover, who has offered the shack he owns next to his store as the site for the future health house. "I need to see a doctor about my foot. Can't hardly walk. They say I need surgery, but I can't afford it. Everybody here got dental problems 'cause no one teaches them how to take care of their teeth. A lot of people over here really need to see the doctor and just can't afford to."

"I got it all," says Charles Griffis, 73, sitting on his porch across from Hoover's store. "High blood pressure, diabetes, and I'm a prostate cancer survivor." Griffis says he's been putting off a visit to the rural health clinic in Mound Bayou—a 100-mile round trip. "That type of service is needed really bad. I think people would accept something like that."

Unlike the Iranians, Shirley, Shahbazi and Miller are trying to establish the Mississippi health houses on a song and a prayer, using volunteers along with donated buildings and medical supplies. The plan is to eventually train single mothers currently on welfare to staff the health houses in their communities, giving them skills they can use to get off government assistance.

So far, support for the project has come from the Jackson Medical Mall Foundation, which supports Shirley's large community clinic in Jackson. Shirley's group is applying for a $20 million grant from the US Department of Health and Human Services to fund 10 health house pilot programs in Mississippi, Arkansas and Louisiana. And though it sounds expensive, Miller is convinced it will actually save money in the long run.

"This is one of the things that can address the cost of health care," says Miller. "Preventive care keeps people from getting sick in the first place, and postoperative care will save billions in readmissions. This really could be an answer for what ails the US health care system. But forget the dollars, what about the human suffering? The value of taking a healthy, productive human being out of society? We've got to change the way we think. If you look at the health disparities for minorities in the US, we look like some undeveloped countries in how we treat our citizens."

And in fact, a number of countries have flourishing primary health care systems. Brazil, Chile, Costa Rica and Cuba all have such care systems, as do Spain and Portugal. Canada and the United Kingdom also have systems that cost less and provide better health outcomes than the current system in the United States.

"Primary care makes a lot of sense," says Hernan Montenegro, M.D., of the World Health Organization. "It's not just for poor countries. If you cover everybody and everybody has some access to health care, they get less sick and are more productive. Kids who aren't sick do better in school and become more productive adults. Investing in health has numerous benefits."

But it's the people-to-people aspect that inspires LaTania Sci, M.D., an internist from Dayton, Ohio, and the fact that she sees more and more Americans falling through the cracks of the current health care system. Sci is one of half a dozen health care professionals who have volunteered to travel to Iran for a six-week crash course at Shiraz University, so she can set up a training center for community health workers in Mississippi.

"I really admire the people who developed this concept," says Sci. "They just happen to be Iranian. But on a person-to-person basis so much can occur. I think it's a brilliant model, and I think it will catch on throughout the US."

An Ice Book Floats Down the Karun River

Basia Irland

Basia Irland is an author, poet, sculptor, installation artist, and activist who creates international water projects featured in her book, Water Library. *Through her work, Irland offers a creative understanding of water while examining how communities of people, plants, and animals rely on this vital element. Using ice embedded with native riparian seeds, Irland creates sculptures of books, which she then releases into watersheds around the globe.*

Raheleh "Minoosh" Zomorrodinia, a photographer and ecological artist from Tehran, came to the United States to study her craft. When she first arrived in 2010, she had an exhibition of photographs in Durango, Colorado, and after the opening of her show Minoosh came to New Mexico to stay with my husband and me for ten days. We had such a fun time enjoying art galleries in Santa Fe, attending a sacred Native American dance at the Pueblo of Taos, and photographing the Rio Grande on cold winter afternoons. Several days before she left, I threw a party for her with twenty friends and tasty Iranian food during which time Minoosh shared images of the work she does with an environmental group in Iran called the Persian New Art Group.

Minoosh described the growing environmental art movement in Iran in an essay for the Women Environmental Art Directory, an online journal published in California.

> Sometimes economic, political, social and religious issues are reflected in the works of these environmental artists, however they focus mostly on urgent environmental issues. Because of the vast physical geographic variations and cultural differences in all of Iran, this movement presents a rich diverse body of work. Many works are ephemeral and are constructed (in part or all) with natural materials such as soil, stones, water, leaves, moss, and/or branches. These works are designed for a particular place (site-specific) and frequently involve collaborations between artists and others, such as community groups or university students. Because final public presentation of these temporal installations is through documentation– photography or video art–collaboration with a photographer is necessary. Also the majority of presentations are on websites and web blogs in order to avoid the expense of exhibitions and to reach large audiences.

Love and Pomegranates

Minoosh e-mailed images of my environmental artwork to her friends in the Persian New Art Group, so that we could collaborate, via the Internet, on an art project during the 30th Environmental Art Festival in Shoushtar in 2010. The artists decided that they wanted to create one of my sculptures, which are hand-carved ice books embedded with native riparian seeds. This project emphasizes the need to deal with the complexities of climate disruption and the importance of efforts to restore watersheds.

To create an ice book, river water is gathered and frozen, carved into the sculptural form of an open or closed book, and placed back into the creek. The closed books have seed patterns on the covers. The open books have a riparian "text" consisting of local seeds, embedded in rows in the ice. This "ecological language," of sorts, releases the seeds as the ice melts into the current. When the plants regenerate and grow along the river, they help sequester carbon, hold the banks in place, and provide shelter.

For our collaborative project in Iran, Tarhere Goodarzy molded and carved an ice book, then Esfahan artist Nooshin Naficy arranged the seeds, which she had found growing along the riverbank. After placing the book into the Karun River in Shoushtar, Shahmaz Zarkesh took exquisite photographs. The images show the local seeds forming a magical text as the ice book slowly floats out beyond the riparian plants of the river bank, and into the current. The tall emerald grasses and the nearby hills can be seen reflected in the water.

Nooshin e-mailed me: "I'm really grateful that I could participate doing your work in Iran. It was a very joyful process and I appreciate it and the concept behind it."

Someday soon, I hope to join this great group of artists in Iran and work collaboratively with them in person.

A Persian Picnic, with Plants

Barbara Ertter

Kicking back above timberline, enjoying a laid-back picnic lunch with a group of congenial companions—does life get any better? Granted, the conversation was mainly in Persian, the slopes had been well-grazed by village sheep, and few plants were currently in bloom. Still, it was a botanist's treat to find lamb's ear in its native haunt, and the view over the precipitous valleys of the northern Alborz Mountains and cloud-shrouded Caspian plain was downright awesome.[1]

This, my second trip to Iran, was the brainchild of an earlier visit hatched by Fosiee Tahbaz. Fosiee, the first female professor at the University of Tehran College of Agriculture, was a visiting scholar at the University of California at Davis when the Iranian Revolution took place. She opted to remain in the United States with her family and eventually found a new professional home at UC Berkeley. She and I began work on the same day at the University and Jepson Herbaria, which houses preserved plants from around the world. The stories Fosiee shared of the natural beauty and botanical riches of her beloved country made me hope that I could one day travel there myself.

This wish became reality when relations between Iran and the United States softened following Mohammad Khatami's election as president of Iran. In response to the new president's challenge for renewed scholarly exchange between the two counties, Fosiee sent a seemingly audacious letter proposing that a delegation of distinguished botanists be invited to Iran. Contrary to the expectations of those of us recruited as aforesaid "distinguished botanists," formal invitations to do exactly that began arriving from several Iranian universities in January 1999.

Since we could expect the best floral displays between January and May, we had scant time for preparations. In the end, only Fosiee and I managed to go. Excitement mixed with anxiety as I boarded the plane, casting myself on the beneficence of unknown hosts in a country of dubious repute. My initial misgivings were quickly set aside during a two-week whirlwind tour of botanical diplomacy, as we were wined and dined (or, more accurately, "tea'ed and kebab'ed") by university after university.

After this initial trip, Fosiee and I determined that the best way to repay the generosity and hospitality we had received was to bring an array of American botanists into contact with their Iranian counterparts. Because of sanctions, our goal of fostering ongoing collaborations was not directly fundable, but the biogeographical similarities between Iran and western North America made it possible to get grant support on scientific merit alone.

Iran's central plateau, with its interior-draining deserts and isolated mountains, is comparable to the western North America's Great Basin. The plateau lies in the rain shadow of the Alborz and Zagros ranges, where alpine wildflowers (and the occasional ski resort) flourish on the highest peaks. Dense deciduous forests, remnants from when such forests spanned the northern hemisphere, persist at the base of mountains facing the Caspian Sea.

These mountains and deserts are home to over 8,000 species of flowering plants, with new species being discovered on a regular basis. Many genera, including wild onion, fritillary, and clover, have numerous (though different) species in both Iran and western North America. Because of the biogeographic similarities, plants from one area—ranging from beneficial crop plants to pestiferous weeds—often grow readily in the other.

The stated scientific goal of our proposal was to amass as complete a set as possible of Iranian plants for use by researchers worldwide, collected by teams of American and Iranian botanists. In our experience, the secondary goal of fostering congenial relationships among participants was inevitable after time spent together on flower-covered hillsides, supplemented by discussions while pressing plants, sharing meals and rooms, and traveling from one site to another.

This second trip, in October 2002, was essentially a trial run, with colleagues from Berkeley as the only American participants. With a nervous eye on current events in the Middle East, Dan Norris, Fosiee, and I boarded the plane to Tehran. We were soon on the road to Hamadan, accompanied by three of Fosiee's former colleagues from the University of Tehran's College of Agriculture: Hussein Lessani, Marzieh Mahdavian, and Teimour Ramak Maassoumi.

At Bu Ali Sina University we were given the red-carpet tour of research laboratories and the local herbarium, after which the local botanist was thrilled to take us to nearby collecting sites. The next day we continued west to Kermanshah and Razi University, where we received an equally enthusiastic welcome. The team was also taken to an oak forest near the Iraqi border, reminiscent of counterparts in California.

Our next destination was the northern edge of Dasht-e Kavir, one of Iran's great saline deserts. The long drive took us through starkly beautiful scenery comparable to the Mojave Desert, with colorful sedimentary bands twisted into barren mountains. We stayed at Semnan field station, a rustic facility reminiscent of counterparts in the Great Basin (except that it was jackals, not coyotes, that provided twilight serenades!) The next day was spent collecting along a tamarisk-lined salt wash, originating at an enclosed hot spring. A side trip into the Alborz Mountains allowed us to collect along a mountain stream above the town of Shahmirzad, popular as a tourist destination. One visiting family, delighted with the presence of Americans, invited us to share their afternoon tea.

Our return trip to Tehran took us through the southern slopes of the mountains, where the occasional stands of juniper made the area look just like northern Nevada. Unfortunately we had only the merest glimpse of iconic Mount Damavand, the nearly 19,000 foot dormant volcano whose snow-capped peak is a popular symbol of Iran.

Back in Karaj we were welcomed into the home of Mahdavian and her family, where we were joined by our herbarium director Brent Mishler. In spite of the 24-hour transit from Berkeley, Brent's stamina carried him through a full day at the College of Agriculture, including a formal presentation on plant evolution under the visage of Ayatollah Khomeini. His talk generated a spirited round of questions, and we were all swamped by enthusiastic students of both genders asking for our business cards and signatures.

With Brent on board, we headed to the relict deciduous forest on the northern flanks of the Alborz Mountains. A full day in Golestan National Park treated us to breath-taking waterfalls, wild boar rooting in the forest floor, rocky scrub in brilliant fall color, and a rich forest consisting of oak, maple, and the endemic parrotia.

From Golestan we drove west across the Caspian plain, through misty fields and innumerable towns and villages, into progressively wetter realms. At Sisangan National Park we wandered through a forest of Hyrcanian box, where moss-carpeted rocks covered the forest floor. The next day was a transect up the Alborz Mountains, passing through sun-dappled alder forests scattered with wild cyclamen, and ending with the aforementioned picnic. The open high country made me yearn to come back in July or August, when the flowering plants would be at their peak.

To our delight, Lessani and Mahdavian later managed to visit the United States. By the end of our time together, Mahdavian and I had taken to calling one another *khoharam* ("my sister"). A follow-up expedition in May 2004 was so successful in fostering relationships among American and Iranian botanists that tears were shed when it came time to part. Although our early high hopes of future collaborations have been tempered by political affairs and other complications, I hold strong to the belief that this is only a transient setback, and that I will yet again enjoy a picnic with my Iranian friends, both human and floral, in the Alborz Mountains overlooking the Caspian Sea. ■

From Tehran to Missoula
An Interview with Artist Rashin Kheiriyeh

Elizabeth Moore

Q: You have said in previous interviews that your mother was an artist, which informed your passion for art, and that you were afforded the opportunity to attend one of the best art schools in Tehran. This bit of information would surprise some people, because there is a perception in the United States that an Iranian woman would have had difficulty attending university and making a career for herself, especially a career as distinguished as yours has been. Please tell us a little bit about your journey as an artist, and about the obstacles or the lack of obstacles you encountered as your pursued your education and your career in art world.

A: I encountered almost no obstacles while pursuing my education in Iran. People in Iran respect art, and there are great art education centers where anyone, men and women both, can pursue their interests. Today, there are many talented, young, Iranian artists who are very active and successful in the international art events all over the world.

I began my education in Azadegan Art School in graphic design in 1996. I then continued studying graphic design in Azad University of Tehran in 2000, and finally went to Alzahra University in 2006 for my MFA. Meanwhile, in 2000, I started my career in illustration and animation, and continued to work as a professional animator and illustrator as I completed my MFA. Now I am studying Visual Art in the School of Visual Art of New York (SVA). I have illustrated 40 children books so far, and I have directed three animated films in Iran and France. The most recent awards I have received are first prize in the AYACC 2012 China animation contest for character designing of the Iranian animation series *Sugarland*, and The Golden Apple from the Bratislava illustration competition for one of my books, *If I Become a Mayor*.

Q: Please elaborate a little bit on attending university in Tehran. What was the application process for getting into the university? How exclusive were the art programs you attended? How demanding were your classes? Did men and women study together? Can you us tell a little bit about university social life at the schools you attended?

A: The application process for entering a university in Iran is complex and very competitive, where very few get a chance to get into a good school, especially in visual arts. First you have to pass the entry exam which is a 2-3 part exam. Hundreds of thousands of people apply and only a few hundred may pass and be accepted. The classes were very demanding in my major (Graphic Design) because of the research and practical art projects that we had to create, such as book art, video art, print making workshops, photography, graphic designing and illustrations for books and magazines. Upon reaching the university level, the classes are mixed but there are a lot of limits placed on the relationships between male and female students, and they are closely watched. Yet, the social life of the students is very active and full. Men and woman get together daily, either in artistic groups or to participate in various activities, such as visiting galleries, theaters and attending social debates, or at coffee shops to discuss their work and new concepts.

Q: Illustrations for children's books make up a large percentage of your body of work. What were some of your favorite books when you were a child? Did you have access to many books in translation?

A: I used to be interested in the Tintin series of comic books when I was a kid. I have read them hundreds of times and I still love them very much. The international folktales were very interesting to me as well, such as Little Red Riding Hood, Pinocchio, Jack and the Beanstalk, and so on.

These fiction stories made my imagination full of colors and images. They were really magnificent literature. All of them were translated and published in Iran. As you know, the Iranian book printing industry is very active, always trying to update itself with new books from all over the world. Iranian publishers try not to miss taking part in international book fairs abroad, and they aim to introduce the great international authors to Iranian readers by translating their novels. For example, Shel Silverstein's books had been translated in Persian and had great fans among the Iranian people. Of course, I was one of them.

Q: In 2007, you participated in a gallery exhibition in Washington, D.C., called *Wishes and Dreams: Iran's New Generation Emerges*, featuring the work of 30 young Iranian artists. One idea the exhibition brought to mind is the way visual art possibly can transcend cultural barriers in ways that language sometimes struggles with. Do you think it's true that art can help bridge barriers between cultures, and how do you see this concept at work in the illustrations you create for children's books?

Love and Pomegranates

A: I do believe that Art is capable of bridging barriers between cultures. As a matter of fact, the artists can communicate easily with a wide variety of people only by using the language of art, which understandable to everyone. No matter where you are from or what religion you practice, or the politics with which you live you can share your feelings about real life with each other. So the concept or theory I use with my own art is to be myself, and to maintain my personality and tell my story. As an illustrator sometimes you have to tell someone else's story, but in my paintings I try to tell mine. My story is that of an artist who came from the Persian culture, with a lot of stories for kids and adults. That is what I'm trying to convey by blending traditional and modern elements.

I love traveling just because traveling allows for a deeper understanding of the meaning of human beings, and it fills my imagination full of new images from nature.

Q: Much of the news coverage of the *Wishes and Dreams* exhibit focused on the politics of bringing Iranian artwork to the US capital. When you agree to display work in certain galleries or exhibitions, are you thinking of the political? In other words, what do you hope your work will achieve when you send it out into the world to be viewed by diverse audiences?

A: When I am in my studio creating a piece of art, like picture book or paintings, and when I'm using my favorite colors, characters, elements, patterns, etc., my hope is for them to fly far away to send my message to other people. That is my ideal.

Of course, I have no political purpose when I send my paintings to the galleries; I just love to exhibit them in new places for new audiences. And I always respect the comments people from Iran or people from other countries leave for me regarding my artwork because they're really helpful. Sometimes they pay attention to a special aspect of my paintings that I have not considered before. For me, exhibiting my work internationally teaches me and shows me new things and new ways to think about my work. That's why I'm always excited to have exhibitions in different countries. I really need their feedback.

Q: You have said that feedback from average people is as important to you as the praise and awards you receive from professional critics. In late 2011, when your work was displayed at the Dana Gallery in Missoula, MT, how did gallery visitors respond to your work? What was the response from people who possibly did not have an understanding of ancient Persian literature, traditional Persian culture, or of some of the other culturally specific elements you incorporate in your work?

A: I had a great experience showing my work in the Dana Gallery in Montana. I exhibited twelve figurative decorative paintings, acrylic on canvas. The concept of the show was to be a woman, which referred to my personal experiences, and is something that I convey by using both traditional and modern elements in my work.

The warm, welcoming people of Montana showed their interest in Persian culture by coming to my opening night and supporting an Iranian artist. The traditional elements, symbols, Persian patterns, and Persian calligraphy were the aspects of my painting that they really liked and responded to.

Q: I also understand that you recently made the decision to live in the United States. What prompted this decision?

A: Last year, I decided to start a new chapter in my professional life by changing my geographical location. That's why I moved to New York from Tehran. To me, it was like taking a big risk because I had a completely stable place in the art society of Iran and was very successful, so this change could be a real challenge for me.

I just was wondering what I should do in a great city like New York where I don't know anybody and will get lost within the huge, famous artists community where nobody has any idea about my work and my background. It seems that I have to start all the way back at the beginning and try to find a way to introduce myself to the art world and learn new things in art. I like challenges anyway. Fortunately, little by little I am moving forward and getting back on track.

Q: What has the transition been like for you on a personal or social level? Is your life in the United States very different from your life in Tehran?

A: In Iran there weren't many international students, and when there were international students, there weren't many opportunities for us to get to know them personally or learn more about their culture. So my transition to the US was a big one, because suddenly I was able to meet and connect to many people from various cultures in one setting. Even when I traveled to other countries I met only people within that culture. But here in the US I am able to meet many people from different cultures all in one room, which I love. This is the biggest difference between the United States and Iran.

My life here is different because of the language barrier. It takes me longer to make new connections and to fully explain who I am and what I have done. Sometimes this gets very frustrating, however, my experiences have been good so far.

Q: In all of your travels in the United States, you must meet a lot of different people. What has the experience been like? Do you have any thoughts about the similarities or differences between people in America and people in Iran?

A: As I mentioned above, I *am* meeting a lot people here in America. The biggest similarity between people in America and people in Iran is kind of general: in the end people are people and we all share the same human feelings and experience the same joys and struggles. The difference is that people in the US are much more open and expressive about their lifestyles, but their privacy is still respected in their personal and business lives. In Iran you don't enjoy the same level of privacy as an artist, due to the various laws and more traditional lifestyle.

Q: What is next for you? What projects are you currently working on and what do you see for yourself in the near future?

A: Currently I am working on some book and animation projects, such as writing and illustrating a children's book titled *A Tale of Two Parrots* for Enchanted Lion Books in New York. I am also making an animated film titled *The Golden Axe* for Lirabelle in France. I also had a group painting show in M Gallery in Santiago last month, titled "Fresh Air."

My next plan is to work on two new book projects from Spain and South Korea, and to do some illustration and comic book work for Fukuinkan (Japan). I also plan to do work for *Life and Style* (Mexico) and *Le Monde Diplomatique* (Germany) magazines.

Q: You seem to have a lot going on in your professional life. How do you find time for it all?

A: I enjoy what I do professionally so it doesn't feel like it interferes with my personal life. For the most part, I am able to mix both together. If you love what you do, then you find time for it all.

Who Is It We Fear?

Judith Ernst

Judith is an artist whose ceramic work is influenced by her life and travels in Asia. She wrote this piece after returning from her first trip to Shiraz, Iran, in the spring of 2007, where her husband Carl Ernst was presented an award for his book Following Muhammad: Rethinking Islam in the Contemporary World.

My wheel spins the clay as I shape the pot. Spinning and shaping. As I reflect on the wonderful week I have just spent in Shiraz I am puzzled by the bizarre stereotypes of Iranians and Iranian culture that I face daily in the United States. If you believe what you read and see in the American media, all Iranians are, at best, religious zealots, and at worst, would-be terrorists. How can this be, given the week that I've just experienced?

Memories surface of our hosts' extended family, three generations of whom just saw us off in the airport after taking us to a park on the side of a mountain. Who are these Iranians seemingly so feared by the journalists and pundits who create the negative images of people in Iran?

Is it the woman guard wrapped in a black chador, staffing the security x-ray machine in the airport? The one whose intense stare caused me to worry if I had been dressed appropriately enough to enter Iran, a country which mandates that my hair, arms and body are well-covered. Just when I thought I would be scrutinized in ways that I didn't wish to imagine, the guard asked, "Where are you from?" When I tepidly answered the United States, she said, "Would you help me with my pronunciation? You, see, I have a recitation to present tomorrow in my English class and there are many words I don't know how to say properly." When I emerged several minutes later from the "ladies only" area with a smile on my face, my husband and our host looked perplexed. "What took so long?" they asked. "Did they search you?"

Are American fears represented by our host, a religious scholar whose professional attire is a white turban and a flowing brown robe? He is a philosopher, a teacher, and a translator of Thomas Aquinas and other Western writers into Persian. He is a progressive thinker, a generous host, a caring and sensitive husband and father, and a kind and gentle man. Yes, he is connected to the government by his theological vocation. But he is not easily categorized by our usual notions of "progressive" or "fundamentalist."

Or perhaps it is the youngest daughter of our host of whom we should be afraid. She represents the future of Iran's nearly 60 percent who are under the age of 30. A serious woman of twenty, she studies biology and art at the university, and combines the qualities of intellect and curiosity, earnestness and innocence. At one moment she'll quote Persian poetry to make a point, the next moment she'll dissolve into laughter at a joke. I was puzzled initially by her habit of pulling her chador over her chin. But finally it dawned on me that while deep in thought, she would draw in her chador to make a stark V around her face. At those moments she created for herself a contemplative space in which she could consider the conversation and what she might contribute. Though a student of the sciences, she also studies the ancient art of manuscript illumination, the complex floral and arabesque paintings that frame calligraphy.

Consider the son, a handsome 19-year-old with a ready smile. While in England for nine months he became good friends with a British scholar, an old man in his eighties, whom he visited every day and whom the young man misses now that he is back in Iran. This son showed up at our hotel to present to my husband three complete collections of mp3s of classical Persian music simply because my husband had mentioned that he wanted to update his collection for use in his classes.

It was such fun to interact with these young people because they aren't disconnected from the continuum between youth and old age. Their earnest self-reflection and optimism made me feel as if I had been in the midst of a Jane Austen novel, with chadors, of course.

I am reminded of their beautiful mother. Is it she whom we should fear? A woman in her early forties who could easily pass as her daughters' elder sister. A woman whose smile lights up her whole face and radiates to all those around her. She and the youngest daughter took me shopping one morning in the old bazaar. There I was, running errands through the covered market with two women clutching chadors under their chins. At a jewelry store I tried on a traditional turquoise and silver necklace and I needed to see how the length looked on my neck. In a storage room off of the main stall hung a small mirror for just such purposes. So, in the privacy of the little room, I took off my scarf and tried on the necklace. Just then the daughter came in and saw me with my head uncovered. To my amusement, she was just as surprised to see what I looked like without a scarf as I would have been to see her minus her hijab.

Was the man I sat next to at dinner to be feared? The one now in his early sixties, who at the age of 26 translated Aldous Huxley's *Brave New World* into Persian. He proudly told me that it was in its third printing, and he revealed what an intense and fulfilling experience it had been for him as a young man to be immersed in such a project.

Perhaps we are to cast a wary eye on the helpful young receptionist at the hotel with bleached blonde hair spilling out from under her headscarf and wearing a touch of bubble-gum pink lipstick. Or maybe the short, plump woman in the lobby with the twinkle in her eye, whose embroidered Indian dress and striped socks peeked out from under her chador.

The wheel has stopped spinning now, and I lift the plastic bat holding my finished pot, shaped as I imagined it would be when I began. I'm reminded of the woman with whom I spoke after the talk at the university, on the last day before our departure to Istanbul. She didn't look like a student. She was older, a bit frumpy, perhaps someone's mother who had heard about the lecture. She pulled an antique lapis lazuli and silver bracelet off her wrist and presented it to me, insisting that I accept it. She said to me in halting English, "Iranians love Americans. Americans used to know this, but they don't anymore."

So who is it that we fear? Apparently it is not the real human beings that I encountered in Iran. Perhaps we need to change the question and ask, Who is it that shapes our fears and who benefits from that spin?

This Sane Idea

Hafiz
A rendering by Daniel Ladinsky

Let your
Intelligence begin to rule
Whenever you sit with others

Using this sane idea:

Leave all your cocked guns in a field
Far from us,

One of those damn things
Might go

Off.

Tens

Azin Arefi

I am ten.
I am a perceptive girl,
Antennae as keen as a praying mantis,
So I must be 15. Perhaps even 20.
I am growing up during war.
How old does that make me?
30?
40?
Not old enough to die.
Not old enough to die.

I am hidden under the table.
The red alarm is still going, going,
Drowning in my ear.
I am ten and I am scared.
Would I not be scared if I was more?
If I was 50? 60?
Or are they scared too?

I am hidden under the table.
But even at ten I know that bombs can see tables.
(Or is it that they can see people past the tables?)
Others must be under their tables too,
Some down in their basements,
Some underneath the stairs.
Don't bombs see through all of that?
They, too, possess keen antennae.

Love and Pomegranates

My heart is beating, fast.
It sounds like soldiers marching.
It sounds like buildings falling.

I am ten
Yet suddenly I want to run out from under the table,
Fly the door open and run up,
Up the stairs to the rooftop,
And wave, wave at the man in the airplane with the bombs
And make him see me.
See me.

Why are we hiding?
What if all of us tens got up on our rooftops?
And our brothers and sisters?
Our moms and dads?
Uncles and aunts.
Cousins.
Second cousins.
Tens and tens and tens of us.

And we all waved at the man in the airplane with the bombs.
And maybe if he sees us,
One of us, me,
If he sees that I am
Ten
He might remember the time he was
Ten
Then maybe, just maybe, he will give me
A chance to grow up.

The Lover Who Saw a Blemish in His Beloved's Eye

Farid ud-Din 'Attar

Translated by Afkham Darbandi and Dick Davis

The following excerpt is from an epic poem Conference of the Birds *written in the twelfth century about a journey inward undertaken by the birds of the world in search of a king, Simorgh.*

A lion-hearted hero met defeat—
Five years he loved, and slavery was sweet.
The girl for whom he was content to sigh
Had one small blemish lurking in her eye,
And though, as often as she would permit,
He gazed at her he never noticed it.
(How could a man possessed by frenzy see
This unimportant, faint deformity?)
Then imperceptibly love ceased to reign;
A balm was found to ease his aching pain—
The girl and all her blandishments
Became a matter of indifference;
And now the blemish in her eye was clear—
He asked her: "When did that white speck appear?"
She answered: "As your love began to die,
This speck was brought to being in my eye."
How long will others' faults distract your mind?
Your own accuse you, but your heart is blind.
Your sins are heavy, and while they are there,
Another's guilt is none of your affair.

How Do I Despise Thee? Let Me Count the (Many) Ways

Ambassador John W. Limbert

The following is an excerpt from John W. Limbert's Negotiating With Iran.

The depths of mutual hostility, ill will, and suspicion that have prevented dispassionate and reasoned discussions of policy for almost 30 years are obvious even to those new to the subject of American-Iranian relations. I recently asked my political science students—who had been studying US-Iranian relations for only a few months—how they believed, on the basis of the recent history they had learned in the class, the United States and Iran viewed each other. In their responses, the students went straight to the heart of the matter of how mutual antipathy has clouded judgment. Based on the last 30 years of history, and our disastrous relations with the Islamic Republic, they believed most Americans saw Iran and Iranians as:

* Emotional. Iranians let their hearts rule their heads. Even Iran's leaders cannot calculate their country's interests and had become captives of their own fiery rhetoric.

* Devious. Iranians have lived up to the stereotype of the mendacious oriental. They will cheat and deceive if it suits their purpose—or sometimes even to no apparent purpose.

* Obsessed with the past. Iranians cannot put past events behind them. They are still fixated on events of 50 or 60 years ago (particularly the 1953 coup) and even on seventh-century conflicts in Islamic history.

* Obsessed with religion. Iranians are attempting to establish a theocratic state in the 21 century based on a version of Mohammad's seventh-century community in Arabia. They are using religion as a pretext to mistreat their women and religious minorities.

* Unreliable. Iranians cannot be trusted to keep their word. They will tell you anything to gain a short-term advantage even if the long-term result is a complete loss of confidence.

* Incomprehensible. Many Iranian actions are inexplicable. One cannot begin to understand or predict how they will act in a given situation.

* Vindictive. Iranians will harbor grudges for decades and even for centuries. They overreact against opponents or critics, imprisoning and even murdering those who think for themselves or ask embarrassing questions.

* Fanatical. Inspired by the stories of their martyred saints, Iranians will embark on suicidal missions. During the mourning days of the Shia calendar, Iranians will work themselves into a frenzy of self-flagellation.

For these students this part of the exercise was easy. They had only to repeat many of the caricatures the popular American media have been propagating for the past three decades. With most American audiences, a simple word-association test of "Iran" and "Iranian" would have yielded about the same results.

I then gave the students a more difficult problem and asked them to put themselves in the place of the other. I turned the original question around, and asked them how they thought Iranians, in light of that same history, might view Americans and American policy. Their answers included:

* Belligerent. Americans cannot tolerate opposition and will react violently when they believe their country's hegemony is being challenged. The American government is always looking to teach someone a lesson and to make other nations change their behavior.

* Sanctimonious and hypocritical. Americans deliver sermons to others on upholding human rights and democracy, yet their government has supported many corrupt, undemocratic, and oppressive regimes.

* Calculating. Americans are forever weighing the material profit from courses of action, without regard to any ethical or religious scruple. Americans are always willing to sacrifice humanity for some strategic advantage.

* Godless and immoral. Americans export and glorify a corrupt culture that transforms women into sex objects and undermines family, religion, and tradition.

* Materialistic. Americans have no spiritual values. They believe that human beings are ruled only by their desires for material goods and have no interest in higher ideals other than the latest fashion or electronic gadget.

* Bullying. If Americans can't get their way, they will resort to threats, subversion, and direct intervention. The American government has never stopped bullying the Islamic Republic because Iran has chosen its own path and has refused to submit to Washington's demands.

* Arrogant. The United States insists that all parties must play by its rules. Iranians thus label the United States as "global arrogance" (*estekbaar-e jahaani*). Americans claim that their political, economic, and cultural system is the only valid one for humanity.

* Meddling. Americans have been meddling in Iranian affairs for decades. The Bush administration labeled Iran a member of the axis of evil and decided to overthrow the bothersome Islamic Republic and install a more compliant regime in Tehran.

Endless Enemies?

The cumulative effect of all this mythmaking—so obvious even to outsiders such as my students—has been to build an enormous wall of distrust between our two countries. In such a setting, Washington's simply sending a representative in July 2008 to join multilateral talks about Iran's nuclear program became in the press a huge, symbolic reversal of policy, even when the American representative apparently neither met with an Iranian counterpart or even participated in the multilateral discussions. Even when one side makes a tentative offer to explore a way out of the impasse, the other side assumes the worst, reacts with suspicion, and immediately asks itself, "What do they mean by doing that? Why are they making this offer now? What trap are they laying for us? What devious plan have they devised? Are they admitting a weakness that we can exploit?"

These suspicions and preconceptions have led both sides to make short-sighted decisions and to miss opportunities. In 1998-99, for example, the Iranians rejected the Clinton administration's offer of talks without preconditions on all issues in dispute to create (as Secretary of State Madeline Albright put it) "a road map to better relations." At the same time, she addressed a basic Iranian grievance by expressing regret for American actions in 1953. Not to be outdone, in April 2003 the Bush administration, while riding a wave of illusory triumph on Iraq, ignored a proposal from the Iranians to open talks on all subjects of mutual interest.

Why should both sides remain stuck in this downward spiral? How can they escape it? The United States and Iran—if one applies a reasoned analysis to the two countries' interests—should not be condemned to be endless enemies. Despite the myths and rhetoric, the number of actual casualties in our three-decade-old conflict—in Beirut, the Persian Gulf, and even in the suburbs of Washington, D.C.—has so far been relatively small, in the hundreds on each side. If we compare those numbers with the hundreds of thousands of victims on both sides of the Vietnam War, for example, it is hard to understand how the United States can today enjoy normal diplomatic relations with the Republic of Vietnam while the United States and the Islamic Republic can think only of new ways to insult and punish each other and appear helpless to find a way out of a quagmire of myths, stereotypes, and grievances, both real and imagined.

Have Low Expectations, Have High Expectations

When entering negotiations with Iranians, we should follow the wise counsel of the thirteenth-century Persian poet Sa'di, who, in his stories in the *Golestan*, advised,

> *Har kera jameh-ye-parsa-bini, parsara dan va nikmard engar.*
> Whomever you see in the dress of an ascetic,
> Consider him an ascetic and assume he is virtuous.

In the same vein, the poet tells us to be wary of assumptions:

> *Ta mard sokhan nagofteh bashad, eib va honarash nohofteh bashad*
> *Har piseh gaman mabar nahali, shayad palang khofteh bashad.*
> Until a man speaks, his faults and virtues are hidden.
> Do not assume that every strand of hair is a sapling;
> It could well be a sleeping panther.

In other words, in our encounters with Iran and Iranians, we should keep our expectations realistic—and anticipate progress will be difficult and slow. At the same time, however, we should put aside those prejudices that have convinced us—before a dialogue has even begun—that no accommodation (short of surrender) will ever be possible. Expect negotiations to fail through the fault of the other side and they probably will. Expect better and success becomes possible.

Love and Pomegranates
The Impact of US Meddling
Reese Erlich

The following is an excerpt from Reese Erlich's The Iran Agenda: The Real Story of US Policy and the Middle East Crisis.

Every opponent of the Iranian government that I spoke to criticized the disastrous impact of US policies. When the United States periodically threatens military attacks, funds dissidents, and sponsors terrorism, the administration helps fuel anti-American nationalism, said journalist and opposition leader Akbar Ganji. "Passing this $85 million budget has made our work much more difficult and the work of the democratic forces much more cumbersome in Iran," Ganji told me.

Shirin Ebadi explained that Iranian activists also opposed unilateral US economic sanctions that began under Jimmy Carter. The sanctions prohibit most trade, investment, and many cultural exchanges.[1] "Economic sanctions hurt people more than the government," said Ebadi. "Americans shouldn't start a military attack. And they shouldn't interfere with the internal affairs of the country."

Iranians rally round their government when faced with an external threat, just as Americans did after September 11, according to former Iranian foreign minister Ebrahim Yazdi. He heads the social democratic Iran Freedom Movement. I met Yazdi at his home in north Tehran. Now in his seventies, Yazdi was the éminence grise of the Iranian opposition. He had a private collection of birds that chirped loudly in the background as we sat down to drink strong, black tea and munch pistachios.[2]

Yazdi told me, "The United States doesn't understand Iran." By threatening possible military action and funding terrorist groups, the Bush administration tosses a lifesaver to the Iranian government, he said. Iranians understand that Bush's talk of "democratizing Iran" is code for overthrowing a sovereign government and installing a US-friendly regime, Yazdi said. Iranians went through that experience once with the 1953 CIA coup. "Democracy cannot be imported or exported," said Yazdi. "American soldiers don't carry democracy in their backpacks. It has to come from within."

Leading Iranian activists argue that the United States could play a positive role if it changed policies. The United States should stop focusing on Iran's alleged nuclear program, according to Ebadi. "The Americans should pay more attention to the human rights issues in Iran," she told me. Lest human rights violations also end up as an excuse for future military action, opposition leaders call for joint international activities.

Yazdi said the United States should cooperate with other countries to hold hearings before the UN's Human Rights Commission and other international bodies. He saw such actions as a tactic to organize international support to strengthen internal opposition, while avoiding unilateral US action. "The US government as an individual member of the UN can back pressure on the Iranian government to observe their human rights obligations as part of a multilateral effort," he said.

US policy toward Iran since the 1979 revolution has failed. The United States must radically shift its policies, according to Ganji. "The United States is a superpower using its military power to force its will on the people. Everyone knows I oppose the Iranian regime. But it is we, the Iranians, who must change it."

The United States doesn't appear likely to change policy anytime soon. Both Republican and Democratic leaders prefer to fish in troubled waters. ■

Jailed in Tehran

Jessica Ramakrishnan

Below is an interview conducted by ASMALLMAGAZINE's Jessica Ramakrishnan with Iason Athanasiadis, a Greek photojournalist and ASMALLWORLD member after his release in 2009 from Iranian prison during the post election protests. It was Iason's first interview after his release. What struck me the most about this interview was Iason's answer to the question, "Will you go back to Iran?"

After three weeks in Iranian prison cells, Iason Athanasiadis, a photojournalist and ASW-er was released by the country's authorities. Only days after he walked free in Tehran and returned to Greece, Iason spoke first to *ASMALLMAGAZINE* about his experience of being caught up in the tumult of present-day Iranian politics.

Q: From press reports, we read that you were on your way out of the country when you were arrested. Tell us what happened.

A: I had passed passport control in the last hours remaining on my seven-day press visa and was walking to the gate of my Emirates flight from Tehran to Dubai when a man (not in uniform) approached me and asked me if I was Iason Fowden, my passport name. I said yes and he asked me to follow him as "you won't be flying tonight." That sounded ominous.

Q: But this is not the first time you've been arrested on the job. And I am sure as a correspondent in war zones, you've considered something like this happening. But how did it feel when it became a reality?

A: It's the second. The first arrest was by Hezbollah shortly after the 2006 Lebanon War but they held me for only an hour. They released me after realizing that I obviously am a journalist. Detentions in sensitive political environments such as conflict zones are absolutely to be expected and the best thing one can do is cooperate with one's captors and get a sense for whether they're pragmatic, practical men or ideological and with an axe to grind. Obviously, I prefer the former.

Q: Media reports indicated that the authorities thought you were a Brit and the implication was that you were part of the British plot behind all the post-election protests. What did your interrogators ask you about this?

A: They tried to use their British spy allegations as a method of discouraging the Greek ambassador from lobbying for my release. To his eternal credit, he stood by me as a Greek citizen and supported my release to the fullest. Also very involved were His Holiness the Greek Orthodox Patriarchate Bartholomew, Greek Foreign Minister Dora Bakoyianni, who personally handled the case, and a host of other political, business, and religious actors who worked behind the scenes to secure my release.

Q: You speak fluent Persian. Did this make you more suspicious in their eyes?

A: Apparently, even though I explained that the reason for this was that I had studied in Iran, a fact backed up by three years of student visas in my passport. The guards quite liked being able to chat with a foreigner in Persian and my skills were certainly rejuvenated by several hours-long interrogations conducted in Persian.

Q: What were the conditions of your detention? Where were you held? What did it look like?

A: I was held in solitary confinement throughout with ample food, which I opted to desist from in preparation for a possible hunger strike in the event that the espionage allegations be taken to trial level. I was moved around a succession of four cells, two of which were in Evin Prison's Section 209, an Intelligence Ministry-controlled prison, and one was at Imam Khomeini International Airport. In all cells, the lights constantly shone and in one, there were no windows or clocks, creating a confusing and disorienting effect.

Q: How much were you interrogated? Were you mistreated at all?

A: I was beaten on the evening of my arrest for engaging in passive resistance. The occasional cuff was administered by my first interrogator but the last pair were gentlemen, sophisticated and enough in control of their questioning to not have to strike me to get answers. Not that hitting me worked. It made me more donkey-headed and unlikely to collaborate. Us Greeks must be won over and convinced to cooperate—beatings make us stubborn.

Q: What did you think of when you were alone?

Love and Pomegranates

A: I dived deep into my past and dredged up memories and images that had lain fallow for years. I went back to childhood a lot and favorite places such as Evia and Aegina, islands to which my parents took me as a child. I relived 'perfect days' and read the Qur'an, which was the only reading matter the guards provided me with. I sang old Greek leftist resistance songs, which I had been taught at school, and watched the shifting daylight reflect off the bars of the window. I counted the journo friends I had in every Greek TV and print outlet and wondered what they were doing about my case in their media.

Q: You were the only foreign reporter arrested, but many Iranian bloggers and press people were also rounded up. Were you held together and what are your hopes for their freedom?

A: I was in isolation throughout. But from the educated tenor of the prisoners' voices that I heard from my cell during mealtimes, I could judge that I was probably surrounded by political prisoners and was not in a criminal ward. They lack the support that I had as a foreign citizen and also the good treatment afforded by captors worried about their testimonies when they are returned to society. I pray for their release. No one should have to suffer those conditions merely for a set of political beliefs.

Q: What are your thoughts about the Iranian situation now, especially since it's been knocked off the news (in the US at least) by the death of Michael Jackson?

A: It's an internal Iranian political affair that will be resolved by the Iranians themselves. The West should not wade into it. I'm a great fan of natural evolution. When a society is ready in its majority, it will shift.

Q: You've got a long and deep connection with the country. Do you think you'll ever go back to Iran? Will you even be allowed back?

A: I was not told that I won't be allowed back and I certainly have thoroughly been filtered now by the Intelligence Ministry for them to know exactly who I am. I love Iran and have lived, loved, and laughed there. It has shaped me as a person in a way that only my home country and my British education have managed. But before going back I'd like to have an assurance that I won't be arrested again.

Q: You're quite the quintessential nomad. How did coming home this time feel?

A: It wasn't so much the coming home as the walking under clear blue skies without a blindfold on and a guard steering you that was a breath of fresh air. Freedom never felt so good. You don't know how good it is until you've lost it.

I Am Neda

Sholeh Wolpé

Leave the Basiji bullet in my heart,
fall to prayer in my blood,
and hush, father
—I am not dead.

More light than mass,
I flood through you,
breathe with your eyes,
stand in your shoes, on the rooftops,
in the streets, march with you
in the cities and villages of our country
shouting through you, with you.
I am Neda—thunder on your tongue.

Is There Another Way?

Reese Erlich

The following is an excerpt from Reese Erlich's The Iran Agenda: The Real Story of US Policy and the Middle East Crisis.

Mainstream policy makers argue that the United States can't live with a clerical government in Tehran. They think the Iranian government will never give up its nuclear ambitions, seek peace with the United States, stop supporting terrorism, or agree to a Palestinian-Israeli settlement. Well, in fact, Iranian authorities once offered to do just that.

In the spring of 2003, Iran contacted Swiss Ambassador Tim Guldimann, who represented the USA diplomatically in Tehran, and proposed comprehensive negotiations that could resolve many of the outstanding US-Iranian issues. The United States had just invaded Iraq, and Iran was worried. In a proposal approved by Supreme Leader Khamenei, Iran agreed to provide intelligence information from al-Qaeda suspects being detained in Iran, agreed to stringent international inspections of nuclear sites, offered to stop military support for Hezbollah and Hamas, and agreed to support a two-state solution to the Israeli-Palestine issue.[1]

The written proposal from Ambassador Guldimann was both faxed and hand delivered to the US State Department. The Bush administration promptly ignored it. The neoconservative faction argued that the United States shouldn't have any dealings with supporters of terrorism. Condoleezza Rice and other Bush officials later denied ever receiving the offer, but receipt of the proposal was confirmed by Flynt Leverett, an analyst with the National Security Council, and by Lawrence Wilkerson, Colin Powell's chief of staff.[2]

We can't know if the Iranians would have negotiated in good faith in 2003. But the Bush administration didn't even try. It has a history of similar blunders. Starting from its opening months in power, at a time when North Korea did not have nuclear weapons, the Bush administration unilaterally undercut a 1994 US-Korean agreement that had been negotiated under Bill Clinton. In February 2007, Bush officials went back and negotiated essentially the same agreement—except by then, North Korea had the bomb.[3]

Successive Democratic and Republican administrations have made a mess of US-Iranian relations since 1979. The United States has tried economic embargoes, UN resolutions, propaganda broadcasts, covert terrorist attacks, detainment of Iranian diplomats living in Iraq, and strident military threats. None have resulted in significant changes inside Iran.

A number of leading experts suggest an alternative. The people of Iran must be left alone to change the government as they see fit. Meanwhile, the United States must negotiate with Iran as part of lowering tensions throughout the Middle East.

Former national security advisor Zbigniew Brzezinski told the Senate Foreign Relations Committee that the United States must leave Iraq "in a reasonably short period of time," start an energetic effort to reach an Israeli-Palestinian peace, and hold a conference on regional stability that includes Iran. In an unusually frank statement for a former National Security Advisor, Brzezinski said, "Practically no country in the world shares the Manichean delusions that the Administration so passionately articulates. The result is growing political isolation of and pervasive popular antagonism toward the US global posture."[4]

Former CIA official Paul Pillar told me, "I believe it is a big mistake not to engage the Iranians. . . . Among the parallel interests are overall stability in their neck of the woods. We worked together in Afghanistan after the overthrow of the Taliban. The Iranians wanted to have something like that happen in Iraq."[5]

Sane voices in Washington can help lower tensions with Iran. But I personally don't trust mainstream politicians, lobbyists, and think tank gurus to resolve anything soon. Nor do I trust the clerics in Tehran to stop their belligerence. A pro-peace, pro-democracy movement exists within Iran. I think people in the United States need to build one as well.

Veterans of the anti-Iraq War movement have already begun educating people about Iran. We need more educational events, people-to-people exchanges, demonstrations, and anti-intervention votes by city governments, all of which can build grassroots pressure to change US policy

If the governments of the United States and Iran won't make peace, the people of our two countries must. ■

Weaving Peace in Tehran

Meghan Nuttall Sayres

*E*aster Sunday I awoke to Tehran traffic outside my hotel window. Women and children in colorful headscarves and men in suits wrestled the tangle of cars and pedestrians, some of whom were on their way to mass at the nearby Orthodox church. I prepared for my own spiritual journey, the reason I had traveled through eleven time zones and half way around the world: to weave a knot on Iran's World Peace Carpet, a project sponsored by UNESCO and the Cultural Heritage, Tourism and Handicraft Organization of Iran. For a tapestry weaver and author (my first novel was inspired by an Afshar tribal rug), tying a goodwill knot on this carpet, along with 700 others from 89 nations, seemed every bit as reverent as attending Easter Mass.

My desire to participate in the Peace Carpet stemmed from a long-held appreciation for Iranian culture, in particular its carpets and poetry, which are often literally woven together. On a visit to the carpet dealers' bazaar in Tehran, I discovered several carpets with phrases of Hafiz, Ferdowsi and Sa'di, or pictorial images of these poets incorporated into the design. I have always admired, if not romanticized, the lives of nomadic peoples and, like Iranian nomads, I learned to raise sheep, spin and dye wool with natural materials, and weave tapestries that are much like Persian *gelims*. I discovered that colors have meanings and rugs contain amulets against the evil eye. Themes such as these inspired my novel, which in turn led to an invitation in 2005 to participate in Iran's First International Children's Book Festival. I remember how elated I had felt that February morning when my plane touched down on Iranian soil. In love with Iranian culture, I could hardly wait to meet its people, with whom I bonded readily during that trip. Thus, when I heard about this UNESCO peace project, I couldn't think of a more perfect excuse to revisit these friends. It was also a way to appease my long-held frustrations over the poor foreign relations between our countries and the palpable mistrust of Iranians among many Americans. I wanted to weave peace in Tehran.

The Peace Carpet stood in the Negaristan Museum situated within the Saad Abad Historical Complex, formerly a Qajar and then Pahlavi summer estate. After the Islamic Revolution, it became a people's cultural park. The atmosphere in the museum felt more diplomatic than artistic, however. Large posters of dignitaries who had tied knots on this carpet hung on the walls beside rugs made in all the provinces in Iran. The Peace Carpet was woven under the direction of Jafar Shahabi, a master weaver and manager of his family's respected carpet business, established nearly a century ago. The rug depicts an image of Cyrus the Great. It was under Cyrus, a Persian king of the sixth century BC, "that Iran became the core of the first universal, multiracial, multi-faith empire."[1] He was famed even among the Greeks for his justice, mercy and generosity. Persians called him the Father of their Nation. The clay cylinder bearing Cyrus's declaration of human rights is kept in the British Museum. The rug contains excerpts from this charter proclaiming religious freedom, elimination of slavery and equal rights for all woven into a bed of flowers along with the words UNESCO and universal peace and friendship in several languages. The now completed Peace Carpet is made of silk and the finest merino wool, and it consists of five hundred shades of naturally-dyed colors and four million knots.

But the carpet was not completed the day I entered the museum and was greeted by Fahimeh Naderinejad the director of the Peace Carpet project. She told me the idea for this carpet was conceived by the current Saad Abad Cultrual Center Director, Eshrat Shayegh. Ms. Naderinejad invited me and my translator to have tea at a table beside the loom along with Mr. Shahabi. Several times my hosts expressed their appreciation of having an American participate. They hoped the Peace Carpet would provide a forum for both diplomats and citizens to gather unofficially and foster new dialogue. It was then that I learned that I was the first American to travel here to weave on this rug. This surprised me since the inaugural ceremony had taken place over six months prior, in November 2008. While I was honored to be the first American, I was saddened that no one else had yet participated.

I asked why the Cultural Center chose to create a peace carpet, as opposed to some other form of art from Iran. They said that tying knots is something many people are capable of doing and most of the world is familiar with Persian carpets. They explained that this project also had an economic component because so many people in Iran are dependent on the strength of the rug industry—the shepherds who grow the wool, the dyers, the weavers, the rug restorers, the dealers and exporters. In this economically difficult time, celebrating this particular kind of art could help renew global interest in Iranian culture and perhaps help boost the carpet industry. But most of all they wanted to export their friendship and a message of peace to the world.

"Art is a universal language," Mr. Shahabi said. "It cuts across political ideologies to touch the soul." I looked at him and smiled, knowing exactly what he meant, as indeed it was their ideal that inspired me to journey here so that I could be a part of it.

Mr. Shahabi turned to the Peace Carpet. "What are we waiting for?"

Time seemed to stand still for a moment when I sat beside the head weaver at the loom. I ran my palm across the silken warp threads in front of me, admiring the subtle hues of the earth-toned yarns dangling above my head on the loom frame. It seemed that not much had yet been woven, only the selvage at the bottom of the rug and six inches or more of the design, knots that would rise toward the ceiling to make up the body of this medium-sized *qalicheh*.

Like every guest I was invited to write down my thoughts, which were later compiled and published when the carpet was completed. After traveling to cities around the world, the book and the carpet were housed in the United Nations office in Geneva. Flags representing each of the guest's home countries were displayed on a round table in the room. "Unfortunately," my hosts told me, "it is illegal to display an American flag in our country, so we cannot put one on our table for you."

I never thought of myself as nationalistic; however, I felt disappointed and slightly offended. But rather than let this one omission damper the respect and friendship we'd forged, I decided to turn the other cheek that Easter morning and let the issue rest. Days later, I received a similar explanation by an apologetic waiter in a restaurant, where visitor nationalities were celebrated by setting flags on diners' tables. He pumped my hand as he greeted me. "It's very regrettable," he said, as he ushered me toward a carpet and pillow-laden platform, an Iranian-style "booth," and then handed me a menu written in both Persian and English. It seemed that everyone I had met—hotel clerks, henna mill workers, merchants, museum employees, students, bookstore owners—either gave me a high five for coming to visit Iran or a thumbs up for Barack Obama. They all praised his recent Norooz greeting. Some Iranians even exclaimed when meeting me, "I love Americans and America!" It seemed these Iranians could do or say anything they wished in reference to America, except display the flag.

After my visit to the Peace Carpet, I met a second personal guide and toured Shiraz and Yazd, driving hundreds of miles between the two cities through a high desert, dwarfed by the Zagros and Shirkuh mountain ranges. In Shiraz I made a pilgrimage to shrines of the classical Persian philosophers and poets, Sa'di and Hafiz. At Hafiz's shrine my guide showed me a ritual the locals perform when they come here. Sitting on the stairs beneath the columned cupola that shelters his tomb from the relentless sun, we opened a book of his poems to the page the wind chose. My guide said that reading his words in this random fashion should help people find solutions to problems or fulfill their dreams. Maybe it was the mood of the sanctuary or the *narenj*-scented air, but I had not a worry at all and felt in need of nothing. In fact, I felt almost drunk, giddy with gratitude. Therefore after reading a few passages, nothing struck me as pertinent at that moment, just a few lines such as: *(O Beloved!) With him, my heart is fellow traveler. In every place where he goeth, be / The blessing of people of liberality the guide of his soul and body.*

Not so for my guide. He gazed into the distance after he read the poet's wisdom and a smile spread across his face.

"Were Hafiz's words relevant for you?" I asked.

"I cannot answer that," he said. "Or my wish may not come true."

At the Persian philosopher Sa'di's shrine, my translator read me a story that we found inscribed in blue tiles on the walls encircling Sa'di's alabaster tomb. The tale seemed strangely familiar. "Once there was a traveler who watched a Sufi leave a caravan and go off weeping in the hills. The Sufi's reason? He noticed all other forms of life were crying to God and he was simply sitting there." One reason I embarked on this trip was that I felt my soul would go to ruin if I simply sat idle while heads of governments continued to speak indirectly at each other. Yet, I also sensed something else, a force pulling me toward this journey: plans fell easily into place; the Iranian government readily granted me a visa; everyone in my family was in good health. Standing inside Sa'di's domed shrine, a space opened inside me. A flicker of knowing. Perhaps, I had thought, my coming to Iran served—or will serve—a larger purpose than simply appeasing my own impatience. Maybe the answer lies within this tale of Sa'di or the words on that random page of Hafiz, which I initially failed to see.

On the road to Yazd, we stopped to visit the ancient site of Persepolis, the vast valley where Darius the Great and other Zoroastrian kings made their spring and fall homes. Before leaving the United States, I hadn't realized how my itinerary directly related to the Peace Carpet. However, while visiting this central region of Iran, I noticed my tour seemed to be unfolding added layers of meaning and purpose. I had not known the Carpet would hang in the United Nations, inside the headquarters of which Sa'di's famous poem greets all who enter. "The sons of Adam are limbs of each other..." I couldn't have guessed that Cyrus the Great would be depicted on the rug. The news I had read about it was that the design would be kept secret until its unveiling.

I had more friends to meet at the Peace Carpet in Tehran, and after exploring Yazd, I returned for a second visit, where I was joined by my Iranian friend Manda and Iran's most well-known dye master Abbas Sayahi. Mr. Sayahi is an author, a former teacher and actor in the film *Gabbeh*, about a nomadic carpet weaver. Sitting beside the Peace Carpet, he recited poetry of his own. The mood in the room was so convivial among us all, some who wove, others who didn't, that it gave me pause. It seemed so natural to be an American inside Iran, gathered amongst new friends discussing art, sharing stories, jokes, wishes for peace, and copious cups of tea served in gorgeous blue and white hand-thrown cups.

This visit to the Peace Carpet closed with a meeting with Eshrat Shayegh, the director of the Saadabad Historical Center and a former member of parliament. Seated around a large oval table, Ms. Shayegh thanked me for traveling so far to weave just one knot. She also expressed her appreciation that I had spent many years learning about Iran to write a novel that celebrates the richness and beauty of her culture. "You are not like others who produce movies such as *300*, which are derisive and insulting to Iranians."

Ms. Shayegh denied that the weaving project was her idea alone. "It was of the people, this is why we held the grand opening ceremony in Tabriz, a city known for its excellent weavers and far away from the halls of diplomats. This carpet, with its humble and simple message of friendship, got its start in a natural setting. People who share this fundamental belief in peace will weave it. It is not only today that Iran is seeking peace. We want others to understand that we have always stood for peace, dating back to Cyrus the Great."

Ms. Shayegh also said that women must show the world how to create peace. "Men have had their chance and it's time for women to get involved and seek positions of leadership." This is a woman, I thought, who refuses to sit idle. When she saw that my camera ran out of batteries, she reached for the clock on her desk and removed its batteries and handed them to me. It was a small but kind gesture, but her generosity didn't stop there. She loaded my arms with books and CDs about Iranian culture and told me to e-mail her anytime.

I gave my Peace Carpet hosts a copy of my novel, which they placed on their peace table. They also accepted skeins of my sheep's wool as keepsakes. Mr. Shahabi hung my yarn on the Peace Carpet loom and said that he would weave it into the rug. My sheep Eiley's and Lydia's wool, *American* wool. It tickled me to imagine what my sheep would think if they understood that their wool is not only working for world peace but would be part of a masterpiece, which in a year or two, would hang in the United Nations.

Before departing, I glanced again at the table where all the flags stood. Despite my new friends' gracious welcomes and generous offer to weave my yarn into their carpet, it still bothered me that it appeared that no American came to express hope for reconciliation.

I realize now that this flag incident has provided an opportunity for introspection. I am grateful for having experienced this "shunning" first hand. Bred in American culture, I have had little experience with being "unheard," and have been steeped in the notion that on these shores there is always a possibility that we might eventually have it our way. The Sufis offer another view. *If every door is always open, is there room for the growth that must come?*

I deeply appreciate the Iranians who helped me take this journey and shared with me my quest of weaving one small knot. This peace knot that is joined with so many others in this lustrous silk carpet, whose wondrously, multi-surfaced fibers are so suited to its mission—to refract and reflect hope and light. To shimmer with Cyrus the Great's vision of dignity for all, and to illume Sa'di's reminder of truth—that harmony in this world lies in the realization that we are interdependent, of one body.

> *The sons of Adam are limbs of each other,*
> *having been created of one essence.*
> *When the calamity of time affects one limb,*
> *the other limbs cannot remain at rest.*
> *If thou hast no sympathy for the troubles of others*
> *Thou art unworthy to be called by the name of a human.* ∎

The Jasmine, the Stars, and the Grasshoppers

Fatemeh Keshavarz

The following excerpt is from Fatemeh Keshavarz's book Jasmine and Stars: Reading More Than Lolita in Tehran.

In Shiraz of the 1960s, where I grew up, summer nights were a journey with a few clear stops. We slept in the courtyard under a sky full of stars, away from the orange, persimmon, and pomegranate trees, but still in the yard. Wooden beds would be brought out at the beginning of the summer. They would be covered first with light textured rugs and then the bedding laid on top. The first station in the night was the cotton mattress on the wooden bed a few steps away from the trees. I would lie there and just look at the sky with wonder, trying to do the hardest thing: fight off sleep just a bit longer. How could the whole neighborhood be sleeping? Most nights, there was the regular crowd of stars overhead. But once in a while there was such an outburst of glittering spots that I would just lie there enveloped in light. Then my gaze would wander around the sky in search of empty patches until my eyes could not stay open anymore. I was very young, and the problems I had then look insignificant now. Still, I did have things to sort out, and it was much easier to put them into perspective under the sky. Most things looked small by comparison anyway. Many years later, when I studied in England for my graduate degree, I missed a lot of things, most of all sorting problems out and putting things into perspective under the stars.

The next station was not a place but a voice. It was not there every night either. Some nights, close to midnight, a particular passerby walked through our alleyway and sang. I never got up to take a peek through the door to see what he looked like. I imagined him to have long hair and to wear a white cotton robe. Perhaps he was a wandering dervish, but certainly not a beggar. Had he meant to beg, he would not have come at midnight when no one was awake to give him anything. He must have gone to school, I thought some years later, because he sang poems that I recognized from my school books and my father's recitations. They were mostly about love, God, or both. But it was not the words alone that stayed with me; he sang them with a voice that was full of urgency and yet untroubled. That is what I loved most. He sang every word as if it carried the secret of the universe, and yet he sang to a neighborhood that was mostly asleep:

Love and Pomegranates

I am glad to be, for being is gladdened by you
I am in love with the world, for the world is in love with you

I must have been seven or eight then. I did not know much about philosophy or mysticism. For a while I did not even know that the words the singer sang were a celebrated verse by the master *ghazal* writer Sa'di of Shiraz, who lived in the thirteenth century. But I knew that he was singing about me, of that I was sure. In his singing, there was a sense of peace with the night that made me grateful for being who I was and where I was. It felt right. Some nights, just as I began to think he was not coming, his voice would start in the distance. The combination of the stillness of the trees, the pale moonlight, and his voice was magical. I would keep still and wait to hear the whole verse then drift into sleep. I never asked anyone the next day if they had heard my passing dervish the night before. It was too risky. What if they said, "Which dervish?" and somehow jinxed him out of existence? Or, worse still, they could say, "O, the dervish," and he would not be magical anymore. As long as no one talked about him, he remained my secret door to a world of comfortable sleepy thoughts.

The next station was just before dawn, and sometimes I missed it completely. I would wake up to the sound of my parents—and my grandmother if she was staying with us that night—performing their ritual wash before the dawn prayer. I had seen the ritual many times during the day. There was nothing mysterious about it. You washed the hands, face, arms, and feet. But before dawn, it was different. First, came the sound of water, then very gentle footfalls—so as not to wake us up—and then the soft whispers of the words of prayer spreading in the early morning air. This was such a short stop that I was never sure if I had really woken up. But it was an important one, particularly if I had argued with someone the day before, done badly on a test, or been scolded for something I should not have done. The sound of prayer said all was back to normal. I would turn softly—careful not to disperse the prayers in the air—and go right back to sleep.

The last station I should call the jasmine station. It was bright and fragrant, and I got the pleasure of it only if my grandmother was staying with us. She would not go back to bed after the dawn prayer. She would walk around the yard, quietly water the plants, and pick little, white jasmine blossoms from the tree that had climbed one wall of the yard all the way to the top. In summertime the tree, covered in white star-like flowers, many of which also covered the ground, looked like a bride standing on a white carpet. My grandmother somehow associated these flowers with prayer and collected fresh jasmine to keep inside her prayer rug until the next morning. But she always collected a few extra flowers for us children and left them on our respective pillows right under our sleepy noses. I would wake up first to their scent, then to their white smiles, and finally to the softness of their petals. They were not just jasmines. They were inseparable from grandma and her prayer rug. They were the gateway to busy summer days.

There were less desirable stations too. One was the arrival of the grasshoppers. Sometimes during the summers in Shiraz the sky would suddenly go dark, and worry would spread over the faces of the grown-ups. It was the migrating grasshoppers. The grown-ups worried because they knew that the wheat or vegetables in some nearby field were about to be destroyed in a matter of hours. A few days after that, many small farmers would be broke, and a few later the price of fresh produce would double. I mourned the attack of the grasshoppers, even when I was not old enough to know the full sad story. I had my own reasons. I was afraid of their long, green bodies and springy legs. Plus, I hated the fact that no one understood my fear. Children in the neighborhood played with the grasshoppers, and my youngest uncle used all the psychological tricks he knew to convince me to touch them so I would lose my fear. But it did not work. Once the insects invaded the sky, I knew there would be lazy ones who would land in our yard to rest and tired ones who would fall despite their will to get to the fields. I would go inside, keep the windows closed, and be suspicious of every green spot that appeared to be moving. It took many days before sleeping in the yard would be safe, bright, and fragrant again.

If I told you about the grasshoppers, you would never look for the stars or the jasmine of my summer nights. Especially if all you had ever heard about was the attack of the grasshoppers. This is why I am writing this book. I am piecing together a colorful tapestry of events, people, and books to give you a new picture of the place in which I grew up. Too many good things fall through the cracks in many books written about the country of my birth and the people who nurtured me. So I have decided to write one that focuses on the good things, one that gives voice to what has previously been silenced or overlooked. Ideally, it should be easy to point to the stars or to give you a handful of my jasmine so next time you think of Iran, you will remember things other than grasshoppers. But in fact it is not easy. The prevailing perceptions make it very hard for me to give you my gifts. It is as if a voice in the background, a master narrative, has told us how to imagine each other.

If God Invited You to a Party

Hafiz
A rendering by Daniel Ladinsky

If God
Invited you to a party
And said,

"Everyone
In the ballroom tonight
Will be my special
Guest,"

How would you then treat them
When you
Arrived?

Indeed, indeed!

And Hafiz knows
There is no one in this world

Who
Is not upon
His Jeweled Dance
Floor.

The Source ~ Negar Ahkami

Acknowledgments

First, I'd like to thank my publisher at Nortia Press, Nathan Gonzalez, for his eagerness to publish this collection. Few mainstream presses are willing to publish anthologies let alone one that offers alternative views on Iran. As a professor of political science, his understanding of Persian language, politics and culture was invaluable in editing and considering pieces for *Love and Pomegranates*.

This anthology wouldn't be the collection it is without the help of Brian H. Appleton, whose network of Iranian friends and colleagues has no bounds. Persis M. Karim suggested writers who contributed to her own anthology Let Me Tell You Where I've been: *New Writing by Women of the Iranian Diaspora*.

My freelance editors, all graduates from Eastern Washington University Master of Fine Arts program, deserve a pomegranate award. Lisa Frank, Laura Ender, Elizabeth Moore and Ericka Taylor, I cannot thank them enough for their years of commitment to this book and the professionalism they brought to the work. The anthology would not have come together without their time and expertise.

I am indebted to the contributing authors, many of whom have been on board since the inception of this anthology seven years ago, and without whom *Love and Pomegranates* would not exist. They have all taught me much about Iran as well as about life. It has been a pleasure getting to know each of them.

I am greatly appreciative to the artists and photographers who contributed their work and time in designing the book: Gaelen Sayres, Aphrodite Désirée Navab, Iason Athanasiadis, Fahimeh Amiri, Laurie Blum, Rashin Kheiriyeh, Sina Nayeri, Negar Ahkami, and Judith Ernst.

As always, my writing group in Spokane, Washington, is indispensible. Thanks to Mary Douthitt, Mary Cronk Farrell, Claire Rudolf Murphy, Beth Cooley (for her swift response to numerous last minute edits), Kris Dinnison, and Lynn Caruso for years of listening and editing and encouragement. Thanks to other friends and readers who offered support and made suggestions on this manuscript, including my husband Bill, Laurie MacMillan, Marianne Sullivan, Suzanna Sanborn, and Kristina Rice-Erso (who read it cover to cover). Knitting friends and neighbors Marian Peterson and Cindy Andrade lent a needed ear. In Moscow, Idaho: Sarah Swett, Rochelle Smith, and Bob Greene, former founder of Book People of Moscow, for their careful reading and input on the book title along with Michelle Humphrey.

Thanks to Manda Jahan and Dominic Parviz Brookshaw for helping me with Persian words, classical Persian poets' biographies and more, and to Sholeh Wolpé for her expertise on the life of Forugh Farrokhzad. I'd like to thank Fatemeh Keshavarz and Shahrokh Ahkami, at *Persian Heritage Journal,* for their help with various cultural questions, as well as Reese Erlich and Dr. Carl Ernst for their initial feedback. Any misspellings or factual errors within the text are mine alone.

Not least, many, many thanks to Russel Davis at Gray Dog Press for his focus, typesetting and suggestions, which made *Love and Pomegranates* tighter and lovelier.

About the Artwork

Title page calligraphy by Sina Nayeri.

Cover image by Aphrodite Désirée Navab. *Re-collecting Iran*. Photograph.

p.xix Iason Athanasiadis: A nightingale framed against a period tile in the Masjed-e Imam in Esfahan. Photograph.

p.5 Fahimeh Amiri. *Bazaar*. Acrylic, 16" X 20".

p.33 Rashin Kheiriyeh. *Persian Lady*. Acrylic on canvas, 72" X 58".

p.99 Iason Athanasiadis: A woman pushes a cart early one morning on the beach in Ahwaz. Photograph.

p.115 Iason Athanasiadis: A man jumps across a sand dune in central Iran's Mesr desert, close to Naeen. Photograph.

p.173 Iason Athanasiadis: A female skier takes time off from the slopes to smoke a *shisha*. Photograph.

p.197 Judith Ernst. *In the Reed Bed 2*, a commemorative piece for Rumi's 800th Birthday. Glazed Stoneware, 19" x 16".

p.249 Negar Ahkami. *The Source*. Acrylic and glitter on gessoed panel, 54" x 48". Photo by Adam Reich. Collection of Jasanna and John Britton.

p.273 Laurie Blum. *Peacocks-Surrendrance*. Gouache on paper, 21.5" X 29".

Mohammad Abolfazli was born in Iran and is a renowned expert in Nutrition Science. He completed his Masters degree at California State University Hayward, and his Ph.D. education from Westbrook University. He is a former athlete and model (for companies like Levi's) and currently hosts several popular TV programs (in Persian) on natural nutrition and healthy lifestyle. He lives in Northern California with his wife and family.

Mehdi Afshar is a writer and translator from Tehran.

Negar Ahkami is an Iranian-American painter based in New York. She has exhibited her work in the US and abroad. Her work has been reviewed in *The New York Times* and *ArtNews*, and is included in the collections of The New Britain Museum of American Art, Depaul University Art Museum, and the Farjam Collection in Dubai.

Fariba Amini is a human rights activist and an independent journalist who has written widely on Iran in various publications and online websites, including the *Guardian*. Her articles have been translated into Persian and published in Iran. She is the publisher of the book *Letters from Ahmad Abad*. She has recently profiled 12 accomplished Iranian Americans in a book called *Faces of Successful Iranian Americans* published by the US Department of State.

Fahimeh Amiri studied as a child under the tutelage of Hussein Behzad, a prominent miniaturist, and attended the High School of Fine Arts in Tehran and the School of The Museum of Fine Arts and Tufts University in Boston. She has illustrated children's books and her work has been exhibited in international art expos, and the National Art's Club in New York. She is a member of the National Woman's Association of Artists. Visit her at: www.amirifinearts.com.

Ryszard Antolak is a writer and teacher specializing in Iranian and East European Literature and History. He lives in the Central belt of Scotland.

Brian H. Appleton is author of *Tales From the Zirzameen* (2008) and *Shamshone; Sun of Assyria* (2012). He writes for *Persian Heritage Magazine, Iranian Times, Zan Magazine, Payvand News,* and *Payam Javan* as well as TV appearances and events pertaining to Persian culture. Visit him at: www.zirzameen.com.

Deniz Azime Aral is from Istanbul, Turkey. She holds a BA in graphic design and an AAS in marketing communications. Deniz has worked in journalism, education, art and non-profit international institutions. She was the assistant to the New York Times' Istanbul Bureau Chief, and the founding director of the Museum of Innocence, Istanbul.

Azin Arefi was born in Iran and moved to the United States as a child. She holds English and creative writing degrees from UC Berkeley and UC Davis. Azin's stories and poems predominantly navigate the Persian culture. She teaches English Literature and Creative Writing at De Anza College in Cupertino and at San Jose City College. She is at work on her first novel. Visit her at: azinarefi@yahoo.com.

Iason Athanasiadis is a Greek writer, photographer and documentary filmmaker who lived in Iran between 2004 and 2007, and returned several times before being imprisoned for three weeks by the Iranian government during the post-election unrest of 2009. Athanasiadis earned degrees in Arabic and Modern Middle Eastern Studies at Oxford University (BA), and Persian and Contemporary Iranian Studies at Tehran's School of International Studies (MA), and was a Nieman fellow at Harvard. Currently based between Istanbul, Kabul and Tripoli, he is eternally grateful to Iran for the wonderful truths it taught him. Visit him at: www.theglobalexperts.org/experts/area-of-expertise/religion/iason-athanasiadis.

Farid al-Din 'Attar is a twelfth century Persian poet born in the same town as 'Omar Khayyam, Nishabur in the province of Khorasan. He studied at a theological school in Mashhad, traveled widely in the Islamic World and India and settled back home, where he ran a pharmacy. His most noted work is the mystical poem, *Conference of the Birds*.

Jeff Baron is a writer and editor living in Arlington, VA. He was a reporter for the State Department's Bureau of International Information Programs, worked as an editor and writer for *The Washington Post*, the *Associated Press*, as well as other newspapers.

Afarin Bellisario was born and raised in Tehran. She moved to the United States in 1974. She has a doctorate from MIT, and is currently a technology licenser officer at MIT. She lives in Boston, MA, with her husband. Visit her blog: http://farawaylandsblogspot.com.

Laurie Blum attended the New York Studio School of Painting, Drawing and Sculpture and the Philadelphia College of Art. Her work of Iran was exhibited at the United Nations, and at the Tomb Shrine of Hafiz, sponsored by the Shiraz Cultural Institute. She is at work on a book, *Language of the Birds—It Is All the Mirror of God*. Visit her at: www.laurieblum.com.

Joel K. Bourne, Jr. is an award-winning environmental journalist whose work has appeared in *National Geographic*, *Audubon*, *Science*, *Outside*, *National Geographic Traveler*, and many other publications. He is a former senior editor and currently a contributing writer for National Geographic magazine.

Love and Pomegranates

Dominic Parviz Brookshaw son of an Iranian mother and an English father, was born in Europe and raised in Britain. He holds a DPhil in medieval Persian poetry from Oxford. He has taught at the University of Oxford, McGill University, and the University of Manchester. He is now Assistant Professor of comparative literature and Persian literature at Stanford University. Contact him at: dominicb@stanford.edu.

Richard Francis Burton (March 19, 1821 - Oct. 20, 1890) was an English explorer, linguist, author, and soldier. In addition to translating "The Golestan of Sa'di," he was an early translator of *Arabian Nights*.

Roger Cohen was Foreign Editor of the *The New York Times* from 2001 to 2004. He has written a column for The Times-owned *International Herald Tribune* since 2004, first for the news pages and then, since 2007, for the Op-Ed page. In 2009 he was named a columnist of *The New York Times*. His books include *Soldiers and Slaves: American POWs Trapped by the Nazis' Final Gamble* (Alfred A. Knopf, 2005). He is at work on a family memoir for Knopf, "The Girl from Human Street."

Afkham Darbandi was born in Tehran, where she trained as a nurse and then as a translator. She and Dick Davis were married in 1974; they translated *The Conference of the Birds* in the early 1980s.

Jasmin Darznik is the author of *New York Times* bestseller *The Good Daughter: A Memoir of My Mother's Life*. She has contributed to the *New York Times, Washington Post*, and *Los Angeles Times* and is a professor of English and creative writing at Washington and Lee University. www.jasmindarznik.com.

Dick Davis retired in 2012, from his position as Professor of Persian and Chair of the Department of Near Eastern Languages and Cultures at Ohio State University. He has published numerous translations from Persian, scholarly works, and books of his own poetry.

Taha Ebrahimi received her M.F.A. from the University of Pittsburgh where she also taught writing for three years. Originally from Seattle, Washington, she currently lives in New York City. Visit her at: www.iranianamericanwriters.org/index.html.

Laura Ender helped edit many of the pieces in this anthology. She holds an MFA in fiction from Eastern Washington University, where she served as an assistant managing editor for Willow Springs. She contributes weekly to Bark (thebarking.com) and writes a food blog (aperfectomnivore.blogspot.com). Her fiction has appeared in *Iconoclast* and *Tomfoolery Review*. She is currently working on a collection of short stories.

Reese Erlich is an investigative reporter, foreign correspondent, and Peabody award winning broadcast journalist who reports regularly for Marketplace Radio, Canadian Broadcasting Corp. Radio, and CBS Radio. He is the author of four books, including

Conversations with Terrorists: Middle East Leaders on Politics, Violence and Empire. Visit him at: www.reeseerlich.com.

Judith Ernst received her BA from Stanford. She has created two illustrated books, *The Golden Goose King* (1993) and *Song of Songs* (2003.) Her article, "The Problem of Islamic Art" appeared in *Muslim Networks: From Hajj to Hip Hop* (UNC Press, 2005). Presently, her artistic medium of choice is ceramics. Visit her at: www.earthembracingspace.com.

Barbara Ertter is curator of Western North American Flora at UC-Berkeley's herbaria. She has been to Iran three times as part of the American-Iranian Botanical Program (www.ucjeps.berkeley.edu/main/research/iran) enjoying natural areas throughout the country with fellow American and Iranian botanists.

Shideh Etaat is a writer/educator who received her MFA in creative writing from San Francisco State University. Her poetry can be found in *Flatmancrooked's Slim Book of Poetry*, the *Atlanta Review*, Iran Issue, and the recent anthology *The Forbidden: Poems from Iran and its Exiles*. She is a 2010 Semifinalist for the Nimrod Literary Award's Katherine Anne Porter Prize in Fiction and a 2010 Glimmer Train Fiction Open Finalist. She is a 2011 Breadloaf Work Study Scholar and is in the process of completing her first novel.

Forugh Farrokhzad (1935-67) is arguably Iran's most significant and controversial female poet of the 20th century. She died in an automobile accident at the age of 32. The translations in this anthology are from: *Sin:—Selected Poems of Forugh Farrokhzad* (Univ. of Arkansas Press).

Farnaz Fatemi is a first-generation Iranian-American poet, writer and writing teacher. She teaches writing at the University of California, Santa Cruz. In addition to regularly publishing poems in journals and anthologies, she is also the author of the libretto for the internationally-produced opera, *Dreamwalker*. Visit her at: sasqi@mac.com.

Tanya Fekri was born in Tehran, Iran, and moved to the United States at the age of two. She graduated from University of Washington, majored in Political Science and Law, Societies, and Justice, and minored in Diversity Studies. She is the founder and president of Interfaith Voices of Youth, and was chosen to interview His Holiness, the Dalai Lama and Archbishop Desmond Tutu on stage at UW in 2008. She attends Seattle University School of Law.

Abo'l-Qasem Ferdowsi was born in the mid-tenth century and died c.1020. He is best known as the author of the epic poem the Shahnameh ("Book of Kings") which he completed in 1010. Written in an archaic style, Ferdowsi's masterpiece (which comprises almost 60,000 couplets), synthesizes pre-Islamic Iranian history, lore, and myth to tell the story of the Persian Empire up to the Arab invasion of the 630s. Within two centuries of the poet's death, the Shahnameh had established itself as the national epic of the

Persian-speaking world. In 2010 the millennium of the completion of the Shahnameh was celebrated with conferences and exhibitions around the world. Ferdowsi is buried at Tus, near the holy city of Mashhad.

Susan Fletcher is author of ten novels for young readers including *Alphabet of Dreams, Shadow Spinner* and, in 2013, *Falcon in the Glass*. Among her books' numerous honors are the American Library Association's Notable Books and Best Books for Young Adults lists. She teaches at Vermont College of Fine Arts. Visit her at: www.susanfletcher.com.

Edward FitzGerald (1809-83) was born in England and graduated from Trinity College, Cambridge. He was a poet and writer best known for his translation of *The Rubáiyát of 'Omar Khayyam*.

Sarah S. Forth has visited Iran twice. She holds a doctorate from Northwestern University, is the author of *Eve's Bible: A Woman's Guide to the Hebrew Bible*, and lives in Los Angeles with her partner Joe. Visit her at: sforth48@gmail.com.

Lisa Frank holds an MFA in creative writing from Eastern Washington University and helped edit many of the pieces in this anthology. Her poems and short stories have been published in the US and abroad. She lives in Galway, Ireland, where she is co-publisher of Doire Press. Visit her at: www.doirepress.com.

Robyn C. Friend, Ph.D. is a dancer, choreographer, linguist, and author. She specializes in the traditional dance of Iran & Central Asia. Her work has taken her throughout the US, Europe, the Near East, Central Asia, and Iran. Her performances and recordings have won awards and rave reviews all over the world. Visit her at: www.robynfriend.com.

Jamila Gavin was born in the Indian foothills of the Himalayas and now lives in London. Her book, *Coram Boy,* won the Children's Whitbread Award, and was shortlisted for the Carnegie Medal. Adapted for the stage, it had two highly successful runs at the National Theatre in 2005/6, followed by a season on Broadway. Her charitable projects include abridging *Measure for Measure* for the Shakespeare Schools Festival. Visit her at: www. davidhigham.co.uk/clients/Jamila_Gavin.htm.

Shaghayeh Ghandehari was born and raised in Tehran. She received her B.A. and M.A. in English literature at Allameh Tabatabaei University, and Shahid Beheshti University. She is currently at work on her Ph.D. She has translated over 60 books for children and adults, and has won awards for her work.

Jahangir Golestan-Parast was born in Isfahan, raised in a family of restauranteurs. He studied and worked in London and Paris before moving to Orange County, California and studying film at UCLA. His documentaries include, *Esfahan: A City Known as Half the World; Iran: A Video Journey*; and *Bam 6.6*. The film *Not Without My Daughter*, which starred Sally Fields, compelled him to make films that informed and educated the world about the true texture of the Iranian culture and people.

Nathan Gonzalez is part-time lecturer of international studies and political science at California State University, Long Beach, and founding publisher and executive editor at Nortia Press. He is author of two books on the Middle East, *Engaging Iran* (2007) and *The Sunni-Shia Conflict* (2009). He holds a Master of International Affairs from Columbia University and is currently finishing a doctorate in political science at UCLA. Visit him at: www.NathanGonzalez.com.

Shams al-Din Mohammad Hafiz was a fourteenth-century Persian lyric poet from Shiraz whose verses are widely known in Iran and other parts of the Persian-speaking world, and quoted orally to this day. His poems often deal with sincere faith and the exposure of hypocrisy. Hafiz wrote almost exclusively in the *ghazal* form. The poet's tomb in the Musalla Garden in Shiraz is popular with both Iranians and tourists alike.

Kabir Helminski has traveled to Iran to speak on world peace. He is co-director, with his wife, Camille Helminski of the Threshold Society, a Sufi organization of the Mevlevi Order of dervishes, which traces back to Rumi.

Shervin Hess is a half-Iranian half-American whose cause is protecting wildlife. He helped establish a Nevada wilderness area, restored a derelict marsh in New York City and collaborates with Iranian conservation NGO Plan4Land. A former PBS TV producer, he now serves as multimedia specialist for the Oregon Zoo in his hometown of Portland.

Basia Irland is an author, poet, sculptor, installation artist, and activist who creates international water projects featured in her book, *Water Library*, University of New Mexico Press, 2007. The book focuses on projects the artist has created over three decades in Africa, Canada, Europe, South America, Southeast Asia, and the United States. Her website is basiairland.com.

Persis M. Karim was born and raised in the San Francisco Bay Area by her French mother and Iranian father. Her poems have been published in numerous national literary journals. She is co-editor of the forthcoming *Tremors: New Fiction by Iranian Americans* (University of Arkansas Press) and a professor of literature and creative writing at San Jose State University. Read about her other books at: www.persiskarim.com.

Mahmood Karimi-Hakak is a theatre artist, filmmaker, poet, author and translator with over 50 stage and screen productions, six plays, four translations and numerous articles and essays to his credit. A Professor of Creative Arts at Siena College, Mahmood is the recipient of five artistic and scholarly awards including Fulbright. Mhakak@siena.edu.

Rashin Kheiriyeh received her MA from Alzahra University of Tehran, Iran. She is an animation director and painter whose work includes 40 illustrated books for children published in Iran, France, Italy, South Korea, Spain, India and the United States. Rashin received first prize for best character designer at the China Animation & Comic Contest 2012, and was winner of the Golden Apple Prize from the Bratislava Illustration Biennial, Slovakia, 2011.

Fatemeh Keshavarz is the author of *Jasmine and Stars: Reading More Than Lolita In Tehran*, University of North Carolina Press, Chapel Hill (2007), among other books. She is a poet, writer and the director of the Roshan Institute for Persian Studies at the University of Maryland at College Park. Visit her at: www.windowsoniran.wrodpress.com.

'Omar Khayyam was an eleventh-century Persian poet, philosopher, and scientist. His poetry has had a major impact on literature, and was popularized in the English-speaking world through the translations and renderings by scholars such as Thomas Hyde (1636-1703) and Edward Fitzgerald (1809-83).

Daniel Ladinsky was raised in St. Louis, traveled the world and spent much time in a spiritual community in India. Among others, his books include *The Gift: Poems By Hafiz; A Year With Hafiz: Daily Contemplations; The Purity of Desire: One Hundred Poems of Rumi*.

John W. Limbert is a U.S. Ambassador and was held in Iran during the 1979 hostage crisis. He is a Distinguished Professor of International Affairs at the U.S. Naval Academy, following a 33-year career in the United States Foreign Service. Ambassador Limbert has taught in Iranian high schools and at the University of Shiraz. His books include *Iran: At War With History; Shiraz in the Age of Hafiz;* and *Negotiating With Iran*.

Damon Lynch loves photography, peace building, and writing free software. He is at work on a Ph.D. in cultural anthropology at the University of Minnesota, and has an MA in Peace Studies from the University of Notre Dame. He is from Aotearoa, New Zealand. Visit him at: www.damonlynch.net.

Rosemarie Brittner Mahyera is the founding director of the English Language Institute at the University of Utah. She taught ESL to international students and has had the privilege of coming to know many of them as friends. In 2001, she was a Fulbright Senior Scholar to Indonesia.

Aidin Massoudi was born in Tehran, Iran, but calls San Francisco his home. He holds an MFA from City University of New York, Brooklyn College and is working on the completion of his manuscript, *Field Song*.

Nancy Matthews a graduate of Connecticut College, has spent most of her adult life in the international field, first as the wife of H. Freeman Matthews, Jr. a senior Foreign Service Officer, and then as Vice President for the Arts at Meridian International Center in

Washington, D.C. She currently resides in Missoula, MT, where she is a Visiting Scholar at the University of Montana.

Amir Haeri Mehrizi is a tour guide and translator living in Iran. Contact him at: amirhaerimehrizi@yahoo.com.

Javad Mohsenian, M.D. is a psychiatrist in suburban Philadelphia. He wrote "Wave in the Wheatfield," while in high school, and "A Guide to University Entrance Exams," and "To-day is Also Late" while in medical school. His two novels in English, *Persian Moonlight* and *9/11 Children* were published in the United States. Forthcoming with Gorgias Press is a collection of stories in English and Persian entitled *Gold for Sugar*.

Elizabeth Moore helped edit this anthology. She holds an MA in literature and creative writing from Southern Illinois University Edwardsville, and an MFA from Eastern Washington University. Her fiction has appeared in *42Opus*, and *Sou'wester*.

Neilufar Naini is a 5th degree black belt and Shidoin in Aikido under Birankai International and currently is the Chief Instructor at Clallam Aikikai (a.k.a. Port Angeles Aikikai, www.portangelesaikikai.com). Her Aikido path led her to Sequim, WA, where she works on an organic farm. She holds a B.A. in Physics and an M.S. in Education.

Manijeh Nasrabadi received her MFA from Hunter College in 2007 and is now a Ph.D. student in American Studies at NYU. Her essays and articles have appeared in *Comparative Studies of South Asia, Africa and the Middle East*, *Social Text online*, *About Face* (Seal Press), *Tehran Bureau*, vidaweb.org, jadaliyya.org, and *Callaloo*.

Joan Nathan is the author of ten cookbooks including the recently published *Quiches, Kugels and Couscous: My Search for Jewish Cooking in France* (Knopf, November 2010). She is a regular contributor to the *NYT Food Arts Magazine* and *Tablet Magazine*.

Aphrodite Désirée Navab Dr. Aphrodite Désirée Navab is an artist and writer of Iranian and Greek descent (born in Esfahan, Iran). She earned an Ed.D. in Art Education at Columbia University (2004), and a BA magna cum laude from Harvard College (1993). She is currently writing a novel, *The Homeling*. Visit her at: www.aphroditenavab.net.

Sina Nayeri was born in 1981 in, Esfahan, Iran, and graduated with a BFA in graphics from New York Institute of Technology. He is a multi-media specialist for advertisements and television shows.

Angella M. Nazarian is the author of two best-selling books: *Life As a Visitor (2009)* and *Pioneers of the Possible: Celebrating Visionary Women of the World (2012)*. She has a background in psychology and is a speaker at various national women's conferences. Her Persian-Jewish family recipes appeared in the *New York Times* last year as a cover piece on March 24, 2010.

Shahrokh Nikfar led a Friendship Delegation to Iran in the spring of 2009 in which Americans were hosted by families in Iran who shared the same interests and professions. Nikfar hosts a weekly radio show called *The Persian Hour* on Thin Air Community Radio in Spokane, Washington, in 2004. His program promotes understanding of Iran and the Iranian culture through music, book and movie reviews, the sharing of Persian recipes, and interviews with people who have traveled to or lived in Iran.

Jaleh Novini is a translator who lives in Tehran. She studied English Literature at Allameh Tabatabi University and worked for The House of Translation For Children and Young Adults. Her published translations include, *White Water,* by P.J. Peterson; *House of Dies Dreir,* by Virgina Hamilton; *Light on Snow,* by Anita Shreve; *Historian,* by Elizabeth Kostova, among many others.

James Opie is author of two books on tribal rugs, the most recent one is *Tribal Rugs:Nomadic and Village Weaving of the Near East and Central Asia*, which was published simultaneously in England and the United States in 1992. His current essays have appeared in *Parabola* magazine. He and his wife Catherine reside in Portland, Oregon. Visit him at: www.jamesopie.com.

Talie Parhizgar was born and raised in Mashhad, Iran, and came to America in 1976. She received her B.A. from American University of Beirut, Lebanon, and her Ph.D. in Human Behavior and Leadership at US International University in San Diego. She has translated 'Omar Khayyam's Rubáiyát into English, and shares his philosophy of life. Talie has taught students from nearly all grade levels, including university. She lives in Spokane, Washington.

Shahrnush Parsipur was born in Iran. She is author of eleven books of fiction and memoir. She was the first recipient of Brown University's International Writers Project Fellowship. She now lives in California.

Jessica Ramakrishnan is a writer and editor. A graduate of the University of London's School of Oriental and African Studies and Columbia University's Graduate School of Journalism, her reportage has appeared in the *Chicago Tribune, Harper's Bazaar,* style. com, amongst other publications.
Ahmad Rezwani is a scholar who lives in Mashhad, Iran.

Karen G. Ruffle is an Assistant Professor in the Departments of Historical Studies and Religion at the University of Toronto. She has conducted field research in India, Pakistan, Iran, and Syria. Ruffle is the author of *Gender, Sainthood, and Everyday Practice in South Asian Shi'ism* (University of North Carolina Press, 2011).

Jalal al-Din Rumi was a thirteenth-century Persian poet, theologian, and Sufi mystic who lived most of his life in Anatolia. His poems have been translated into many languages, and in 2007, he was described as the "most popular poet in America." His works often deal with the divine, and the quest to be reunited with the Beloved.

Sheikh Mosleh al-Din Sa'di was a thirteenth-century poet from Shiraz. His work is widely quoted and recited by Iranian schoolchildren. Sa'di's work is best known for its social reflection and approachability. The poet's shrine in Shiraz is a great attraction for lovers of poetry and literature.

Susan Safa was born in Ventura, California. She received a master's degree from the University of Southern California. She enjoys reading, listening to music, ancient Persian history, home decorating, being in nature, and takes great pride in making a positive impact in other people's lives.

Meghan Nuttall Sayres conceived and edited this anthology. She feels privileged to have met many of its contributors and hopes to meet them all in person. Read more about her on page 275. Visit her at: www.meghannuttallsayres.com.

Roger Sedarat is the author of two poetry collections: *Dear Regime: Letters to the Islamic Republic*, which won Ohio UP's 2007 Hollis Summers' Prize, and *Ghazal Games* (Ohio UP, 2011). He teaches poetry and translation in the MFA program at Queens College, City University of New York. Visit him at: www.sedarat.com.

Farnoosh Seifoddini received an MFA in creative writing at San Francisco State University. She is a published poet who lives in San Franscico, where she enjoys collaborative projects and destination workshops with fellow poets. Farnoosh recently joined the Squaw Valley Community of Writers. Visit her at: http://iranianamericanwriters.org/member-profiles-s.htm#p7APMc1_3.

Sohrab Sepehri (1928-1980) was a poet and painter who traveled the world only to return to his hometown of Kashan, where he is buried. The beauty of nature permeates his work.

Shahriar Shahriari was born in Iran, educated in England and Canada, and currently lives with his wife and son in Los Angeles, California. He is a mechanical engineer by training, and a lover of Persian mystical poetry. For more information, go to www.Shahriari.com.

Rick Steves hosts the public television program "Rick Steve's Europe" and the public radio show "Travel With Rick Steves," and is also the authors of numerous travel guides. His "Rick Steves Iran" public television special has received international praise. Visit him at: www.ricksteves.com.

Rowan Storm is recognized internationally as a frame drum designer, performer and educator of traditional Middle Eastern hand drumming and singing. She studied the ancient Persian frame drums *Dayereh* and *Daf* with the master of classical Persian music,

Love and Pomegranates

Mohammad Reza Lotfi. Rowan performs in venues including San Francisco's Asian Art Museum and Greece's Epidavros Ancient Amphitheater. Visit her at: www.rowanstorm.com.

Ericka Taylor holds an MFA in Creative Writing from Eastern Washington University. While pursuing her master's, she served as Assistant Managing Editor at Willow Springs Magazine. She graduated from Cornell University with a B.A. in English and her non-fiction has been published in *Human Ecology News, Cornell Political Forum*, and *Ark Magazine*. She has an as yet untitled novel in progress and contributed to the editing of several pieces in this collection.

Bill Wolak is a poet who has just published his eighth book of poetry *Whatever Nakedness Allows*. He recently co-translated with Maria Bennett *My Voice Seeks You*, the first translation of the Italian poet Annelisa Addolorato. Mr. Wolak teaches creative writing at William Paterson University.

Sholeh Wolpé is a poet, and literary translator. Her books include three collections of poetry, two books of translations, and four anthologies. Her most recent books are: *Keeping Time with Blue Hyacinths* and *Breaking the Jaws of Silence*, both forthcoming in 2013 from the University of Arkansas Press. Born in Iran, she lives in Los Angeles.

Permissions

First Impressions and Persian Hospitality

"Stones In A New Garden," the words the author chants to herself in the taxi first appeared in a short story by Aphrodite Désirée, Navab "Tales Left Untold," in *POWWOW: Charting the Fault Lines in the American Experience, Short Fiction from Then to Now*, edited by Ishmael Reed & Carla Blank, Da Capo Press, Perseus Books, 2009.

The Golestan of Sa'di - Chapter 2 - Story 26, by Sheikh Mosleh al-Din Sa'di, translated by Richard Francis Burton, found on the website: www.iranchamber.com/literature.

Finding Ourselves in the Other

"A Friendship of Words," by Susan Fletcher first appeared in *The Horn Book Magazine*, March/April 2009.

"Fly, Howl, Love, A Tribute To The Life Of Forugh Farrokhzad," by Shideh Etaat is based on a "A Brief Biography" in *Sin—Selected Poems of Forugh Farrokhzad* translated by Sholeh Wolpé, as well as on excerpts from a letter written to Ebrahim Golestan and "Sin" also found in the same book published by University of Arkansas Press, 2007.

"Let Me Tell You Where I've Been," and "Beyond," by Persis M. Karim, first appeared in her book *Let Me Tell You Where I've Been: New Writing by Women of the Iranian Diaspora*, edited by Persis M. Karim, Fayetteville: University of Arkansas Press, 2006.

"Masquerade," by Jasmin Darznik first appeared in the *The Washington Post Magazine*.

"Forty Days in a Wilderness of Heartland," by Brian H. Appleton (L&P e-book edition), first appeared in *Tales of the Zirzameen*, 2008.

"Not Iranian, Not American, but Definitely A Full-Blood Granddaughter," by Susan Safa. The Rumi poem within this piece was translated by Majid M. Naini in *Mysteries of the Universe and Rumi's Discoveries on the Majestic Path of Love*, Delray Beach: Universal Vision and Research, 2002, p. 212.

Love and Pomegranates

"Merging of Three Poets." The five poems in this section by Bill Wolak and Mahmood Karimi-Hakak were first published in *Love Emergencies*, published by Cross-Cultural Communications, NY, 2010, and in the collection *Your Lover's Beloved*, published by Stan Barkan, Cross-Cultural Communications, 2009.

Tasting Home

"Love and Pomegranates," by Mohammad Abolfazli, is adapted from an article that originally appeared on www.kodoom.com/en/search/?q=abolfazli&qw=United+States.

"An Iranian Seder in Beverly Hills," by Joan Nathan (L&P e-book edition), first appeared in Dine & Wine, *New York Times*, March 23, 2010.

"The Laughter of Pomegranates," a poem by Rumi translated by Kabir Helminski and Ahmad Rezwani, first appeared in *Love's Ripening: Rumi on the Heart's Journey*, Shambhala Publications, Boston, 2008, p. 56.

Art and Culture

"Journey Into Iran's Literary Landscape," by Meghan Nuttall Sayres, was first published in *The Spokesman Review*, August 21, 2005.

"On Loving," "Rebellious God," and "Only Voice Remains," poems by Forugh Farrokhzad, first appeared in a collection *Sin— Selected Poems of Forugh Farrokhzad* by Sholeh Wolpé, published by University of Arkansas Press, 2007. www.uapress.com.

"Bam 6.6, The Movie," an interview by Brian H. Appleton of Iranian-American film-maker Jahanghir Golestan, was previously published in *Persian Heritage Journal* and Payvand.com.

"Persia Primeval," an essay by Shervin Hess, first appeared in *Persian Heritage Journal*, Winter 2010, in a longer version as "Iran's Other Ancient Heritage."

"'A Bold Hand' Making A Mark on the Art World," by Jeff Baron, was first published by the State Department's Bureau of International Information Programs, featured on America.gov, and also by *Persian Heritage Journal*, Summer, 2010.

"The Festival of No-Ruz," an excerpt of "The First Kings" from *Shahnameh: The Persian Book of Kings*, by Abolqasem Ferdowsi, foreword by Azar Nafisi, translated by Dick Davis, copyright © 1997, 2000, 2004 by Mage Publishers, Inc. Used by permission of Viking Penguin, a division of Penguin Group (USA) Inc.

"Welcome, Nooroz, Welcome," by Azin Arefi, first appeared in Iranian.com, March 2007.

"Conversation With Composer Behzad Ranjabarab," by Fariba Amini, first appeared in Iranian.com, and then Payvand.com.

"Iran's Literary Giantess is Defiant in Exile, But Missing Home," by Mohammed Al-Urdun, first appeared online in *Camden New Journal-Middle East Eye,* June 19, 2007.

Quatrains XLVI and LXXVII of 'Omar Khayyam, translated by Edward Fitzgerald, *The Rubáiyát of 'Omar Khayyam*, Quality Paperback Bookclub, Random House, Bertelsmann, New York, 1996.

Islam and Other Faiths

"Ripened Fruit," a translation of Rumi by Kabir Helminski and Ahmad Rezwani, first appeared in *Love's Ripening: Rumi on the Heart's Journey*, Shambhala Publications, 2008, p.1.

"Ghazal 374 – Hafiz," translated by Shahriar Shahriari and contributed by Jaleh Novini, first appeared on the website: www.hafizonlove.com.

"What Iran's Jews Say," by Roger Cohen reporting from Iran for *The New York Times*, February 22, 2009.

"I Have Learned So Much," a rendering of a poem by Hafiz by Daniel Ladinsky in *The Gift: Poems by Hafiz The Great Sufi Master*, Penguin Compass, 1999, p.32.

"The Reapers of Dawn," the poem by Sohrab Sepehri, translated by Mehdi Afshar, was first published in *An Anthology of Sohrab Sepehri's Poems*, by Zarrin Publications, Tehran, Iran, 2004. The poem within this anthology was edited lightly for punctuation.

A New Path Forward

"Travel As A Political Act," is a blog excerpt from Rick Steves, the acclaimed travel writer and television and radio travel host, and was first featured on his blog at: www.ricksteves.com.

"Iranian Cure For The Delta's Blues," by Joel K. Bourne Jr. Reprinted from the July/Aug issue of AARP Bulletin, a publication of AARP. Copyright 2010 AARP. All rights reserved.

"A Persian Picnic, With Plants," by Barbara Ertter. An adaptation of an article printed in the newsletter of the Jepson Herbarium, University of California at Berkeley.

Notes

Preface

1. On Xenophon's reported conversation with Socrates, see *Anabasis* (Book III, 1). For Xenophon's fictional accounts of Cyrus the Great (who was not his contemporary), see Xenophon's *Cyropaedia*.

2. Despite the fact that Cyrus's cuneiform cylinder, which outlined protections for his conquered subjects in Babylon, was not a new practice at the time, it is considered by many Iranian nationalists to represent the first human rights charter. See "Cyrus cylinder, world's oldest human rights charter returns to Iran on loan," *Guardian* (September 10, 2010).

3. Amnesty International, *Annual Report, 1974/75* (London: Amnesty International Publications, 1975), p. 8.

Introduction

1. The study mentioned in this introduction was reported in *Persian Heritage Journal* (Jan. 09) and was conducted April 2008. The poll about "Americans Are More Afraid of Muslims Now that Bin Laden Is Dead," appeared online at www.aslanmedia.com, July 28, 2011.

2. Citation about Cameron Powers from: www.musicalmissionsofpeace.org/mm/cameronpowers/index.html.

Finding Ourselves In The Other

"Fly, Howl, Love: A Tribute to the Life of Forugh Farrokhzad" by Shideh Etaat Based on a "A Brief Biography" in *Sin: Selected Poems of Forugh Farrokhzad* translated by Sholeh Wolpé as well as on excerpts from a letter written to Ebrahim Golestan, and the poem "Sin" also found in the same publication.

"Marteza Varzi" by Robyn C. Friend, Ph.D.

1. The *kemanche* is a small, violin-sized bowed musical instrument. It is held so that the strings are vertical to the ground. At the base of the body is a brass spike that sits on the musician's knee or thigh, stabilizing the instrument as it is played.

"Not Iranian, Not American, but Definitely a Full-Blooded Granddaughter" by Susan Safa.

Love and Pomegranates

1. Literature cited. Naini, Majid M. *Mysteries of the Universe and Rumi's Discoveries on the Majestic Path of Love*. Delray Beach: Universal Vision and Research, 2002. Page 212.

Art and Culture

"On Loving" by Forugh Farrokhzad
Sholeh Wolpé notes in this poem Farrokhzad speaks of a kind of love that no longer seems to exist and says, "Today people measure love with the tick-tick of their watches. They register it in books so that it is respectable. They subject it to laws. They put a price on it and limit it with 'faithfulness,' or 'deceit'."

"Bam 6.6, The Movie" by Brian H. Appleton
1. To read about the Tobb Dell'Oro Friendship Fund, a nonprofit project building a school in Bam, Iran, go to www.tobbdelloro.org. To read the unabridged version of this interview go to: www.payvand.com/news/07/feb/1161.html.

"Persian Primeval" by Shervin Hess.
To learn more about efforts to protect Iran's wildlife, visit the Persian Wildlife Heritage Foundation at www.persianwildlife.org.

"The Oldest Living Iranian" by Ryszard Antolak
1. In this way we can better understand legends of cypress trees singing in human voices. Two cypresses speaking in a human voice are said to have foretold the death of Alexander. And in the Testament of Abraham, a cypress tree prophesies the patriarch's death, etc.

2. When the latter tree was cut down in 847 AD on the orders of the Abbasid caliph al-Mutawakkil, earthquakes shook, buildings fell and a swarm of birds filled the night sky screaming with rage. It was cut down in sections and transported on more than 300 camels to Samarra. The Abarkuh cypress is older than the cypress of Kashmar.

3. Two hills of ashes in Abarkuh were once associated with the "Fires of Nimrod" into which Abraham was thrown. The patriarch is also said to have prophesied that rain would never fall within the walls of the city, and that its inhabitants would never raise cows.

"Norooz" by Farnoosh Seifoddini
From Ahmad Sahmlu's "Pari-a."

"Welcome, Norooz, Welcome!" by Azin Arefi
The *haft-seen* is a traditional table laid out by Iranians during Norooz, or new year, comprised of seven (haft in Persian) items that begin with "seen" the Persian letter for "s." Each of the items has symbolic significance and represents triumph of good over evil, and the hopes Iranians have for the New Year. The laying of the *haft-seen* goes back thousands of years.

Islam and Other Faiths
"Bagh-e Eram" by Aidin Massoudi
Bagh-e Eram means "Garden of Paradise."

"What Iran's Jews Say" by Roger Cohen
For more discussion and insights related to this article please see the following web links:
JTA, *The Global Newspaper for Jewish People* (www.jta.org/news/article/2009/03/16/1003749/roger-cohen-spars-with-iranian-jewish-expats) *The New York Times* (www.nytimes.com/2009/03/02/opinion/02cohen.html?_r=2&th&emc=th).

"Baba Kuhi and Hafiz of Shiraz" by Damon Lynch
1. The translation of "Only God I Saw" is from Reynold A. Nicholson, *The Mystics of Islam*. London: Arkana, 1989.

A New Path Forward
"A Persian Picnic, With Plants" by Barbara Ertter
1. Our deepest appreciation to the University of Tehran College of Agriculture, which served as our primary host institution for the first two trips, and the National Geographic Society's Committee for Research and Exploration, which provided funding. For more on the various expeditions, and biogeographical similarities between Iran and western North America, see ucjeps.berkeley.edu/main/research/iran.

"The Impact of US Meddling" by Reese Erlich
1. For a listing of all US sanctions against Iran, see Kenneth Katzman, "Iran: US Concerns and Policy Responses," Congressional Research Service Report for Congress, January 5, 2007.

2. Ebrahim Yazdi, interview with author, November 16, 2006, Tehran.

"I Am Neda" by Sholeh Wolpé
On June 20th, 2009, Neda Agah-Soltan, a 26-year-old Iranian woman and a student of philosophy, while attending a demonstration in Tehran protesting the vote-count in the reelection of President Mahmoud Ahmadinejad, was targeted and shot in the heart by a Basij. The name Neda in Persian means "the Call."

"Is There Another Way?" by Reese Erlich
1. Gareth Porter first broke the story in "Burnt Offering," *The American Prospect*, June 6, 2006. The story was confirmed by Glenn Kessler, "US Missed Chance with Iran, Ex-Officials Claim," *Washington Post*, June 18, 2006.

2. Gareth Porter, "First Rejected, Now Denied," *The American Prospect*, February 9, 2007. See also Kessler, *Washington Post*.

3. Charles Scanlon, "The end of a long confrontation?", BBC News, February 13, 2007 (www.news.bbc.co.uk/2/hi/asia-pacific/6357853.stm).

4. Brzezinski testimony.

5. Interview with the author.

6. Some groups working against intervention in Iran and related issues include Campaign Against Sanctions and Military Intervention in Iran (www.campaigniran.org), Just Foreign Policy (www.justforeignpolicy.org), Global Exchange (www.globalexchange.org), United For Peace and Justice (www.unitedforpeaceandjustice.org), and Jewish Voice for Peace (www.jewishvoiceforpeace.org).

"Weaving Peace in Tehran" by Meghan Nuttall Sayres
1. Paul Kriwaczek *In Search of Zarathustra*, Vintage Books, 2002. pp. 171 and 184.

Peacocks-Surrenderance - Laurie Blum

About the Editor

Meghan Nuttall Sayres is a writer and tapestry weaver from Washington State who raises sheep, spins and colors the yarn for her tapestries with natural dyes. She has traveled in Iran, Turkey, Qatar, Syria and Uzbekistan, where she has met with scholars, carpet weavers, dyemasters and merchants to study the age-old techniques, symbolism, and Sufi poetry that infuse many rugs woven throughout the Middle East.

On her first visit to Iran in 2005, she attended their First International Children's Book Festival to speak about her debut novel, *Anahita's Woven Riddle*, a story about an Iranian nomadic carpet weaver (Harry N. Abrams, 2006, and Nortia Press, 2012). This book is an ALA Top Ten Best Books YA 2007, A Book Sense/Indie Pick Winter 2006/2007, and an ALA Amelia Bloomer Project Feminist Book Selection 2008. The novel has been translated into European and Middle Eastern languages and CRS Libri/ Rizzoli chose *Anahita el'enigma del tappeto*, as the featured book at the 2008 Bologna International Book Fair. Among other books, Meghan is also author of *Night Letter*, a new novel set in Iran and Uzbekistan (Nortia Press, 2012) and co-author of *Daughters of the Desert: Tales of Remarkable Women from the Christian, Jewish and Muslim Traditions* (Skylight Paths Press, 2003).

In 2009 Meghan traveled back to Iran as the first American to weave on Iran's first World Peace Carpet, sponsored by the Saad Abad Historical Society and UNESCO. She holds a graduate degree in international rural development and has given talks and workshops on Iran, weaving, interfaith dialogue and creative writing throughout the US, Ireland, the Middle East and Central Asia. Please visit her at: www.MeghanNuttallSayres. com, Facebook, Goodreads and Twitter.